Between Two Fires

⏤⟫⟳●⟲⟪⏤

The African Saga of Margarete Trappe

Dallas, 08 January 2012

For Maruca & Frank,
With warm
regards and with every good wish for
a splendid future.

Between Two Fires

The African Saga of Margarete Trappe

Fiona Claire Capstick

Margarete Trappe

ROWLAND WARD PUBLICATIONS

JOHANNESBURG

ISBN Standard copy 978-0-9814424-4-0
ISBN Collectors copy 978-0-9814424-5-7

First Edition 2011

Rowland Ward Publications
P O Box 2079, Houghton 2041 South Africa
Tel: (27 11) 646 9888
email: sales@rowlandward.com

www.rowlandward.com

Design and reproduction, L W McMurray
Lithographed and bound, Tien Wah Press (Pte) Ltd
Collectors' edition bound by Graphicraft

Dedication

Dedicated with pride and love
to my husband, Adelino Serras Pires,
who also came out to Africa,
lived between two fires
and fought havoc.

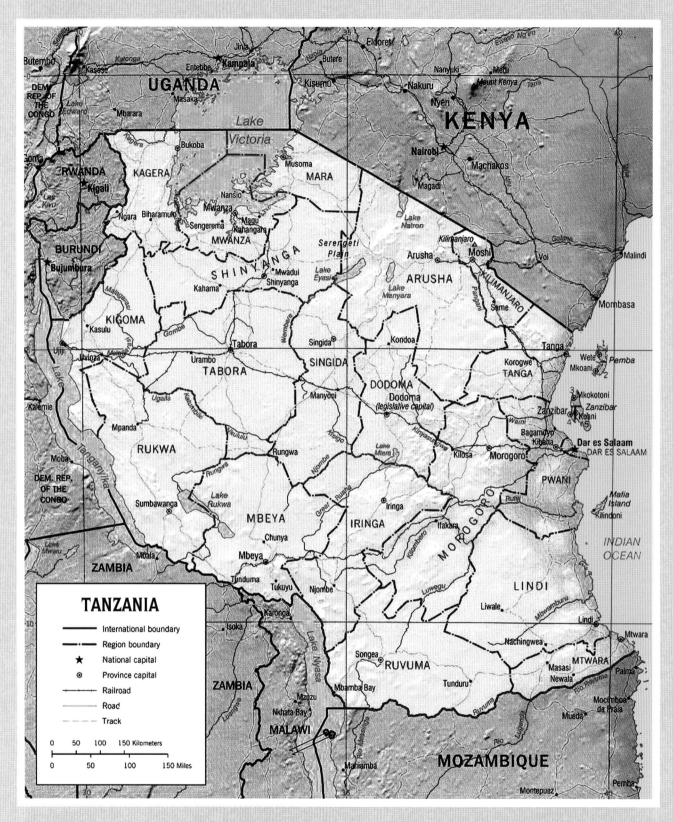

Map of present day Tanzania

*"The generation to which I belong
has seen Africa yield up her secrets; and the
survivors of this generation, who have witnessed the passing
away or transformation of many of the great game regions,
alone can tell of what our generation has done
and seen, and which those who come after
can never do or see again."*

The Book of the Lion
By Sir Alfred E. Pease, Bart.
London, John Murray, 1913)

Margarete in her mid-teens. [Yorck-Michael Trappe]

Contents

Guests on the Trappe estate, against the magnificence of Mount Meru. [Emil Karafiat]

Acknowledgements

Many people contributed towards the eventual publication of this book, but Margarete's grandsons played the decisive role in bringing this story to the attention of the Anglophone world in the new millennium. Emil Karafiat of Switzerland, Dr Jobst-Ulrich Trappe and his brother Yorck-Michael Trappe of Germany gave unstintingly of their time, knowledge and advice over the years it took to research the remarkable life of their grandmother. The grandsons provided a wealth of photographs and documents, sharing certain off-the-record details to facilitate greater understanding of the events and people of the day and how they influenced Margarete's life. This entire undertaking would have been impossible without the profound goodwill, co-operation and knowledge of Emil Karafiat, Dr Trappe and Yorck-Michael Trappe.

Bernd Reufels, the noted German independent documentary filmmaker who produced the script and directed the 2007 documentary film on Margarete Trappe, was a very significant factor in the writing of this book. He, on behalf of The Ziegler Film Company of Berlin, invited the author to take part in the filming on location in Tanzania, indeed, on part of what was once Margarete's legendary farm. Those magical days amid the astounding beauty of the Mount Meru and Mount Kilimanjaro region ignited the desire to finally share Margarete's story with a new world and a new generation. Bernd facilitated introductions to Emil Karafiat and the Trappe brothers, thereby ensuring authenticity. Regina Ziegler, the founder of The Ziegler Film Company, is warmly thanked for her Company's great hospitality and generosity.

Richard Curtis, veteran literary agent of New York City, displayed his customary flair in seeing to the paperwork and in helping reveal a fresh chapter on the huntress/pioneer in Africa;

Jane Halse, Managing Director of Rowland Ward Publications of Johannesburg, exhibited great tenacity, courage and vision in the production of this book;

Gabriële Löhrl, a cousin of Dr Trappe, for permission to reproduce material. Mrs Löhrl, who died in Germany in November 2010 at the age of 83, took part in the 2007 documentary film and was the guardian of valuable family documents, including personal letters to her from Margarete. May their spirits rejoice together;

Lionel McMurray, a truly gifted graphic artist, who has once again excelled himself.

The following is a list in alphabetical order of all the other people who contributed in a variety of ways to this project:

Dr Rolf D. Baldus, an expert on human/lion conflict in Tanzania;

Jim Casada, an internationally recognized authority on books devoted to African hunting and exploration literature;

Bambi Chilvers-Lubin, noted huntress and writer, with a special insight into the world of the African safari, for agreeing to write the Foreword;

Laurian Coughlan, my sister, for her proofreading skills and for gathering a great deal of historical facts needed for this book;

Gerhard Damm, who comes from a strong German hunting tradition, and who is a key figure in the international hunter/conservationist community;

Tom Fassaert, the prize-winning documentary filmmaker from The Netherlands, for his still photography;

Peter Flack, erudite international hunter/conservationist with vast experience of the game fields of Africa in particular;

Marlies and Jörg Gabriel, the owners of the superlative Hatari Lodge on part of what was once Margarete's farm, for their wonderful hospitality and permission to use some of their wildlife photographs;

David Grayling of Cumbria, Great Britain, leading antiquarian book dealer, for excellent service in providing elusive research material;

Lars Hauck of Germany, a member of the documentary film crew, for permission to reproduce important photographs;

Robin Hurt, one of the most prominent and respected personalities in the African safari industry;

Rosemary Malcomess of The Wilderness in the Southern Cape of South Africa who is related by marriage to Margarete Trappe and who was the source of much fascinating detail;

Klaus Mielich, Production Manager for the Trappe documentary film by The Ziegler Film Company, Berlin;

Paul Mills of Clarke's Africana and Rare Books of Cape Town, the noted antiquarian book dealer, for tracking down important reference works;

Jack Rosewitz of Sotheby's/Stephan Welz & Co. of Johannesburg, an expert on vintage vehicles, for identifying Margarete's car;

Count Hubertus Saurma-Jeltsch, a direct descendant of Count Samuel Teleki, for sharing historic material from his personal collection of photographs;

Anja Seela, The Ziegler Film Company, Berlin;

The late Professor Ilsa Scmidt-Ihms, head of the Department of German at the then University of Natal, South Africa, for her inspiration;

Louise Schweikerdt-Alker, dear friend of many years and enthusiast of Africa's history and wilderness areas, for unstinting assistance concerning the German language, her mother-tongue;

Petra Staab, The Ziegler Film Company, Berlin;

The late Harry Tennison, founder of Game Conservation International, for unforgettable conversations in his home in Fort Worth concerning his meeting with Margarete Trappe in Arusha in 1955;

Stephanie Thomas, Production Assistant for the Trappe documentary film by The

Ziegler Film Company, Berlin;

Emil Tudor, of The National Library of Romania, Bucharest, who shared very important, out-of-print material, available only in Romanian, from the National Library concerning Margarete Trappe and for his excellent translation of this material;

Charles Urio, former Head Guide of Hatari Lodge, for taking the author to Margarete's grave where he spoke of his family's memories of her;

Baroness Marissa von Firks, a great friend of the Trappe family, for permission to reproduce photographs;

Baron Christian von Lettow-Vorbeck of Düsseldorf, direct descendant of General Paul von Lettow-Vorbeck, and grandson of the noted German author Gerd von Lettow-Vorbeck, for permission to reproduce a historically important image of Margarete;

The late Ada Wincza for sharing her wonderful experiences concerning Margarete Trappe;

Gregor Woods, the noted authority on African hunting rifles, for permission to quote from his book *Rifles for Africa*;

And finally, Adelino Serras Pires, my husband, whose courageous spirit and lifelong experience in many African countries proved invaluable throughout the years it has taken to bring this project to fruition.

Cattle enclsures on Ngongongare in 1913. [Dr Jobst-Ulrich Trappe]

Margarete at home on Momella in the 1930s. [Baroness Marissa von Firks]

Author's Notes

The purpose of this book is to share with the Anglophone world for the first time the remarkable life of Margarete Trappe against the backdrop of German and British colonial Africa. The story spans fifty momentous years, from 1907 until mid-1957.

Germany's own 'scramble for Africa' is studied in order to better understand how her colony in East Africa came about, giving the reader a keener awareness of the era into which Margarete Trappe was born and the period during which she lived. The word 'discover' is avoided when speaking of European exploration in Africa. Europeans documented for the literate, scientific outside world what the indigenous peoples of the continent had already known for generations immemorial concerning geographic features, wildlife and its habitat.

The focus of the book is the pioneering life of a young woman who lived through two world wars, raised a family in the very heart of uncontaminated African wilderness and forged a reputation as one of the most remarkable women of 20th century colonial Africa. Farmer, equestrienne, livestock breeder, skilled amateur veterinarian, healer of humans, transport rider and intelligence operative during the First World War, formidable first full-time professional big game huntress in Africa, photographic and eco-safari leader, and protagonist of goodwill among the tribal peoples of her African home, Margarete Trappe gained legendary status during her extraordinary lifetime.

Any debate about the colonial era as such is the preserve of scholarly works. Every effort has been made, however, to give a balanced picture of the Africa Margarete knew and of the ways in which she strove to survive. History is what it is and not what one would like it to have been.

Margarete Trappe and Colonel August von Spiess, retired Chief Hunt Master to the Royal Court of Romania, with the Colonel's buffalo, taken on an extensive big game safari shortly before the outbreak of the Second World War. [Emil Tudor, The National Library of Romania]

Foreword

Brooke Chilvers Lubin

L'Isle Adam, France, September 2011

"The minute we laid eyes on each other, we knew we were going to be the best of friends!" wrote American folksinger Emily Lou Harris about one of her pals. And so it was with Fiona Claire Capstick and me, despite our first conversation being amid the din of a safari convention floor rather than around a campfire in the company of hunters or while digging through dusty bookshelves, looking for a treasured tome about Africa.

But whenever and wherever our minds meet, the same parts of our brains light up. Both multi-lingual, both passionate readers and travellers, both daughters of strong, busy, single mothers (and unforgivably absent fathers), both enraptured with European culture as girls and with wild places as women, both married to professional hunters, both authors, we strive to capture the spirit of Africa's places and the soul of its people, whether yesterday's or today's.

But Fiona's energy and excellence have taken her much further with three important books on Africa: *The Winds of Havoc, A Memoir of Adventure and Destruction in Deepest Africa*, written with her second husband, Adelino Serras Pires, safari pioneer in Mozambique and beyond; *The Diana Files: The Huntress/Traveller Through History*, for which she was awarded the CIC Literary Prize in 2005; and now, *Between Two Fires, The African Saga of Margarete Trappe*.

But let me tell you Fiona's saga first.

Her very horsey/hunt-country, High Church of England mother came out to South Africa in 1939 for a holiday with *her* best of friends, the then lady-in-waiting to the wife of the Governor-General of South Africa. There she met and married a debonair, wealthy, Irish Catholic playboy. He soon drifted away, as playboys do, at the world's worst of times, just two months before Fiona's startlingly blue-green eyes first saw light in Durban, Natal on November 3, 1945 – Saint Hubert's Day. The hunters' Patron Saint must have inscribed something on his heavenly agenda that day, for he surely has played a role in directing her destiny.

If Fiona's first words and thoughts were in her nanny's Zulu, they were followed by studies and degrees in English, French, Afrikaans and German, and a post-graduate teaching diploma for high school education. She added Italian and Spanish while continuing her studies at various universities in South Africa and abroad.

After teaching modern languages in private schools in South Africa, Fiona did para-diplomatic/public relations work, refining her skills as an interpreter. Soon she was recruited by the then South African Defence Force and seconded to Military Intelligence

Elephant
[Marlies and Jörg Gabriel]

as a translator and interpreter, holding the rank of Major in the Army! Today, she is admitted to the High Court of South Africa as a very active sworn translator in five languages.

No wonder she was so appealing to the appealing Mr. Peter Hathaway Capstick, whom she met in 1981 in the hunting grounds close to the Mozambican border. "That brief meeting in the bush changed my life forever," tells Fiona. They married, she learned all about hunting, and when Peter died in 1996, she inherited his fine library of Africana, and likely read it all.

My role in her providence began with my review of *The Diana Files* for *African Sporting Gazette* in 2004, commenting that the chapter on the life of the most remarkable huntress and courageous white lady in Africa's colonial history – Margarete Trappe – deserved being expanded into a book of its own. Fiona had first absorbed the outlines of this extraordinary life story during her friendship with East African safari pioneer and Polish huntress Ada Wincza, who had known Margarete until her death in 1957.

Two years later, while on my own pilgrimage to the sacred grounds of Momella and

Hippo
[Marlies and Jörg Gabriel]

Mount Meru and what was once part of Margarete Trappe's magnificent estate, girl-talk with Hatari Lodge's Marlies Gabriel led to my recommending that Fiona be contacted by Bernd Reufels of the Ziegler Film Company in Berlin, whose plans for a two-part documentary on Trappe's exceptional life were already well underway.

Ziegler flew Fiona up to Arusha – on her St. Hubert birthday in 2006. There, while taking part in the documentary being made in the foothills of Mount Meru, she gazed at Kilimanjaro and visited Margarete's grave to pay her respects to a woman of singular courage and accomplishment, whose story she is telling for the first time in English.

After Margarete's 1928 divorce, she became the first full-time professional huntress in Africa, guiding the cream of European aristocracy in Tanganyika, developing a formidable reputation for her hunting skills and knowledge of wildlife. She suffered through the hardest knocks of nature and war, farming, breeding, training and nursing horses and raising her children with the devoted assistance of her beloved sister Tine. Revered by her African workforce and safari staff who stuck by her through terrible times, esteemed by German and British soldiers alike for her veterinary and hunting skills, and greatly valued by General Paul von Lettow-Vorbeck for whom she carried out intelligence missions during the First World War, few white males on African soil can claim to be her equal.

The sustained assistance and advice of Margarete Trappe's grandsons – Dr Jobst-Ulrich Trappe in Germany and Professor Emil Karafiat in Switzerland – proved invaluable as Fiona dug into the facts and heart of 'the little lady', as she was known.

Margarete Trappe is an example of intelligence, excellence, endurance and courage, whose faith and kindness remained despite incomprehensible repeated losses through two World Wars played out on the game and farm fields of Africa. She deserves our respect and admiration, and Fiona's own gifts have done them both right on every page.

I am honoured to have played my part in Saint Hubert's plans for bringing about this important book.

Dr Jobst-Ulrich Trappe

Preface

Jobst-Ulrich Trappe

Meinerzhagen, Germany, September 2011

Ngongongare, Momella, Tanganyika – these resonant words as well as stories about my grandmother have accompanied me since my earliest childhood and have become part of my family identity. Although Margarete had already left on her last great safari by the time of my birth, my father succeeded in instilling her presence in my innermost world.

I often sensed her proximity when hunting and also in my professional life. I had the following experience as a young student of veterinary science: the examination in 'general agricultural science' was being held by a professor whom the students thought thoroughly unpleasant. As our examination group entered and my name was called, the professor asked if I knew of Margarete Trappe. I replied that she was my grandmother.

The professor's stern expression relaxed into a friendly smile and he said: "Do you actually know where I shot my first oryx?"….. We all enjoyed a very pleasant and successful examination! I remember feeling at the time an unbelievable surge of pride in my grandmother.

I have had many similar experiences down the years with people who had known Margarete personally or who had become acquainted with her through books and newspaper articles. Even in 1985, when I participated in a *rinderpest* vaccination campaign in Tanzania, people came up to me time after time, welcoming me and asking after the family. I never heard a single negative or critical comment about my grandmother.

Margarete's positive work is the only explanation for how she managed to fulfil her dream. Against every imaginable impediment, she created a paradise on the slopes of Mount Meru over a period of fifty years and through two world wars.

A letter that Margarete wrote in December 1946 during difficult times to 'My dearest darlings' ends with the words:

> 'Never lose your faith in God's righteousness. Always remain my devoted children and God grant that you regain all your cheerfulness and sense of humour that help one pull through so much.'

Margarete with her granddaughter Yvonne. [Emil Karafiat]

Prelude

"Mrs Trappe, you are to collect some extra clothing and get into the police vehicle. As British Custodian of Enemy Property I am authorised to order you off this land with immediate effect. It is no longer yours. You are to be interned indefinitely at the Shinyanga Internment Camp in Central Province. Do not enter the house alone. I shall accompany you."

October 1940. Tanganyika. The renowned Trappe estate in the foothills of Mount Meru, with Mount Kilimanjaro looking on. The petite woman of German origin felt dazed, but unsurprised as she saw the entrance to her farmhouse blocked by the vehicle and the British official. In a mere five months she had witnessed at intervals how both her sons, her daughter and sister had been summarily detained and sent off to internment camps. She knew she would be next. The only thing saving her remaining child was her age. Rosie was still at boarding school in nearby Arusha, where her mother had collapsed with nervous exhaustion just days previously. The stiff British official with his crisp orders barricaded the steps leading up to her front door, drumming his fingers all the while on the official document.

Margarete Trappe, still feeling weak but now filled with rage and scorn, refused to enter her own home like some sort of criminal. She refused to pick out clothes and go through all her personal things, watched by this police officer. No, she would simply get into the police vehicle with the bare essentials she had taken with her to see her daughter in Arusha.

Scenes of the last thirty-three years cut into her numbed mind like bits of jagged glass. There she was, with her husband Ulrich, arriving by boat that hot January dawn so long ago, her world plump with happiness and hope as they entered a new life. Decades followed, punctuated by triumph and loss and the birth of four children. She recalled the exhilaration of riding and hunting over vast regions of that wildly beautiful country, of enjoying the goodwill and support of the tribal peoples and of surviving the First World War. Memories of being forced into exile and the years of deprivation and separation from her children sliced into her thoughts as did her return to her ruined home, asphyxiated by debt not of her making. Gradual recovery and peace. Now this.

As the police vehicle prepared to move off, two of Margarete's dogs leapt in beside her and were allowed to stay with her. They were not considered important enough to be impounded as enemy property. The farm employees stared, silent and unseeing, as the person they called *Yeyo* – Mother in the Maasai language – was taken away from them. They too had seen her sister, sons and a daughter all taken away like convicts. Why were the White people fighting one another again? What would happen to them and their families, to the cattle, the horses, the other livestock, the crops, the houses and everything else that was their world too? Who would help them now in times of hardship and ill health? What would happen to *Yeyo*? Who would help her now?

A new kind of silence descended as the sky went dark and the sun disappeared.

Margarete and Ulrich Trappe on board ship, bound for German East Africa, with one of their dogs, December 1906. [Dr Jobst-Ulrich Trappe]

PART ONE

"Bliss was it in that dawn to be alive
But to be young was very heaven!"

WILLIAM WORDSWORTH

Africa at Last

The young woman had been up before dawn as the boat came through the Zanzibar Channel and neared her destination, Dar es Salaam, in German East Africa. First light slid over the Indian Ocean, growing bolder as the young sun rose, the air becoming denser and more humid than anything she had ever experienced. The warm, salty atmosphere filled her lungs, thoughts of her now-distant home in Silesia, far southeastern Germany, with its interminable winters melting away as the coastline drew closer. One memory remained and it had propelled her to Africa: her late father's dream of taking her with him to travel and hunt in this land of many horizons and a profusion of wildlife.

Margarete, second from right, on board ship, December 1906. [Dr Jobst-Ulrich Trappe]

Clusters of rocky islets marked the approach to the harbour, coco palms and beaches becoming more distinct as the day grew stronger. A scattering of wooden dhows with their characteristic triangular sails could be seen hugging the coast, gulls lazing overhead in the morning sunlight. The lighthouse, perched on a coral outcrop, showed the way through a narrow entrance into the Abode of Peace. The long voyage from northern Germany, via the Strait of Gibraltar, across the Mediterranean, through the Suez Canal and Red Sea, round the Horn of Africa and down the east coast of the continent was over at last.

Aboard, the air was joyous with expectation and energy as soldiers of the *Schutztruppe* – the Protection Forces – back from leave, prepared to disembark and resume their duties in the colony. Planters and their young families gathered on deck for last-minute conversations before heading off to their coffee, tea, sugar, sisal, cotton and rubber plantations. Prospective settlers looked about them, trying to absorb a thousand new impulses as they made their way towards the gangplank and down onto the quayside. A small group of obviously important people disembarked first. The men had the bearing of high-ranking colonial officials used to deference. The women, finely dressed, exuded the pride of their station in life.

A band of *Schutztruppe* officers, sprucely turned out in white uniforms, were standing to attention on the wharf, their brass instruments gleaming in the morning sun. The bandmaster took charge and the men struck up with familiar martial music from the home

The Zehe estate in Petersdorf, Silesia where Margarete learned to ride and hunt with her father. [Yorck-Michael Trappe]

country, brightening the atmosphere and spreading a sense of well-being and optimism. It was infectious. Black workers in khaki, calling to one another in Kiswahili, moved about with purpose as they helped passengers with their luggage and saw to the many tasks that made the port function efficiently. Whenever the *Deutsch-Ostafrika Linie* boats docked twice a month, the harbour and town took on fresh vigour as first-timers arrived, news from home came in, people reconnected and fresh supplies of all kinds were unloaded. Two-wheeled rickshaws moved about, conveying people and their possessions out of the harbour area to their accommodation.

The petite, dark-haired woman, Margarete, was joined by her husband Ulrich as they made their way off the boat to the Customs House, both of them absorbed by the light, heat, space and sounds of this new world. Awaiting them was a family friend who had inspired the young couple to come out to the colony and explore opportunities for a new life.

Ulrich Trappe, who came of a family steeped in military tradition, was a Lieutenant in the Silesian Von Podbielski mounted artillery regiment when he started courting Margarete. She accepted his marriage proposal on condition that he request a transfer from his regiment to the *Schutztruppe* in German East Africa so that they could settle in the colony.

From early childhood and throughout her youth, Margarete learned about the natural world from her father who taught her deep respect for it, in keeping with the entrenched hunting and conservation traditions of the German people. She developed great skill at arms as they rode, hunted and wingshot together in the countryside around the family's Petersdorf estate in Silesia. The young girl also acquired a profound love of dogs that would endure throughout her life. Karl Zehe would share his dream with Margarete, namely of going out to German East Africa to hunt and explore, to live and rejoice. It was the time of German Empire when all seemed possible. Letters from friends who had settled in the colony and official publications full of buoyant events fed this desire to go out to Africa.

Her father's untimely death in 1901 was a particularly cruel blow for Margarete. She was

Margarete in the middle with her three sisters and brother. [Yorck-Michael Trappe]

only seventeen years old at the time, but she clung to her father's dream as if he were still alive. Nobody else in her immediate family shared that dream of Africa. When her mother, now widowed, moved some distance away with her four daughters and toddler son to the Silesian town of Sagan, the world Margarete had shared with her father disappeared as well. Fate, however, placed the young woman in the very town where troops were recruited for German East Africa. It was there that she met her future husband.

Ulrich Trappe, seeing his fiancée's iron resolve to go out to Africa, eventually resigned his commission and decided to seek the couple's fortune through farming. A transfer to the *Schutztruppe* could have meant a five-year delay and Margarete was not about to defer her dreams of Africa any longer for the sake of a wedding band. She was already twenty-three years old. The laws of the day were rigid enough concerning couples wishing to emigrate to the colonies. A single woman was at the back of the queue. The same legal and social norms of the day had prohibited Margarete from studying veterinary science, thereby crushing one of her major early ambitions in life. She was not about to see the bloom of her youth dissipate and then disappear while she waited for the military to make up its mind. Margarete's indomitable character would antagonise and intimidate. It would overshadow many who crossed her path. It would also be her salvation in Africa.

The colonial authorities were keen to attract young and industrious people to develop the largest of their four African colonies at a time of quite considerable German emigration, especially to the United States of America. In fact over 6 000 000 Germans emigrated to that country between 1848 and the outbreak of the First World War. In order

Margarete in 1905. [Yorck-Michael Trappe]

Sagan. Frühere Bober-Brücke, gen. Sorauer Brücke,
an deren Stelle im Jahre 1881 die Kaiser Wilhelm-Brücke erbaut wurde.

A. Menzel, Sagan

A historic postcard of Sagan in Silesia where Margarete met and married Ulrich Trappe. [Yorck-Michael Trappe

to encourage emigration to German East Africa, favourable conditions were offered prospective emigrants to acquire land and basic necessities to start cultivation. In many instances, however, no land could be purchased outright until the new farmers had started cultivation and given proof of ability and endurance. Margarete was free of that initial financial stricture because she had received her inheritance from her father's estate. The couple set sail from Hamburg in January 1907. They were young and they were filled with expectation and zeal as they left the north European winter behind them and headed for the African tropics.

First Impressions

First impressions of Dar es Salaam were indeed more favourable than the Trappe couple had expected. The small town boasted a fine esplanade. Beyond the harbour, handsome government buildings rose, some with wooden balconies, their whitewashed walls and red roofs set amid broad, immaculate avenues. The Colony's Governor, Baron Albrecht von Rechenberg, who had recently succeeded Count Gustav von Götzen, resided in a double-storied residence whose huge verandah with its high white colonnades and archways overlooked luxurious gardens and the Indian Ocean. An open carriage drawn by a pair of perfectly matched chestnut horses, groomed until they gleamed like their burnished harnesses, could often be seen entering or leaving the grounds, proudly conveying visiting dignitaries. Indian attendants, resplendent in scarlet turbans and sashes over white tunics, drove the carriage.

To the left of the official residence were the botanical gardens, originally laid out in 1893, where many different kinds of palm trees and exotic cycads flourished. Close by lay the hospital where pioneering work concerning the fight against malaria, the scourge of Africa, was being undertaken. The Lutheran church with its stucco steeple was instantly recognizable on the

Left — Margarete and Ulrich Trappe on their wedding day.
[Yorck-Michael Trappe]

shoreline, as was the impressive cathedral nearby. Between the churches was the mission house of the White Fathers Order that had served as a harem in the 1860s during the rule of Zanzibar's Sultan Majid.

The sense of order, purpose and development was all the more enhanced by the shops and cafés along the pristine streets, graced by flamboyant trees now in full bloom. The Biergarten was another feature from the home country as were the clubs where the settlers could meet and relax away from the heat of day. Spacious private homes with their tropical gardens, the open spaces and surprisingly good roads spoke of industriousness and dedication. Statues of the Kaiser and of the Prussian Prince Otto von Bismarck, the 'Iron Chancellor' and founder of the German Empire, and the large building of the German East Africa Company indicated that the Germans were no mere birds of passage, but were determined settlers with long-term plans in place to develop the country and thrive. As Charles Miller expressed it in his *Battle for the Bundu: The First World War in East Africa* (London: Purnell Book Services Limited, 1974.) on page 22:

> 'Dar as Salaam was the showcase city of all tropical Africa. Any other colonial capital, even Britain's fast-growing Nairobi to the north, was a shantytown by comparison.'

Imperial Germany, under Kaiser Wilhelm II and the black, white and red flag, assumed control by 1891 of 994 996km² (384 170 square miles), heralding the birth of the German East African Protectorate. It shared boundaries with British, Portuguese and Belgian possessions, stretching from the Rovuma River boundary in the south with Portuguese East Africa, northwards to the cutline with British East Africa, westwards from the lengthy coastline to the eastern flank of the Congo basin and the kingdoms of Ruanda and Burundi that were incorporated by the Germans into Ruanda-Urundi. Part of Lake Tanganyika in the far north and of Lake Nyasa in the southwest also came under German rule. A stupendous coastline, the highest mountain in Africa, lush forests, mighty rivers, arid expanses, vast plains of thorn and scrub, limitless savannah grasslands and cool mountain recesses, ornithological and floral richness and an abundance of wildlife that beggared belief comprised the colony. It had it all.

Construction of a railway, begun in 1905, had already progressed from Dar es Salaam for about 260 kms (almost 162 miles) inland to Morogoro in the central part of the country by the time the Trappes had arrived. The ultimate goal was Kigomo on Lake Tanganyika. Up north, flanking the Usambara Mountains on the border with British East

Africa, the first railway in the colony had already connected the port of Tanga with the nearby settlement of Korogwe in the west before turning north to another small settlement called Mombo. One day, it would go all the way up to Moshi in the bracing high country of Mount Meru and Mount Kilimanjaro, linking the cotton, sisal, coffee, rubber and tobacco plantations with the coast.

On the outskirts of Dar es Salaam were the native quarters, surprisingly well laid out and clean, exhibiting order and thorough planning. The houses were made of mud and wattle with roofs of palm leaves. Many had verandahs and there were even whitewashed or painted homesteads, some built of stone, standing out against the luxuriant vegetation and palm trees. A patchwork of shambas or small plots of agricultural land flanked the area where maize, cassava and other vegetables were cultivated, supplementing the abundant diet of fish and fruit. Goats and poultry could be seen among the shambas, as could scrawny village curs with their yellow eyes and grubby coats. Women wearing kangas, brightly coloured cotton wraps, were working the fields while their menfolk sat in the shade of coconut palms, smoking and conversing at leisure in Kiswahili.

The Swahili Culture

Margarete had begun learning basic Kiswahili before leaving Germany. It would become her language of fluent habitual usage in her new home. In fact, the German missionaries Johann Ludwig Krapf and Johannes Rebmann had already translated the entire Bible into Kiswahili by 1853. Krapf's *Outline of the Elements of the KiSwahili Language*, published in 1850, became indispensable to generations of missionaries, explorers, settlers, traders and colonial administrators. The young woman recalled what she had read and been told about the Kiswahili-speaking people who predominated along the East African coastline adjacent to Zanzibar as well as on the other off-shore island of Pemba, north of Zanzibar and on Mafia Island and the Kilwa Archipelago in the south. The name *Swahili*, as Margarete discovered, was derived from the Arabic word *sawahil* meaning 'belonging to the coasts'.

The Swahilis were descended from Muslim merchant-mariners of southern Arabia and from the Shirazi people of southwestern Persia who frequented the East African coastline during the golden age of Arab exploration between the ninth and fourteenth centuries. There had been interaction well before that with merchant-mariners going back to Greek, Roman and Phoenician times and subsequent contact with peoples from China, Ethiopia, India, Indonesia, Malaysia, Oman, Persia and the Persian Gulf. The Arabs and the Shirazi traded and mingled with the coastal-dwelling Bantu peoples, giving rise to the Swahili culture and language through conversion to Islam and inter-marriage. The mosques and the emblem of the crescent moon as well as the dress code of head coverings and flowing robes were strong reminders to the newly arrived Germans of this millennia-old heritage.

Kiswahili was a language that eventually emerged from this fusion of cultures, incorporating large swathes of Arabic, Farsi, Bantu languages, Portuguese and Gujerati. It became the lingua franca throughout East and Central Africa, evolving with the Arab-dominated slaving caravans as they trawled the region for human merchandise and for ivory, the white gold currency of the age. The very word safari is derived from the Arabic word *safara*, meaning to travel or set out. This gave rise to the word *safari*, meaning a journey. The literature of exploration and hunting, anchored in the African colonial era, led to this word's becoming part of the standard English lexicon and, indeed, of all major

West European languages.

The Swahili people, alongside the Arab, European and Indian communities, and the accompanying animist, Muslim, Christian, Hindu and Jainist beliefs, illustrated the richly diverse world the Trappe couple had entered. The Portuguese had ruled over much of the East African coastline in the early 16th century. During the 19th century, a series of European explorers and missionaries, among them Germans, conducted extensive exploration in East Africa in particular, resulting in Germany's eventual 'Scramble for Africa' and the birth of German East Africa.

Germany's Scramble for Africa

Germany was a relative latecomer to the European party that sliced up and shared out the African continent like a *'magnifique gâteau africain'* [a magnificent African cake] to quote King Leopold II of the Belgians in November 1877. The Belgian King triggered the 'Scramble for Africa' when he finally obtained international approval in May 1885 for the creation of the Congo Free State, his personal fiefdom. This gave the Belgian King complete dominion over the region's fabulous resources and some ten million inhabitants. His imperialist ambitions were unmatched at the time as, indeed, was the subsequent barbarity of his regime.

David Livingstone, the Victorian era's iconic explorer-missionary, traversed Africa between 1841 and 1873 in a series of expeditions during which he exposed the slave trade to ordinary Europeans and set in motion an international movement to fight for its abolition. His writings also ignited widespread general interest in the 'Dark Continent', especially in Victorian Britain.

In East Africa, Zanzibar was the main clearing house for slaves and ivory under the Omani sultans who, for generations, had controlled the island, the neighbouring islands, the adjacent coastline and immense regions inland as far as Lake Tanganyika. Zanzibar or *Zayn Z'al Barr* – meaning 'fair is this land' in all its exquisite irony – was also the principal starting point of major European exploration expeditions into an unknown interior. Richard Burton and John Hanning Speke became the first Europeans to enter the East African interior when they left Zanzibar in 1857, crossing over into the mainland to find the source of the Nile River.

Henry Morton Stanley's epoch-making meeting with Livingstone at the slave depot in Ujiji, on the banks of Lake Tanganyika in November 1871 fuelled further interest in eastern and central Africa. Subsequent major expeditions followed. Verney Lovett Cameron became the first man documented to have crossed Africa from the slaving port of Bagamoyo, just north of Dar es Salaam, to the coast of Portuguese West Africa, arriving near Benguela in November 1875. It had taken him over two years and eight months.

The Cameron triumph led to what was termed a 'Geographical Conference' at the Royal Palace in Brussels in September 1876. The Germans were represented by Baron Von Richthofen. Word was out about the extraordinary riches and potential of the African hinterland for the Europeans. The formation of the International African Association arose out of the conference.

From then on Africa became the focal point of European ambition through a series of expeditions. German merchants, in the meantime, had established a presence at a place called *Angra Pequena* [small bay] – today's Lüderitz in the Republic of Namibia – on the southwest African coast. Bismarck annexed the territory in April 1884, inflaming the British. The fight was on for a slice of the African cake.

Portugal, already an established presence in Africa since the 15th century, proposed that an international conference be held to find a solution to the Congo issue that was on the boil. Bismarck stepped in smartly and offered to host the conference in Berlin in order to thwart any attempt by the Portuguese or the British to set the agenda. Thirteen European countries joined the Germans when the conference opened on 15 November 1884. On 25 February 1885, the Berlin Act was signed, recognizing King Leopold's sovereignty over the vast Congo basin and heralding the final stages of the European scramble for Africa. Germany entered these last frenzied days of empire-building, initiated under Kaiser Wilhelm I and the authoritarian, militaristic mindset of his time. Economic power, political rivalry, national prestige and capitalism all combined to feed European imperialism and, with this, the desire for territorial expansion and colonisation.

German Missionaries and Explorers in East Africa

Johann Ludwig Krapf settled in Mombasa in 1844 and became the pioneer Christian evangelist of East Africa. He produced his classic book on the Swahili language in 1850. Johannes Rebmann, a fellow German missionary, had already joined Krapf in 1846. Both men began planning expeditions into the far interior – *terra incognita* – to spread the gospel and explore.

On 11 May 1848, Rebmann became the first European to see the 5 891.6 metres (19 329.16 feet) snow-capped Mount Kilimanjaro, straddling the equator, and to document it for European science, only to be greeted by incredulity and derision. Krapf witnessed the same extraordinary scene in November 1849 and confirmed his colleague's testimony, but was also ridiculed by pillars of the Royal Geographical Society in London. Time would eventually vindicate both men.

In 1862, Baron Karl Klaus von der Decken managed to map the Kilimanjaro region, even climbing up to just below the snowline at 4 267.25 metres (14 000 feet). He was also the first European to record a sighting of the 4 558 metre (14 954 feet) Mount Meru that year, followed by fellow-German, Gustav Fischer, in 1882. These events gave further impetus to European curiosity about East Africa and saw a major British expedition enter the same region in 1883, led by Joseph Thomson of *Through Masai Land* fame. He was followed by the Austro-Hungarian, Count Samuel Teleki, in 1887.

Emin Pasha, one of the most enigmatic and brilliant personalities in the colonial age of African exploration, was born Eduard Schnitzer in Silesia, Germany. A medical doctor by training, his extraordinary life saw him succeed General Charles Gordon in 1878 as Governor of Equatoria Province in Sudan. There, he earned the soubriquet 'a second Gordon of Khartoum' because of the way in which he and his 4 000 loyal troops held out until 1889 against the stringently Islamic Mahdist forces. Schnitzer eventually entered the service of German East Africa in 1890.

That year, he and Franz Ludwig Stuhlmann, a naturalist and zoologist, led an ambitious expedition out of Bagamoyo to Lakes Albert and Victoria in the interior. The purpose was 'to secure on behalf of Germany the territories situated south of and along Victoria Nyanza up to Albert Nyanza' and to place the local populations 'under German supremacy and protection, and to break or undermine Arab influence as far as possible'. Political decisions by Britain and Germany that same year nullified this purpose and Schnitzer subsequently disappeared, reliably reported as having been murdered in the Belgian Congo in late October 1892.

Dr Oscar Baumann, a geographer and hunter, led an expedition between 1890 and 1892 into the interior of what became German East Africa. He was the first European to document the existence of Lakes Eyasi, Manyara and Ndutu. He was also the first European to enter the Serengeti region in 1882 and record the existence of the spellbinding Ngorongoro Crater. It was not until 1901, however, that the first European ascended Mount Meru. While there is still uncertainty as to whether the German, Carl Unlig, did so that year or whether it was his compatriot Professor Fritz Jäger in 1904, there was no doubt about the strong German association with this magical land.

Dr Hans Meyer, a German professor of geology, was the first European to reach the summit of Kilimanjaro. That was on 6 October 1889. His guide, without whom he would not have succeeded, was a Chagga youngster called Yohana Lauwo. The Wachagga were the dominant tribe of the Kilimanjaro region and were known for their prowess as elephant hunters. Until his death in 1996 at the astounding age of 125 years, Lauwo had spent a full 70 years leading expeditions up Kilimanjaro. He recalled Dr Meyer with clarity in advanced old age.

As for the presence of the other major European powers in the region, Belgium, Britain, France, Italy and Portugal all eventually had consular representatives on Zanzibar, as did Germany. The American diplomatic presence dated back to 1837. All the European powers were motivated by trade. Zanzibari trading caravans became synonymous with wealth as they ploughed inland to the lake region. The slave trade and ivory were the crux of this wealth that also saw firearms and ammunition being brought into the wild interior where the blizzard of tribal affiliations and concomitant rivalries posed a danger of their own to any outsider.

Dr Karl Peters and the Society for German Colonisation

Karl Peters was the founding father of German East Africa. He established the Company for German Colonisation [*Gesellschaft für Deutsche Kolonisation*] in 1884. On 17 February 1885, Chancellor Bismarck granted Peters an Imperial Charter, known as a *Schutzbrief*, to found a German Protectorate in East Africa. The Chancellor had already laid claim to Togoland, Cameroon and South-West Africa. This new protectorate, however, was the crown jewel in the German Imperial scheme of things.

Peters and a handful of assistants, among them military officers, then engaged in a relentless, bizarre and even sometimes officially unsanctioned

The notorious Karl Peters in the 1880s. [The Lunatic Express by Charles Miller, New York: The MacMillan Company, 1971. Photo by Culver Pictures Inc.]

campaign to extend the boundaries of the new Protectorate by having a series of chiefs and chieftains sign a rash of so-called treaties, especially in the Kilimanjaro region. In

August 1885, five German warships dropped anchor in the lagoon overlooking the Sultan of Zanzibar's palace to exert pressure and reinforce the German presence in the Sultan's empire. The Sultan succumbed and signed approval for the creation of a German Protectorate over almost half of his empire. The warships then set sail, mission accomplished.

The Anglo-German Treaty of 1886 resulted in the partitioning of East Africa into an Anglo and a German 'sphere of influence', to quote Thomas Packenham in his celebrated book *The Scramble for Africa: The White Man's Conquest of the Dark Continent from 1876 to 1912* (New York: Random House, 1991). The Germans gained Mount Kilimanjaro in the process, the border forming a bulge with British East Africa to accommodate the world's highest free-standing mountain and Africa's highest. Queen Victoria, according to a long-standing popular myth, was reputed to have given Mount Kilimanjaro to her grandson, the future Kaiser Wilhelm II, as a birthday present. Modern scholarship repudiates this in its entirety as a fanciful story, but it is one that is still circulating. The actual reason for the kink in the border cutline was to ensure that the deepwater port of Mombasa remained firmly in British hands.

By 1891, under Kaiser Wilhelm II, the German East African Protectorate came into formal existence, its capital first at Bagamoyo for a brief period before being established in Dar es Salaam, just to the south. Dr Peters was appointed Imperial Commissioner for German East Africa in 1891, his less than clear activities notwithstanding.

These are the bare bones of an intricate, lengthy process that lies outside the scope of this book. The foregoing also gives the barest of details concerning Dr Peters. As colonial records and subsequent research have revealed, Dr Peters was a man of ferocious cruelty. Known in Kiswahili as *mkono-wa-damu* [the hand of blood] this puny little academic with his pince-nez and stiffly waxed moustache had indulged in an orgy of ruthless 'treaty-making' with one chief after another as they signed over their land to the Kaiser. He had maltreated and killed an unknown number of people, also sanctioning the killing of women as he forged his bloody way over the East African hinterland.

His monstrous behaviour saw him appear in court in 1897 and be dismissed from the German colonial service without a pension. In late 1906, literally a few weeks before the Trappes sailed out of Hamburg harbour, more scandals erupted around the disgraced Dr Peters' head. Atrocities directly linked to him had also occurred in the Mount Kilimanjaro region where the Trappes were headed. The image of the *Wazungu* – the White people – had become associated with suffering and death in the minds of many of the tribal peoples because of Dr Peters and some of his contemporaries.

As this young couple made last-minute preparations for a journey that would change their lives irrevocably, they were aware of the dangers in the country where they hoped to make their new life together. There had been several bloody uprisings against the Germans and it is useful to take a glance at some of these occurrences in order to better understand the world where the Trappes intended settling. It had not been a quiet neighbourhood.

Popular Uprisings

Disenchantment with the German rulers had been simmering since the mid-1880s. There had been formidable resistance to German rule from 1891 by the equally formidable Wahehe tribe in the central region until their leader's suicide in 1898. In the meantime, a sugar-plantation and slave-owner called Abushiri ibn Salim al-Harthi, of

Arab-Ethiopian descent, led a rebellion between 1888 and 1890 by Arabs and local tribes against the Germans. This became known as the Abushiri Rebellion or the Arab Revolt. It was triggered after the Germans had concluded an agreement with the Sultan of Zanzibar to lease the entire coast from the Kilwa Archipelago in the south to Tanga in the far north and to take over all administrative matters on behalf of the Sultan who expected a percentage of the takings. The German East African Company was an increasing threat to the dominance of the Arab traders on the East African coastline.

This resulted in heavy taxation, ever more determined efforts to abolish the slave trade, disregard for local customs and sensitivities and other hardships that ignited deep resentment among the Swahilis in particular. A feeling of having been betrayed by the Sultan, of having been handed over to the Germans, took hold. Anger and humiliation spread like a mediaeval plague into the interior where the tribal peoples joined Abushiri in a revolt aimed at encouraging all the coastal settlements and towns to rise up against the Germans. Many fled their posts as some 20 000 men of all factions and many tribes ran amok screaming "Death to all Europeans!" The revolt eventually died out by May 1889 in the face of superior firepower and a joint British/German naval blockade to starve Abushiri and his men of guns and ammunition.

Commandant Hermann von Wissmann, a celebrated explorer who had twice crossed Africa between 1880 and 1887, had been ordered by Chancellor Von Bismarck to crush the revolt. He arrived in the territory with sixty European officers and about one thousand excellently trained African troops. Most of them were from Sudan, from Emin Pasha's forces, including Turks. A mixture of Swahilis, Somalis, Blacks recruited in Portuguese East Africa and even Zulus from South Africa were also under arms. This was the genesis of the Imperial Commissioner's Forces or *Wissmanntruppe*, the military forerunner of the Kaiser's Protection Forces for German East Africa, the *Schutztruppe*.

The Maji Maji Rebellion

More trouble was brewing. In August 1905, about 200 kilometres south of Dar es Salaam, in the Matumbi hill country, violence erupted over official policies of forced labour to cultivate cotton. Wages were often derisory or even absent and the work was tough as official demands for more labour and more cotton escalated. The cotton scheme also went against tribal customs in the south where the people had no tradition of working on communal lands. Each household lived independently as far as agricultural work was concerned yet the cotton fields under the German rulers were strictly communal in their organisation.

It is also a matter of record that Arabs and Swahilis, known as *akidas*, and employed by the Germans to enforce the hut taxation and help run this communal commercial farming scheme, were ever ready with the whip to lash the tribal workers on the government cotton plantations. The southeast of the country in general was still the domain of the Arabs and the Swahilis. They were corrupt and they were brutal towards the tribal peoples forced into the cotton scheme. Dissatisfaction spread and turned into open rebellion in southern and central German East Africa. A prophet in the region, revered for his powers, created a cult following among the masses when he convinced them that his medicine – millet seed mixed with castor oil and water (*maji* in Kiswahili) – would turn German bullets into just that, water. The message was one of uniting the people across tribal lines and of driving the Germans out of the country.

When the call to war came the Germans were taken by surprise. Civilians were murdered, military patrols ambushed and killed and German garrisons burned to the ground. Even the capture and hanging of the prophet did not stop the rebellion. The spreading revolt took on all the appearances of a guerrilla war as German outposts and supply lines were sabotaged, five missionaries were murdered and an Asian trading post attacked. German reinforcements were called in, but the situation worsened.

Unable to quash the rebellion by military means alone, the Germans resorted to a scorched earth policy that saw villages burned to the ground and food supplies destroyed. Leaders and any suspected collaborators were shot or hanged as the people in their tens of thousands succumbed through disease and starvation. By the end of the rebellion in the latter part of 1907, an estimated one third of the population in the central and southern regions had died. Recent scholarship estimates that anywhere between 250 000 and 300 000 people perished.

Between 1890 and the outbreak of World War I in 1914, there were sporadic outbreaks of armed resistance against the German colonists in the interior regions. It is a matter of record that the Germans were able to put down these mini-revolts by deploying African *askaris* from rival tribes.

Cattle Plague

The Trappe couple, intent on creating a new life in Africa as farmers and livestock owners, were aware of the super contagious viral 'cattle plague' – commonly known by its German name *rinderpest* – that had killed between 90% and 95% of all cattle in Africa between 1889 and the early 1900s. Believed to have come to Africa from South-East Asia, it first took hold in British Somaliland in the far northeast, a favoured big game hunting destination and a key port of call for all ships on the long voyage to India, the jewel in the British colonial crown. The plague quickly spread next door into Ethiopia and then on to Sudan and East Africa. By 1896, it had raced into West Africa and southwards through Central Africa into Bechuanaland – today's Botswana – before infecting South Africa at the very foot of the continent. This was the greatest natural disaster ever to strike Africa.

Rinderpest destroyed the most potent symbol of wealth, authority and status in Africa – cattle. Sheep and goats were also not spared, while vast herds of cloven-hoofed animals such as buffalo, all kinds of antelope, giraffe, eland and bush pigs were wiped out. Written testimony exists concerning German East Africa in 1891 where the majority of the famed Maasai people, a nomadic pastoralist people straddling the northern region and neighbouring British East Africa, died as a direct consequence of the *rinderpest*. Cattle constituted the Maasai universe. They believed that all cattle anywhere belonged to them by divine ordinance, The Maasai diet consisted of blood, milk and, upon occasion, meat from their cattle. Nothing was wasted. The hides provided clothing and material for a host of other uses. To lose their cattle to this unknown plague was to lose life itself for they did not touch fish, birds or game.

Human populations were decimated as the cattle plague destroyed a vital ecological balance. Sleeping sickness, always endemic, spread beyond its usual range, mutating into an epidemic. Survivors migrated internally and once flourishing cattle country reverted to tsetse-infested bush, the domain of wild animals. C.G. Schillings, the noted German writer, hunter and pioneering wildlife photographer, recorded in his book In *Wildest Africa* (London: Hutchinson & Co., 1907) on page 12:

'I have often found lying together, in one narrow space, the countless white bleached bones of the cattle and the skull of their former owner.'

The only creatures that rejoiced in this landscape of death were the satiated vultures. Centuries of slavery and all that this horror entailed, drought, disease, revolt and massive loss of human and animal life had scarred the world into which the Trappes were now moving.

Such had been the public outcry back in Germany about the various uprisings in German East Africa and about reports of abuse inflicted on the indigenous peoples that new policies were instituted in 1906 under the new Governor, Baron Georg Albrecht von Rechenburg, in a genuine effort to restore calm and seek a more just way forward. In 1907, the *Reichs Kolonialamt* or Imperial Colonial Office was established to facilitate German emigration to the African colonies. Civilian colonial rule replaced military rule in German East Africa and revised policies of governance were established.

While not remotely denying the overt European imperial ambitions of that age or the feudal-like relationship between the Germans and the tribal peoples, Von Rechenburg nevertheless heralded a period of vigorous reform, economic expansion and sincere initiatives to provide for the welfare and education of the indigenous peoples. They were also encouraged and assisted to grow and market cash crops for which guaranteed prices were paid. In the context of colonial Africa over a century ago, these reforms were unprecedented.

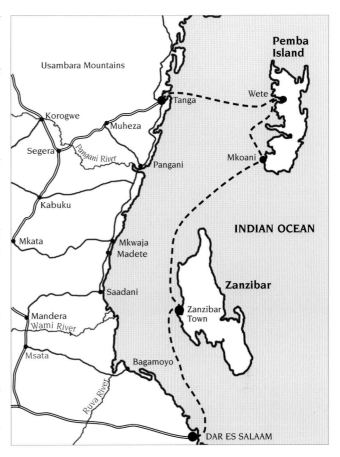

The route the Trappes sailed from Dar es Salaam to Tanga in January 1907.

The new Governor also oversaw the enforcement of measures to curb racially oppressive acts.

Unpaid forced labour became a criminal offence and the wanton expropriation of tribal lands by white settlers was now curtailed by new land laws. Roads, railways, schools, hospitals and clinics as well as boosted agricultural development ensued. Missionary activity increased and, with it, greater access by the tribal peoples to education and medical care, however rudimentary.

The Imperial Government also expanded education for the indigenous population from primary school level to post-school vocational education. In fact, the record shows that German East Africa's progress in all spheres under Governor Von Rechenburg, whatever the failings of the system, was matched with difficulty elsewhere in colonial Africa at that time. Von Rechenburg's successor, Dr Heinrich Schnee, sustained these reforms which also saw the establishment of a biological agricultural research institute in the southern Usambara Mountains that the British themselves described as superior to anything in their vast colonial empire. The medical research into tropical diseases that was conducted in the colony resulted in new treatments that became standard therapies for sleeping sickness and tickbite fever wherever they occurred.

It was at this juncture in German East Africa's history that the Trappes prepared for their first African journey. Ahead lay a foot safari over hundreds of kilometres with a huge retinue of porters who would guide the couple into a region of such astonishing beauty and promise no letter or grainy monochrome photograph could possibly have conveyed.

Setting Out

Mangrove swamps and coral, set against dense bush, coco palms, mango trees and banana groves flirted with the steamer as it chugged up the coast to the port of Tanga in the far north. The Trappes had completed all formalities in Dar es Salaam as prospective settlers and had sought advice in supplementing their supplies before setting sail. The four-hour crossing to Zanzibar to pick up goods and passengers was now behind them and a fresh day lay ahead. Creeks and inlets, interspersed with river estu-

A caravan of ivory in Tanga. [from C.G. Schillings' book In Wildest Africa, London: Huthinson & Co., 1907]

aries, punctuated the shoreline as the fierce February heat and humidity bore down on the passengers that far-off day in 1907. The 'long rains', the *masika makubwa* – commonly referred to as the *masika* – of the Indian Ocean monsoon, were due by mid-March, bringing torrential downpours that could last for days at a time. Tracks would become muddy trenches and watercourses would be impassable on the route up into the high country, often delaying any plans for travel into the interior until after May.

The pear-shaped bay of Tanga finally came into view, the curious Toten Island – Death Island – with its stone ruins of Shirazi-Swahili mosques set just opposite the dock. The bay was flanked by mangroves and the distant plains with their sisal plantations leading into the foothills of the Usambara Mountains, the domain of the Wasambara tribe. The port, founded by Shirazi merchants from southwest Persia in the fourteenth century, was subsequently ruled by Omani sultans from the eighteenth century onwards.

Subtropical multi-coloured croton shrubs with their glossy green, white, yellow, pink, russet and crimson leaves as well as a profusion of lime trees dressed up the settlement under the baking sun. The German Governor's neo-gothic residence dominated the spruce settlement with its whitewashed buildings and the clock tower that overlooked the bay. On most days, an *askari* brass band, smartly turned out in uniform, played vibrant martial music, gaining a degree of fame during German colonial times.

The port's luxuriant beauty belied its recent past: it had served for centuries as an important clearing house for slaves and ivory for onward shipment to Zanzibar. Slave-trafficking in East Africa only ended in the first quarter of the 20th century. The Germans had fought to enforce a ban from 1884 onwards, but so-called 'house slavery', however, was still permitted as late as 1905 as the Germans set about weaning the populace permanently of this practice. All children born of such slaves after 31 December of that year were free of bondage, but records reveal that slavery persisted into the early 1920s. This was long after the Germans had lost their colony after World War I to the British who finally succeeded in eradicating this scourge.

Less than twenty years before the Trappes' arrival, Tanga had served as the main gateway for German conquest of the interior. One of the centres of the bloody Abushiri uprising in the 1880s, Tanga was now the increasingly prosperous springboard for settlers headed for the interior. Accompanied by a Captain Leue of the German East Africa Company, who was there to escort the new arrivals, the couple boarded the train in Tanga, the East Usambara Mountains providing a dramatic backdrop as they rose steeply from the coastal plain. In fact, the word Tanga is reputed to mean 'road beside a mountain' in Persian. The trip covered just over 96kms (60 miles) on the Usambara Line to a place called Korogwe on the Pangani River. The train steamed past that swampy, mosquito-plagued outpost to the terminus in Mombo, in the foothills of the West Usambara Mountains, overlooking the Maasai steppe country, where the safari caravan would be organised.

This was a world away from the enervating heat and soaking humidity of Dar es Salaam. Great peaks, often swathed in mist, soared into the cerulean skies, their flanks covered in lush rainforest. Deep gorges traced through by rivers and waterfalls formed the home of the Sambaa tribe who cultivated a riot of tropical fruit such as loquats, pineapples, coconuts, passion fruit and papaya. In fact, just over 24kms (about 15 miles) inland from Mombo was a beautiful little town called Wilhelmsthal — named after the Kaiser — and set amid forest-clad mountains. German colonial officials enjoyed this African Switzerland as a summer retreat, much like Simla, in the Himalayas, was used in British colonial India during the same period.

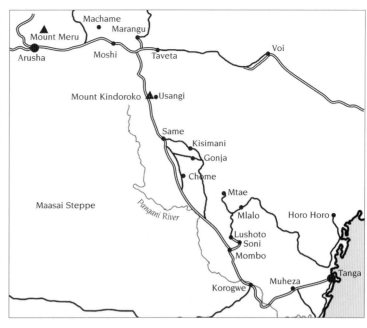

The route followed by the Trappes from Tanga to the foothills of Mount Meru in early 1907.

Margarete and her husband had assembled not only clothing, footwear and household utensils, but also comprehensive kits of medical and veterinary supplies as well as tentage, tools and implements that would be needed to literally carve out a new home in the bush. Margarete's middle sister, Lehne, had married Dr Karl Lindner, a medical doctor in the German Army. He had been invaluable in teaching Margarete what would amount today to a highly advanced paramedic course so that, eventually, she would be able to handle almost any emergency in the bush like a military professional. This could mean anything from malaria and dysentery to burns, snake bite and childbirth. She could administer injections, disinfect and stitch gaping wounds in animals and humans to fend off gangrene and she knew how to treat for shock, remove jigger fleas and stabilise broken limbs. She also had excellent nerves. Just as well.

Unable to study veterinary medicine because of her gender, Margarete nevertheless already had hands-on experience concerning the care of horses, dogs and cattle. She had learned how to shoe horses and to diagnose and treat diseases. This arose from her rural childhood and youth spent hunting and riding with her father and learning by his side how to care for animals. Margarete was equipped to cope with the isolation of the African bush and to improvise under conditions of duress. Africa for Margarete meant opportunity, a new kind of freedom and a chance to exercise her courageous initiative. It gave her a sense of purpose she could not find in her home country and, with that, a life-changing dignity of being.

On Foot to 'The Shining Mountain'

"*Tayari!*" "Ready!" The headman of the entire safari, an imposing Swahili, cast his eyes over the two-hundred-strong retinue, his voice resonating that dawn outside

German officers in the Mount Meru region before the First World War. [Dr Jobst-Ulrich Trappe]

Mombo as he gave the order to pick up the 23kg (60lb) loads. As one, the porters rose, shouldered their boxed loads in three fluid movements and broke into a rhythmic chant in Kiswahili as they began the march to the northern highlands and the fabled region of Mount Kilimanjaro – believed by some sources to mean the 'shining mountain' in Kiswahili because of its snow and ice – and the nearby dormant volcanic magnificence of Mount Meru. A number of donkeys bearing goods in pack-saddles were brought into line behind the porters while a laden oxwagon followed, a youngster herding the extra oxen at the very rear of the column.

Cooks, gun bearers, grooms, personal servants and trackers fell in, accompanied by the German-trained and drilled armed levies, the *askaris*. Every necessity for the journey was included in the caravan – water containers, tentage, bedding and mosquito netting, basic collapsible camp furniture, foodstuffs, cooking and eating utensils, medicine chests and all the personal equipment the Trappes had brought out from Germany to establish their first home in the bush.

Captain Leue had supervised the selection and recruitment of the men in Mombo where safari outfitting for German settlers was already well organised. Ulrich Trappe was riding the horse his wife had bought especially for him in Morocco. Margarete, the only white woman in the safari, was instructed to get into a *machila* – a hammock-like contraption attached to two poles and carried by two Swahilis. It was thought undignified for a white woman to walk. Captain Leue probably also doubted the physical ability of this young European woman to last the pace of several marches per day to cover almost 483kms [300 miles] over several weeks across wild country.

Feeling queasy from the swaying motion of the *machila*, Margarete ordered the carriers to stop after a very short while. She climbed out and informed Captain Leue and anyone else within earshot that she refused to get back in and that the cook's plump wife was to take her place! There was silent amazement in the ranks at this unheard of behaviour and at this dainty *mzungu* with her basic Kiswahili instructing her black counterpart to get in and make herself comfortable! Black women had already become a rarity in safari retinues and it is likely that the said cook's wife was one of very few women on the Trappe safari.

The entrance to the German military garrison in Arusha, photographed in 1903, just four years before the Trappes arrived there. [From John Boyes' book The Company of Adventurers, London: "East Africa" Ltd., 1928]

The Captain bristled with annoyance and spoke out sharply at this unprecedented flouting of safari etiquette in colonial Africa and at the overriding of his authority. He was no match, however, for Margarete's steely will. Neither was Ulrich Trappe. From the first day, Margarete revealed her indomitable character and ability to relate to the tribal people with a directness and courage that would set her against the system on many occasions in the decades ahead.

Depending on terrain, heat and other vital factors, foot safaris were divided into two or more stages per day, the caravan resting up in the middle of the day and aiming to reach known places with access to water before nightfall. At twilight, the far horizons darkened against skies of watered-silk magnificence. Margarete soaked up the sights, sounds and aromas of this new world as the safari left the plateau country of the Maasai steppe with its robust herds of plains game. Grasslands, savannah thorn bush, flat-topped thorn trees and riverine undergrowth on the permanently-flowing Pangani River to the west gave way to the forested foothill country of the misty South Pare Mountains. This was the home of the deeply traditional Pare tribe who were famed for their secrets of healing, but also for their witchcraft rituals.

The chill of night in the higher altitudes enhanced the warmth of the camp fires and the strong smells and flavours of food cooked in the open. Above, skies of blue-black velvet were splashed with millions of stars of a clarity so startling as could not be imagined in northern Europe. The young European woman felt a special relief on hearing her first lion's muffled, staccato calls on the night air, the distant chatterings of hyenas, barks of alarm by baboon and the myriad sounds of the African night as the moon waxed and sleep came. It was the sleep of relief at finally having fulfilled a major ambition.

The African dawn in all its wild beauty heralded strenuous days, but they were passing quickly. The spoor of black rhino and other members of the big five were encountered as were birds of riotous plumage and strange calls that lit up the atmosphere as the safari moved ever forward to the North Pare Mountains and past its highest peak, Mount Kindoroko. Margarete feasted on the sight of African wildlife in its natural habitat and no doubt recalled how much her father had wanted to experience this with her.

After several weeks, the tiny settlement of Moshi came into view and with it, the first dramatic sightings of Mount Kilimanjaro in all its snow and ice-crested grandeur. The highest of its three main peaks – Kaiser Wilhelm Spitze, named after Kaiser Wilhelm II – was free of cloud, glistening in the morning sunlight.

The Trappes passed westwards, through the farming settlement of Arusha where the Germans had established a military garrison and administrative presence in 1886. The instantly recognisable administrative headquarters or *boma* was a handsome white building, surrounded by a moat, with a prominent clock tower on which the German coat-of-arms was emblazoned. John Boyes, the near-legendary English adventurer-author, described Arusha as he found it in 1903, just four years before the Trappes' arrival. In his book *The Company of Adventurers* (London: East Africa Ltd., 1928), Boyes wrote on page 170:

> 'We had discovered a real oasis in the wilderness. The township was spotlessly clean and we saw Natives with small baskets picking up any litter lying about, as though the place were the Tiergarten of Berlin and not the wild interior of the Dark Continent.'

The Trappes took leave of the main party in Arusha and, with a small retinue, left the most-frequented track and headed for nearby Mount Meru in all its forested beauty. They were about to see the setting for their first home in Africa.

Ngongongare and Momella – The Beginning

Having left their wagon, draft oxen and most of their possessions under guard in the foothills of Mount Meru, the party crossed over a shallow river strewn with boulders where yellow-bark acacia trees rose from the moist earth nearby. The vegetation became denser as the Trappes ascended the slopes of Mount Meru. Called *Oldonyo Orok* [Dark Mountain] by the Maasai, this dormant stratovolcano was once higher than Mount Kilimanjaro. A cataclysmic event over a quarter of a million years ago blew apart the eastern slopes and the crown, strewing rocks and boulders, ash and lava for many kilometres distant and creating the rich volcanic soil Margarete Trappe would get to know so well. Lichen, bamboo and ferns grew in profusion, bold strangler fig trees reaching out into the champagne air beside weird trees with aerial roots from which long strands of moss hung down. Rivulets of spring water tumbled over moss-covered rock like crushed ice over dark green moiré silk. High above, patches of indigo sky could be seen through a vast canopy of trees.

An opening was reached on the side of Mount Meru where the Trappes could step out into bright sunlight. From the edge of the clearing, all chronic fatigue forgotten, they saw a panorama of breath-stopping beauty. Below stretched a lush valley of open savannah and acacia woodland. It was enclosed on

The Red River, known as the Engare nanyuki, at the base of Mount Meru.
[Bernd Reufels]

The Trappes' first postal address in German East Africa in 1907. [Dr Jobst-Ulrich Trappe]

Left — One of the many tracks leading up the slopes of Mount Meru. [Bernd Reufels]

three sides by the Mount Meru foothills, with several small lakes scattered about its surface amid gently undulating hills to the east where streams threaded their way through the vegetation. This region was known as 'The Eye of the Waters' in Maasai, while the immediate vicinity of the lakes was known as *Momella*, named after a Maasai chief. East of *Momella* was a steep range of thickly wooded hills known in German as the *Festungsberge* [the Fortress Hills].

Most thrilling of all was the sight of elephant, moving in small herds as they made their way over the valley floor; numbers of buffalo stood grazing while others were lying down, chewing the cud in comfort near mud wallows; giraffe moved fluidly passed in all their languid beauty, stopping upon occasion to survey their untouched world where tawny eagles coasted on the thermals. To the east, Mount Kilimanjaro soared into the skies, as it had done for aeons. Known by the Maasai as *Oldonyo Oibor* [the White Mountain] its mighty magnificence was unusually free of cloud that day, as if to bid a special welcome to this young woman. Margarete was bewitched. This was 'the place of many-sounding waters', N*gongongare* in the Maa language. This would be where the Trappes would start a new life.

The news had travelled with speed into the nearby Maasai Reserve. Two new W*azungu* were in the valley. They had put up some tents and were busy marking out land and making a fence around their home. There were black people with them from another place who were helping them. They were not Maasai. The white people had almost no animals, but they had arrived with a wagon and some oxen, a horse, many wooden boxes and other containers. The small white woman got up before the sun, spoke to the black people slowly, but correctly in the Kiswahili of the coast and not in the simple *shamba Swahili* most white people used. She never stopped working, wore long skirts and seemed to be the leader. The white man, also a hunter, worked hard and knew about growing things.

These white people were good to those who helped them. The woman had guns and was able to use them like her man to bring food home – birds and small buck. She would go out on the horse and come back with the food, placed across the horse, in front of her. She knew how to cut up the birds and the buck before placing the meat on the fire to cook. The black people were also given some of this meat by the white people. The woman laughed readily as she worked with the black people. She was also always asking questions of them about the animals, the birds, the plants and the mountains and seemed to have no fear. The black people addressed her as B*ibi*, the Kiswahili word for lady.

A view of the valley where the Trappes settled, as seen from the slopes of Mount Meru. [Fiona Capstick]

She was already an adult, but had no children, which was very strange. The man also had only her as a wife, which was not strange as these were *Wazungu*. One of the many boxes had magic in it. When somebody was hurt or sick, the white woman would open that box and take out magic things that made the people better. She could become cross very quickly when the work was not properly done, but then she became happy again very quickly. This was a different white woman. She seemed like a mother – worrying about everybody and making sure the people had food and were healthy.

In a matter of days, Margarete and her husband met their first Maasai face-to-face

Masaai at Ngongongare, on the Trappe estate in 1912. [Dr Jobst-Ulrich Trappe]

when a small group came up to their rudimentary home. The men were very tall and slim. They wore their red or purple cloth *shukas*, cloaks tied at one shoulder, with a proud nonchalance, their distorted earlobes adorned with wire and colourful beaded ornaments, their necks with beaded necklaces, their ankles and calves with wire ornaments. All carried long spears and were barefoot. Some of the men had scar patterns on their faces and all had their two front teeth on the lower jaw missing – clearly a tribal custom. A lifelong bond was about to be forged between these special people and the white woman from the far country. These emissaries had come to reconnoitre in person, but they had come in peace, as symbolized by the ostrich feather and leather coverings on the tips of their spears. They left with a message of peace and greetings from these white people for their chief and all his people.

Over the next six months, through the 'long rains' and into the dry season with its very cold nights and luminescent days, the Trappes worked as never before in their lives. They were a formidable team of courage, ingenuity and persistence. Margarete had invested most of her inheritance from her late father in buying from the German Imperial Government 3 800 hectares (9 407 acres) at *Ngongongare*. Ulrich had also invested his

The Trappes' first home in Africa, taken in early 1907. [Dr Jobst-Ulrich Trappe]

more modest inheritance. The Trappes had to supply all the wire for the fencing, but the cost of the actual fence posts was subtracted from the overall purchase price.

Margarete was directly involved in meeting and selecting her first workforce principally from among the Bantu tribes of the Wameru and the Il Larusa, more commonly known as the Waarusha, of the immediate region. With time, members of other Bantu tribes such as the Wachagga from the eastern and southern slopes of Mount Kilimanjaro joined the Trappe workforce. No Maasai, however, were engaged to start clearing virgin bush, loosen the earth, plant seeds and tend the flourishing orchards, vegetable and flower gardens that would eventually emerge. The Nilo-Hamitic Maasai, fiercely independent and proud nomadic pastoralists, never engaged in any agricultural work as it was taboo to break soil because it sustained pastures for their herds of cattle.

Margarete had an innate ability to relate to people. From the outset, she exhibited genuine interest in the tribal peoples whose world she had entered. She embraced every opportunity to learn more about their beliefs, customs and ways of life. With this willingness to learn came a natural respect for the indigenous inhabitants, sincere interest in their welfare and recognition of their profound knowledge of the environment and its stupendous wildlife.

Margarete, left, and Ulrich outside their Banana-leaf house. [Dr Jobst-Ulrich Trappe]

Those first six months at *Ngongongare*, as the first farm was called, laid the basis upon which the formidable reputation of Margarete Trappe as a fearless, honourable human being was cultivated. News travelled quickly among the tribes in the region that this petite lady was indeed different from most of the *Wazungu* from her country who had passed through the region in the last two decades or so. She did not force foreign ways on the people and expect them to forsake their cultures in the process. She also never

Above — The Trappe oxwagon in the very early days. [Dr Jobst-Ulrich Trappe]

Above right — The cattle enclosures on the Trappe estate. [Dr Jobst-Ulrich Trappe]

Right — Part of the Trappe cattle herds. [Dr Jobst-Ulrich Trappe]

spoke about the foreign god of the *Wazungu* who promised fire and suffering to all who did not accept him and who expected a man to have only one wife.

Apart from the boulder-strewn Red River, the *Engare Nanyuki*, at the base of Mount Meru that rose to the rear of the property, another beautiful stream flowed through the property that would cover 6 000 hectares (14 826 acres) within a year. Ulrich was full of initiative as he worked with the increasingly skilled tribal peoples to establish the beginnings of flower gardens that would eventually boast distinctly European varieties such as roses and violets. The crisp climate, abundant sunshine and water also facilitated the cultivation of orchards that would include pineapples as well as an experimental section devoted to grapes on trellises. Cypress trees and colourful shrubs were planted as borders to these gardens and orchards. The well-watered earth was also perfect for the cultivation of weeping willow trees with their graceful foliage and shade.

From tough and humble beginnings, the Trappe farm gradually matured. After six months in tents, the couple built a small house using timber from the surrounding forests and thick layers of banana leaves for the roof. It even had a verandah of sorts and was decidedly 'up market' after the tents. Rudimentary enclosures nearby served as a poultry run that provided food as well as a means of barter.

The Trappes also acquired their first lot of indigenous humped-back Zebu cattle for meat and breeding purposes as well as dairy animals for fresh milk, butter and cheese. A cattle enclosure surrounded by thick thorn fencing was built and new pasture grass planted to improve grazing. Margarete soon had several dogs on the property. They had the run of the Trappe domain and would become an inseparable part of Margarete's existence, as would her horses and cattle.

In 1908, the Trappes were able to buy a further 2 000 hectares (4 942 acres) of land at *Momella*, due east, of *Ngongongare*. This was bought through a hire-purchase agreement with the German Imperial Government and would contain a piggery and much larger cattle enclosures to cope with an ever increasing herd of beef and dairy animals. As seen

Early and very successful farming activities on the Trappe estate. [Dr Jobst-Ulrich Trappe]

in extracts from a letter published in the *Hamburger Nachrichten* on Sunday, 1 May 1910, the Trappe estate already boasted a large cattle kraal and special enclosures for the calves as well as a small dam. Some 10 000 trees, among them European cedars, were planted as well in a sustained effort to protect the soil and enhance the overall environment. The beginnings had been well laid for a stud farm to breed horses, a favourite mare already being in foal that year. Local Maasai sheep and pedigreed merino sheep from Kenya soon made their appearance on the estate.

By late 1912, not quite six years after arriving by oxwagon in totally uncultivated country, the Trappe dairy herd was producing several hundred pounds of butter every month. Shorthorn and Hereford cattle were also bought and crossed with other breeds. In fact, the Trappes were especially impressed with the Hereford breed and imported Hereford bulls from South Africa as well as other breeding stock from neighbouring Kenya.

Specially packed butter and cheese from the Trappe estate were taken twice a week to the Moshi railway station, just over 48kms (about 30 miles) distant, by donkeys led by two Maasai herdsmen. There, some of the produce was taken for sale locally while the rest was conveyed down to the port of Tanga on the coast – a twelve-hour train journey. Tinned butter had been the norm on the coast, but once fresh butter became available, the demand rose. Dairy products were also sold in Arusha and in surrounding settlements. Beehives for the cultivation of honey were introduced for home use and for sale as well as barter. More poultry runs to house ducks and turkeys were established as the estate expanded its livestock activities.

The burgeoning farm soon had special storage structures for livestock feed and farm implements. Stabling was expanded to care for a growing number of horses. Margarete was a skilled rider with a profound knowledge of horses. She would gain renown throughout the region for her expertise not only in breeding and training horses, but especially in successfully diagnosing and treating injuries and illnesses.

Maize was now being cultivated as well as lucerne and other cash crops such as potatoes. In time, a mill was constructed at *Momella* to grind maize. The Trappes also made the mill available to their workforce and to the surrounding tribes so that they, too, could grind their own maize more efficiently. Millet, known as *ulezi*, was a favourite. The ground grain was used to make a nutritious porridge called *uji*. The mill was also a gathering place where news was exchanged. The Trappes seemed to instinctively know about the importance of sound working relationships and good morale. The tribal women loved the mill as it eased their daily slog of handgrinding the family grain and afforded them regular opportunities to meet, gossip and relax, however briefly.

Magarete on her black stallion Comet among some of the Trappe cattle. [Dr Jobst-Ulrich Trappe]

At between 1 650m (5 413 feet) and 1 800m (5 905 feet) above sea level, the Trappe estate enjoyed a very healthy climate where malaria was uncommon. The district's tribes knew they were welcome to come and barter goods and, indeed, to seek the advice and hands-on help of *Yeyo* – Mother, as the Maasai now called Margarete or *Mamma*, as the Waarusha and the Wameru addressed her. She helped them, their children and their cattle when they fell ill, developing a potent reputation as a healer of humans and animals alike.

The first regular interaction between Margarete and the tribal people, especially to provide rudimentary medical care for women and their babies, took place on the veran-dah of the 'banana-leaf house' whose roof and walls were clad in that leaf. There, she would treat for malaria, eye and skin conditions, burns and digestive troubles, including potential killers such as dehydration in babies. She would teach through example about hygiene and correct feeding and she would listen and learn as the people opened up about their troubles. Margarete was trusted and increasingly respected as a 'healer' when adults, children and babies alike responded to her care and often recovered from ailments that routinely killed in the past because of ignorance.

In those early days, as mentioned in Gerd von Lettow-Vorbeck's fine book, A*m Fusse des Meru* (Hamburg und Berlin: Verlag Paul Parey, 1957), a Maasai chief came to Margarete in desperation because newborn babies were dying at an alarming rate in his kraal. She fetched her medical kit, saddled up her horse and rode out to the distant kraal to inspect. An extremely strict regime of hygiene was then enforced in that kraal, especially among the women and midwives, during childbirth and in the ensuing weeks. Margarete was the midwife at one of the births at that time. A boy was born and was named *Ngongongare*, after her home.

The infant mortality rate decreased quite dramatically at that Maasai kraal after Margarete intervened. The news travelled, naturally, as did Margarete's reputation as a 'wonder worker'. The people took particular note of her humanity and willingness to help and to share knowledge. This made a special impression so soon after the traumatic events under Karl Peters a mere two decades or so previously.

Margarete impressed the local people more and more as time passed because she actively sought their knowledge about how they dealt with ailments and disease, both in humans and in animals. The Maasai, for example, taught her about the grasses of the region, which ones caused illness in their cattle and how they treated these illnesses. Margarete recognized that nature possessed a formidable pharmacopoeia and that tribes such as the Maasai who had lived for centuries in harmony with the natural world would know about natural remedies for humans and animals. The young woman soon learned of the bark of a tree the tribal people used to make a tea to combat malarial fevers and she added to that knowledge as the years passed.

The German Government had established a veterinary facility very close to *Momella* where serums were being produced to ward off a repetition of the catastrophic *rinderpest* of the previous decade. Margarete was a frequent and very welcome visitor to the station where she learned an enormous amount about the care of cattle in particular, but also about horses and other livestock. The veterinary specialists shared their knowledge freely with this young German lady who had so wanted to study veterinary science. She developed a high level of skilled knowledge about diagnosing diseases, performing surgical procedures on animals and preventing epidemics. This would prove invaluable throughout her life in Africa. Margarete became famous in the region as an 'animal doctor' and was soon known among the Maasai as 'the woman with many cattle'. This was the ultimate accolade.

Comet

During that first year at *Ngongongare*, Margarete acquired a young, soot-black stallion with a white star she named Comet. He had been sold to Margarete by Abel Pienaar, a Boer immigrant from South Africa. He and his family had arrived in the Mount Meru district in October 1907 to establish a farm on the other side of the *'Ngare Nanyuki* River. In terms of rural Africa, this was quite close to the Trappe estate. Both families became acquainted very quickly, the Pienaars being destined to play a significant role in the lives of the Trappes later on. The Pienaars were merely one of many Boer families such as the Malans, Jouberts, De Wets, Van Dyks, Van Schoors, Vissers, Bothas and Engelbrechts who had emigrated from South Africa after their defeat at the hands of the British Imperial forces in the Anglo-Boer War of 1899 to 1902.

The earliest photographs show Margarete riding in knee-length shorts. They would become her trademark into old age and were no doubt cause for comment at the time. It was not until the mid-1920s in neighbouring Kenya that women started wearing even trousers for the

A young Margarete on her black stallion Comet. [Dr Jobst-Ulrich Trappe]

first time, let alone shorts. This was considered very 'fast' behaviour. As for shorts, they were introduced in Kenya in the 1920s by Lady Idina, the scandalous and much-married Countess Erroll. She and her shorts became one of the features of the debauched 'Happy

Valley' clique in the Wanjohi Valley of the Aberdare Mountains. These moneyed derelicts certainly did not in any way represent the British East African colonists as a whole who were skilled and immensely hardworking.

Margarete Trappe wore shorts for comfort and she could not have been more different from the 'Happy Valley' denizens next door whose every whim was catered to by private armies of servants and who sought escape from boredom through drugs and serial liaisons. Margarete Trappe, like the majority of the Kenyan settlers, worked tirelessly to build and sustain a mini-empire of agricultural, horticultural and livestock excellence. Comet was an inseparable part of that process in those vital early years when she reconnoitered the countryside on horseback.

Horses are not indigenous to Africa south of the Ethiopian Highlands and the Horn of Africa where they have a long history. Before the close of the 19th century, the British began importing thoroughbred and Arab horses into British East Africa, often cross-breeding them with the tough Somali horses to increase resistance to disease. The Germans brought in horses of various breeds as well. Margarete bought an Arab stallion she named Diamond to join Comet as her first stud stallions. A legend was in the making. The Trappe stud farm would eventually have some sixty brood mares and many people in the region experiencing difficulties with their horses consulted Margarete for advice of every kind.

Comet was a hugely courageous animal, but its temperament was such that only Margarete could ride it with any safety. She quickly became known also as 'the lady on the black horse'. During the first few months, she would take along a couple of 'Boys' from her workforce who knew the region in detail so that she could start learning first-hand about the land and its wildlife and about all the essential skills for survival in the bush. This involved knowing where to find secure sources of potable water, how to recognize edible plants, orient oneself in the bush, recognize spoor, especially in difficult terrain, track game effectively, and how to read moods in dangerous game. Margarete learned to live off the land with total confidence concerning her own survival, but also concerning the survival of anyone with her.

The word 'Boy', that appears in many books on African hunting, settling and exploration of the 19th and 20th centuries has an interesting pedigree. It is misunderstood today as having been a demeaning, racist word, used in colonial times in Africa for an adult black man. This is a misconception. The word is derived from British colonial India where 'boy' traced its origins back to the Hindi word *bhoi* and to the word *boyi* in the Telegu and Malayal languages of southern India. Both words refer to a special manservant, a palanquin-bearer. The expression eventually came into use in China and in the British Caribbean Islands. It was inevitable that the word would become colloquial in British colonial Africa and that it would cross the border into German East Africa. Margarete used it and, as this story of her half-century in Africa will demonstrate, she was fair and respectful concerning black Africa. The tribal peoples who worked for her and who had any sort of contact with her came to revere Margarete for her fearless, principled stance on all issues affecting their lives. Her workforce was also always fairly remunerated.

The young woman started going further and further afield with her stallion to become more familiar with the vast bush, forest and lake country where towering mountains, gentle hills, streams and rivers crisscrossed the landscape that was now her home. This would include, for example, the Ngurdoto Crater in the eastern foothills of Mount Meru. This three-kilometre wide crater is known to this day as 'Little Ngorongoro', after the world renowned Ngorongoro Crater to the west, adjoining the Serengeti plains with its

superabundance of wildlife. Ngurdoto was filled to bursting with game of all kinds in the early decades of the 20th century. Margarete would ride down its steep, rocky sides onto the floor where she would spend hours studying the game, especially buffalo, elephant and black rhino.

How well she would also get to know the Serengeti plains with their vast horizons and teeming populations of game animals west of the Ngorongoro Crater and over 300kms (almost 186.5 miles), due west of her home as the crow flies. The equivalent meaning in English of the Maasai word *Siringiti* is 'extended places'. Indeed they were.

Margarete would remember for the rest of her life the first time she saw the annual migration of a couple of million or more game animals through the Serengeti plains. Words on paper to relatives in Germany struggled to describe this largest and most extravagant animal migration anywhere on earth. It took place at the end of the long rains in early June when dominant waves of wildebeest, joined by Thomson's and Grant's gazelle, zebra in their teeming thousands, mighty herds of buffalo and streams of plains game such as waterbuck, hartebeest, eland, oryx and topi joined in the surge northwards in search of grazing and water as the Serengeti dried up under the searing summer sun.

The animals washed over the plains and thrashed their way through the Mbalageti and Grumeti Rivers in the south, some drowning or being snatched by crocodile as they headed for the Mara River in the north and the Maasai Mara sanctuary over the border in Kenya. Great prides of black-maned lion as well as lithe-limbed cheetah, leopard, clans of spotted hyena and wild dog as well as robust numbers of jackal followed this

The Ngurdoto Crater, close to the Trappe estate, where Margarete would often ride on solo safaris to observe dangerous game.
[Bernd Reufels]

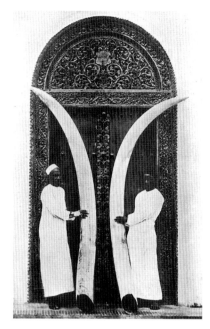

The Kilimanjaro monster tusks. [From C.G. Schillings' book In Wildest Africa, London: Hutchinson & Co., 1907]

moving feast, sure of a meal throughout the migration. Satiated vulture overhead watched and waited, ready to fall to earth in all their gorged glory to resume their gormandizing. Come early November, the animals would start leaving the Maasai Mara to sweep back into the northern and eastern reaches of their Serengeti home where the short rains had transformed the dry landscape as fresh grass pushed through the moistened earth. It was unequalled. It was Margarete's new home.

As for Comet, the stallion was absolutely 'traffic-proof' when it came to wildlife of any kind and under all circumstances. The stallion never baulked, shied or tried to gallop away. It was also completely 'gun-proof'. Quite apart from shooting for the pot in the very early days, Margarete would eventually hunt lion from Comet's back without ever having to doubt her mount's reliability under fire and up close to dangerous animals. As for ordinary shopping in Arusha, Margarete rode over on Comet and stayed in the saddle as she placed her orders! This was serious Big Five country where black rhino were also common and the savannahs home to vast herds of plains game.

In time, Margarete would go out on her own, sometimes staying out overnight with her horse so that she could study game up close and get to know its habitat in all its moods. She would sleep in the open, on the ground, with her horse, seemingly fearless in coun-

Another view of one of the monster tusks. [From C.G. Schillings' book Flashlights in the Jungle, New York: Doubleday, Page & Co., 1905]

try alive with lion, leopard and hyena. It would become a characteristic of hunts with Margarete that time would be invested in observing game, dangerous game included, at close quarters and without firing a shot. Margarete Trappe would become known for responsible interaction with and knowledge about wildlife and its habitat.

As Margarete got to know the environment, she absorbed more and more stories about the peoples and animals of her new home. A mere nine years before she arrived at *Ngongongare*, a black named Senoussi happened upon a bull elephant in the foothills of Kilimanjaro. Its tusks were gigantic, so astoundingly so that the man raised his old muzzle-loader and brought down the bull. The ivory traders in Zanzibar – used to huge ivory – had also never seen the likes. Those tusks can be viewed today in the British Museum in London. They weighed 226 lbs and 235 lbs at the time of the hunt. They remain the largest reliably documented tusks to have come out of Africa and it is now certain that they will never be surpassed. It is far too late in the day in Africa.

Margarete once got wind of an elephant with massive tusks and she set out to try and locate it. Nicknamed the 'Crown Prince', it evaded the most skilled and persistent trackers. Margarete pursued the bull into the region of the Ngurdoto Crater, but it managed to vanish. Nobody ever succeeded in catching up with it. How she must have wondered about its fate over the years.

*A views of
Momella Lakes.
[Bernd Reufels]*

The seven shallow alkaline lakes due east of the *Momella* section of the Trappe estate were awash with birdlife and were free of crocodiles. Masses of wading birds such as candyfloss-pink flamingoes, and a variety of other aquatic birds such as ducks, spur-winged geese, herons, cormorants, ibises and jacanas dressed the astonishing turquoise and emerald green waters. One of the lakes was rich in tilapia that was always a welcome addition to the Trappe cuisine as were guinea-fowl, francolin and other gamebirds. Margarete soon learned that the Maasai never touched fish of any sort.

Margarete's favourite bird was the crested crane, found near swampy terrain. She loved the way it would prance and flap its wings, like an ornithological showgirl. She never tired of riding out to the lakes, just as she loved the much longer trek due west to Lake Manyara on the western escarpment of the stupendous Great Rift Valley. The lake's name is the Maasai word for the Candelabrum euphorbia found there. Although shallow, the lake boasted huge pods of hippo and the immediate surroundings were home, amongst other animals, to bushbuck, waterbuck, reedbuck, hartebeest and plump herds of zebra and wildebeest. Flamingoes and pelicans in their thousands also congregated at the lake.

From the very early days, Margarete exhibited exceptional independence. Some would be tempted to say that she was selfish in her desire to be alone and in charge. She liked being alone in the bush and there is no record of her ever having been lost or of having gone missing and getting into dangerous difficulties as a result of these lone safaris. She was at home in the deep forests of Mount Meru, in open savannah country, in the dry *miombo* woodlands of the central region, and in the swampy country southeast of Lake Manyara in the Tarangire area. This would become a favourite with its intense concentrations of game and birdlife. Flamingoes and storks vied with elephant and eland, fringe-eared oryx and warthog. Tarangire's robust baobab forests were a major feature, Margarete soon learning all about that ancient tree's medicinal and practical uses as she drew closer and closer to the heart of her new home.

After seeing the Mahenge area in the far south of the central region, situated in the spectacular Kilombero Valley, on the western edge of what is today the Selous Game Reserve, Margarete loved to return there, especially alone, to observe and to hunt. This was where she would encounter magnificent specimens of sable antelope with their high-arched, swept-back horns and where she would see extraordinary herds of elephant and buffalo. She would soak up the sound-and-light spectacle of seemingly limitless wetlands and stupendous birdlife, the high-pitched cry of the African fish eagle

Candelabrum euphorbia close to the Trappe estate. [Fiona Capstick]

sounding across the region as it swooped down onto the waters, talons spread, scooping up a fish before regaining height and flying off in triumph. The rivers in the region were also home to huge numbers of hippo and crocodile.

The grass in the Kilombero Valley was often exceptionally high and thick, making a follow-up after dangerous game particularly hazardous. It never ceased to astonish Margarete how an animal as large as an elephant or even a buffalo could remain virtually hidden in such grass. The constant threat of malaria and the risk of serious injury were as nothing when it came to the privilege of being in that untouched paradise of game, birdlife and peace.

Margarete's adventurous nature, the heritage of centuries-old European hunting traditions and, indeed, the outward-looking spirit of German settler and colonial official alike, belie observations made by Steward Edward White, the prolific American author, in his book *The Rediscovered Countary* (London: Hodder and Stoughton, 1915). He had been on a three-month big-game safari at the beginning of 1913 with the famed Richard John Cuninghame during which they spent a protracted period of time in German East Africa. In explaining his difficulty in obtaining information about the relatively unknown, game-rich, mountainous area of the Great Rift Valley well to the west of Arusha and in the arid Lake Natron region on the northwestern border with Kenya, White wrote on pages 4 and 5:

> 'To all intents and purposes we were the first to explore the possibilities of this virgin country ... the German himself, being mainly interested in administrative and scientific matters, is rarely in the technical sense a sportsman. The usual Teuton official or settler does not care for shooting and exploration, and the occasional hunter is quite content with the game to be found near at home. He does not like to go far afield unless he is forced to do so ... from the German side this patch on the map was much too far, from the British side it was practically inaccessible.'

The Banana-leaf House

All was not sweetness and light in those early years. Although the word had spread that the *Wazungu* couple had indeed come in peace and were immensely hard-working, fair people, the Maasai in the neighbouring reserve could not look past the growing herds of cattle. Margarete not only had to cope with frequent attempts by lion and occasionally leopard to invade the cattle enclosures at night – sometimes successfully – she also had to contend with the cattle-rustling Maasai. This meant often standing guard over her treasured cattle with her Wameru and, interestingly enough, Maasai cattle herders and night watchmen in the chill black of night for hours on end, armed and ready, watching and waiting for the first signs of lion, leopard or rustler.

She faced down the Maasai from the reserve and refused to be intimidated by their

Margarete and Ulrich Trappe on the verandah of their Banana-leaf House where Margarete would provide medical care for the tribal peoples. [Dr Jobst-Ulrich Trappe]

actions, their numbers or, indeed, by the tricks they resorted to with the help of their witchdoctors to try to scare this white woman into abandoning her cattle and leaving. Margarete was a born fighter for what she believed in. The message was driven home and, from the outset, she was able to establish a reasonable *modus vivendi* with the warlike Maasai, but she was always on the lookout for the first sign of any attempt at their resumption of cattle-rustling. Some members of the Waarusha also tried to get at Margarete's cattle. They soon learned that this was inadvisable behaviour.

The banana-leaf house was quite flimsy. In fact, it had no solid doors as in a bricks-and-mortar house. The *Ngongongare-Momella* region was alive with insects, spiders and lethal snakes such as puff adders as well as aggressive ants known as *askari* ants or *siafu*, the Kiswahili word for 'biting ants' that Margarete learned to keep at bay with ash and oil. The real concern, however, was lion, leopard and hyena. It became a ritual to take whatever large items were available and stack them against the doors after dark so as to impede any such invasion.

Margarete's many dogs were another line of defence because they would raise a fearful din of howling and barking whenever there was some kind of attempted intrusion after dark. Occasionally, a lone black rhino would come right up to the farmhouse compound at night, leaving its distinctive spoor as a calling card. Margarete would see its cushioned pads with their rounded backs and larger front imprints close to the banana-leaf house. There were impressive numbers of black rhino in the Mount Meru region a century ago. In fact, record has it that black rhino were sometimes seen in among the Trappe cattle on the pastures, quite happily minding their own business as they sought suitable shrubs to nibble. There are no reports of anyone having been killed by black rhino on the Trappe estate. Record also has it that Margarete once saw an elephant trample a black rhino to death. This appears to have occurred elsewhere in the region.

Maximilian von Rogister, a German aristocrat who hunted with Margarete after the Second World War, records in his book *Momella: An African Game Paradise* (London: Odhams Press Limited, 1954), which he dedicated to her, that one of Margarete's house servants, Selemani, had indeed been severely injured by a black rhino. This happened well before the Trappes arrived in 1907. Selemani's broken leg was not correctly set and

*Colobus monkey
[Marlies and Jörg
Gabriel]*

this prevented him from ever going out to hunt again. As Margarete got to know him better, she discovered that he had been sold as a slave in Zanzibar while still a child.

Margarete interacted easily with people and it is certain that she learned at a very personal level from conversations with her workforce about some of the most infamous pages in recent human history. It was this genuine personal interest in people, however humble their circumstances, that set Margarete apart. Von Rogister also wrote of the fearful scars on Tindegari, Margarete's cook. These were the result of a lion mauling long before the Trappes arrived. There is no doubt Margarete asked about this. Danger was all about her in that new world.

Monkeys and baboons were a constant nuisance in the maize fields. They were scared off in routine sorties with shotguns while a variety of antelope would try to sneak in after dusk to nibble the veggie smörgasbord before being chased out. Elephants, however, were the real problem. They would come down from the thickly forested lower slopes of Mount Meru and barge into the Trappes' extensive vegetable gardens, orchards, banana plantations and even flower gardens.

The trouble was that the elephant became Margarete's favourite animal from that first day in the African bush. She would not countenance any use of terminal force on these crop raiders, relying instead on noisy rattles carried by the cattle guards and night watchmen as well as the use of flares and blank rounds later on to act as some sort of deterrent. Elephants would always have a *passe partout* as far as Margarete was concerned. They would also raid the thorn-encircled *shambas* of the Trappe workforce who all had their plots of land on the estate where they grew maize, millet and vegetables. The fear was always there that the great grey creatures would trample the workers' goats and their prized zebu cattle with their distinctive humps and large dewlaps or, much more seriously, that the elephants would tusk a human being.

The nearby forests were home to the very showy black-and-white Colobus monkey with its long sleek coat much prized by some tribes for their ceremonial dress. These beautiful creatures lived high up in the trees in family groups. They very rarely came to ground and certainly did no harm to the Trappe agricultural undertakings. Their curious rattle-like call was often heard at dawn, glimpses sometimes being caught of their black-and-white faces peeping down at the new arrivals before they disappeared into their treed haven.

When the first silky colours of dawn began to backlight the still-dark horizon, generous numbers of doves could be heard already around the banana-leaf house, their liquid calls interspersed with the more strident tones of the emerald-hued turacos in the forests and the sweet song of black-fronted bushshrike. Margarete was long dressed and

Margarete on Comet, exploring her new world. [Dr Jobst-Ulrich Trappe]

out of the house to hear the night watchmen's reports before going off to inspect the cattle. The stables were next and then the dairy where Margarete would check over the butter and milk to be taken to Arusha by donkey cart for sale on certain days of the week. A quick detour to the poultry run for fresh eggs saw this indefatigable woman finally sitting down to breakfast before the real work began.

Baroness Marissa von Firks at home in Germany. [Lars Hauck]

The Hamburger Nachrichten newspaper of 1 May 1910, featuring Ulrich Trappe's detailed description of agricultural progress on Ngongongare. [Dr Jobst-Ulrich Trappe]

The first of the tribal women and their babies would begin arriving early on her little veranda, seeking medical help. Margarete also personally treated as best she could any member of her workforce who was not well. If necessary, she would take a sick worker herself to the nearby mission clinic or, if the condition was that serious, to the hospital in Arusha with its German doctors and nurses. There was never any whisper of any of her workers ever having been treated differently because they were tribal people. Margarete soon acquired the nickname *kiberiti kali*, meaning 'fierce match' in Kiswahili because of the way her temper would flare if something or somebody offended her. It was inadvisable to cross swords with *Yeyo*. From those very early days, she defended her territory and all who shared it at *Ngongongare* and *Momella* with a leonine courage. It was a courage that would be tested again and again in the coming decades.

Margarete was on horseback every day, inspecting the fences for damage, reconnoitering the surrounding countryside or going off alone or with a helper, also on horseback, to shoot for the communal pot. Her husband, Ulrich, was closely and constantly involved in management and development of the farm. An accomplished hunter, he was also a dedicated farmer at heart. The Trappes formed an indomitable partnership in those tough early years in Africa.

One wonders, deep down, however, whether Ulrich ever really wanted to leave Germany in the first place as he was a career military officer from a long line of military officers in his family. He knew that if he remained in Silesia with his regiment, Margarete would refuse to marry him. This was confirmed in 2006 by Baroness Marissa von Fircks, a long-standing friend of the Trappe family. Once Margarete made up her mind about anything, nobody could crack her iron resolve. She had a tremendously strong personality – the original 'iron lady'. As events would prove, it was more often than not injustices from foreign sources that rained down on her and that threatened her family, her workforce and her whole way of life in Africa that forged her resolute character. Women with resolute characters often do not endear themselves to others, even in the new millennium with its remaining glass ceilings still to be shattered. In the pioneering days of German colonial Africa a century ago, it is likely that Margarete's forceful personality annoyed and antagonised as much as it induced respect. A woman who confronted and challenged in an age when women did not even have the vote and who were usually considered 'strange' if they did not marry and live the strictly conventional life of *Kinder, Kirche, Küche* – 'children, church and kitchen' – could easily be branded as 'mannish'.

New Life

In 1909, Margarete and Ulrich celebrated the birth of their first child, a daughter they called Ursula. She was born at the Nkoaranga Mission Station in Arusha, founded by Lutheran missionaries sent by the headquarters in Leipzig. Early photographs show Margarete in long dresses with her first child outside the banana-leaf house. Other photographs show the Trappe children on ponies soon after they could walk. Riding skills were a prerequisite for life in the bush at that time.

As was the custom in colonial Africa, the baby also had a child minder. Margarete was a 'working mother' whose responsibilities not only took her out of the banana-leaf house all day but, as would eventually happen, sometimes off the estate itself for varying periods of time as a professional huntress. The tribal people were totally trustworthy and imparted not only their languages to the children of the *Wazungu*, but also strong identification with and love for Africa. As they grew older, the Trappe children gained insight into the cultures and tensions of the region where they were born. Today, many would be tempted to question Margarete's habit, as a first-time mother, of picking up her rifle, saddling up Comet and heading out into the wilds.

In November 1911, Margarete gave birth to her first son, Ulrich. She had been out hippo hunting shortly beforehand! The mind boggles at the risks she had run in late pregnancy, hunting a notoriously dangerous animal. As it was, Margarete became quite seriously ill afterwards, so much so that she was urged to return to Germany for more

advanced medical treatment. The whole family did just that. There was talk of an operation and of Margarete's never being allowed to ride horses again. Fortunately, none of
this came to pass and the parents and their children returned to *Ngongongare*. Germany,
after an absence of five years, was no longer home.

Too much had transpired in Margarete's life for her ever to want to return there to live.
The sun, the space and the whole experience of Africa had washed over her soul and
effected changes that would be permanent. There was no going back. Margarete's irasci-
ble temper and independent nature no doubt found much against which to chafe in
Germany.

Back home on *Ngongongare* and *Momella*, Margarete resumed not only her daily routine
that stretched from sunrise until well after dark; she resumed hunting. After cutting her
African hunting teeth on plains game and gamebirds, she developed increasing experience with dangerous game. Her first black rhino nearly marked her last day on earth. She
was out on foot with a tracker and one of her dogs, following very fresh spoor through
thick bush when she heard noises. Her tracker assured her they came from monkeys or
baboons. Suddenly, the tracker shrieked "*Faru! Faru!*" meaning black rhino. Without any
warning, a rhino boiled out of the dense terrain and made straight for Margarete. With
an icy calm that became her trademark, Margarete shouldered her 9.3x62mm Mauser and

*Left — Margarete
and her son Ulrich
and her daughter
Ursula.
[Yorck-Michael
Trappe]*

*Right — Margarete
in front of the
banana-leaf house
with her first child,
Ursula, and a child
minder.
[Dr Jobst-Ulrich
Trappe]*

got off the first shot, stopping the
rhino no more than four or so metres
(about 13 feet) from her. By the time
she had fired the second 'insurance'
shot, her tracker had long fled the
scene, but her trusty dog was by her
side throughout. One can but imagine
the post-hunt debrief with the tracker!
Being impaled on the rhino's horn was
perhaps preferable to the rapier-
tongued roasting that Margarete
surely gave the tracker. She set high
standards for herself and demanded

*Margarete on the
grey with her infant
son, Ulrich, and her
daughter, Ursula,
in front going out
for a ride.
[Dr Jobst-Ulrich
Trappe]*

no less of those she entrusted with tasks, especially in the field on a big game hunt.

As for Margarete's Mauser rifle, the internationally recognised authority on the history

Left — *The Trappe homestead that replaced the Banana-leaf house. [Dr Jobst-Ulrich Trappe]*

Right — *Tribal women with barter goods at the Trappe homestead. [Dr Jobst-Ulrich Trappe]*

of firearms in Africa, Gregor Woods, states on page 63 of his book R*Ifles for Africa* (Long Beach, California: Safari Press Inc., 2002):

> 'Undoubtedly, the most successful European medium-bore and all-purpose cartridge for African use was the 9.3x62mm Mauser, introduced in 1905. With full-metal-jacket bullets (286-grain at 2,360fps), it had all the penetration necessary for elephant, rhino, and buffalo, and the softnose version was supremely reliable on all other game … since the Mauser rifles were economically priced, the 9.3x62mm remained the most widely used medium-bore cartridge (German or British) in Africa until the Mauser factory was destroyed following World War II.'

When hunting black rhino, Margarete tried always to shoot over the second horn, something that required good nerves. She learned to recognise the danger signs when a rhino began snorting and stamping a front foot, but she also knew that a rhino could charge with no warning at all. Despite its poor eyesight, the creature's senses of smell and hearing are acute and can prove deadly to the inexperienced or unwary human. Its bulk being no hindrance, a black rhino in full charge is a frightening experience because of its speed.

Margarete would eventually have one of the worst scares of her life years later when her second-born son, Rolf, was nearly gored by a black rhino and she managed to put it down with nano seconds to spare. As for rhino barging into a camp site and going straight for the campfire, this happened more than once to Margarete. It was after such episodes or when recalling similar experiences with her trackers that she would learn of the legends surrounding such creatures. She would then share them much later on with her hunting and photographic safari guests from around the world.

Lion were classed as vermin at that time. They played a pivotal role in the Maasai culture, as is well known, but the Maasai in both German and British East Africa were coming under increasing restrictions concerning the hunting and killing of lion with a spear as part of their ritual in becoming fully fledged warriors or *Olmurrani*. Margarete became well acquainted with lions at night close to her cattle kraals and to those of her workforce where the cats would make repeated attempts to break in and get hold of some fresh meat. Occasionally, they succeeded. Margarete would eventually be called out to help deal with man-eaters in the region and in the far south of the central province.

It was by no means unheard of for a pioneering European woman in Africa during the early years of the 20th century to have to 'sort out' marauding lion on her doorstep. In fact, during the four years Margarete spent in the flimsy banana-leaf house until shortly before the birth of her first son, Ulrich, she would frequently hear lion close by. The next

day, she would find their pug marks right outside the house. This was an early lesson never to slacken her vigilance or rely too heavily on anyone else. The Trappes eventually built a solid house with a corrugated iron roof that was far more secure than their banana-leaf house. Ironically, it was in this house where Margarete had her first near-lethal experience with a poisonous snake.

One night, she was half-woken by a feeling of weight of her chest. She reached out and felt a slimy, cold, long object on her body. Snake! Before Margarete could think another thought, she was bitten in the mouth. Screaming with shock, she leapt out of bed and grabbed a solution of permanganate of potash, plastering it on the two puncture wounds on her lips and then gulping down a vast quantity of neat brandy! It worked! Apart from unsightly swelling for a few days, Margarete made a full recovery.

The snake was thought to have been a green tree snake. Either it had not managed to give a full bite, ejecting a full dose of venom from which Margarete would all but certainly have died, or it had already depleted its store of poison by having bitten some other animal beforehand. Margarete once lost a horse in a matter of minutes to the bite of a green tree snake. Looking back, it was nothing short of miraculous that none of her children was ever bitten. They spent the best part of their childhood and youth out of doors, with their wild animal pets and on their ponies, riding out into the wilderness where snakes thrived.

Margarete came to view elephant as by far the most dangerous big game animal to hunt. She recognized the great difficulty of administering a successful brain shot and the manifold disasters that would result from a botched shot. Margarete had hunted sufficient dangerous game by the time her second son, Rolf, was born in 1913 to be completely confident on her own or with a visitor to the Trappe estate. She was a stickler for correct shot placement, especially when out with a guest later on. Hunting with Margarete was first and foremost instruction in such matters. She never took shooting skills for granted in others. That could be deadly in the field when after dangerous game.

Margarete was out big game hunting soon after Rolf's birth and would always be torn between her profound love of her children and her sense of responsibility towards them and her passion for hunting. It is interesting to note that Margarete started accompanying visitors on hunts out of the sheer joy of living and not for payment. In fact, she also assisted visitors in those very early days who wanted only to photograph or sketch game animals. Here, her bush skills came into full play – the ability to track effectively and bring her guests up close to game.

The Trappe estate was enlarged before Rolf's birth to include 200 hecatares (494 acres) of leased forest in the Mount Meru foothills. The German Imperial Government did not allow farmers to buy actual forest at that time. The Trappes also bought a further 1 500 hectares (3 706.5 acres) between 1912 and 1913 from another farmer on the hereditary leasehold basis, the whole estate now covering 7 500 hectares (18 532.5 acres) of magnificent country where the big five flourished, plains game thrived, birdlife abounded, butterflies in their graceful throngs dressed the landscape and swarms of North European migratory birds such as swallows and nightingales shared space in the

Left — *Tribal women bringing bananas to barter with the Trappes.* [*Dr Jobst-Ulrich Trappe*]

Right — *Margarete with Ursula, her second son Rolf in her arms and Ulrich on her left.* [*Yorck-Michael Trappe*]

summer with Kori bustards and vultures.

The Trappe workforce, representing close on a dozen different tribes, comprised whole family groups, housed in safety on the estate where they could cultivate their own small plots of land and keep livestock. Although the Wameru and the Waarusha predominated, the workers' common language was Kiswahili.

A Farm in Africa

"Ngongongare is a farm in German East Africa on the southeastern slope of Mount Meru…"

So begins a seven-page, detailed article in an official publication that appeared in Germany in 1913. Entitled *German Agriculture under Kaiser Wilhelm II – Motherland and Colonies*,

this illustrated article describes the significant agricultural and horticultural developments achieved on the Trappe estate. It is disconcerting today to note that only Ulrich Trappe's name is mentioned, his wife remaining invisible as did her relentless hard work, courage, skill and ingenuity.

Be that as it may, one learns that the Trappes utilised the Maasai zebu cattle as well as Hereford, Shorthorn and Guernsey cattle, importing stock from British East Africa and South Africa in the quest to breed hardy, disease-resistant animals. Cattle breeding would be the main agricultural activity at N*gongongare*.

The dairy was already fully equipped with all the imported machinery needed, especially to make butter. Within barely six years of arriving in Tanga, the

The extensive vegetable gardens on the Trappe estate. [Dr Jobst-Ulrich Trappe]

Trappes were selling dairy and meat products to the port and providing the livelihoods of dozens of local people. Skimmed milk was also used in barter trade with the tribal peoples, in exchange for maize and bananas. Berkshire pigs were imported from British East Africa to start pig breeding in all earnestness. After a problematic start, the Trappes eventually began selling their pork products not only in Arusha and Moshi but also down at the coastal towns.

Part of the cattle enclosures on the Trappe estate. [Dr Jobst-Ulrich Trappe]

'Salted' horses – those that had survived the dreaded African horse sickness and that had developed immunity – were imported from South Africa to be incorporated into the breeding programme. Maasai sheep and goats were also being bred on the farm as were Plymouth Red poultry, Pomeranian geese and Beijing ducks.

The article described the farmhouses and outbuildings, especially the cattle stalls,

Teil des Hofes, Stall- und Wirtschaftsgebäude.

Ngongongare.

gongongare ist eine Farm in **Deutsch-Ostafrika** am Südostabhang des Meru-
berges zwischen etwa 1700 und 1500 m Meereshöhe. Besitzer ist Ulrich Trappe.
Das Gehöft liegt über 1600 m hoch. Begrenzt wird die Farm im Westen,
Norden und Osten durch den zum Waldreservat erklärten Urwald des Meru, im
Süden durch das für die Ansiedlung der Palästinadeutschen vorbehaltene Gebiet.
Die Entfernung nach Arusha, dem Sitz der Bezirks-Nebenstelle und Standort der 1. Kompagnie
der Schutztruppe beträgt etwa 5—6 Stunden zu Fuß; nach Moschi, dem Endpunkt der Bahn,
zwei Tage. Das Klima ist der Höhenlage entsprechend kühl. Die um Mittag zur heißen Zeit
beobachtete Maximaltemperatur betrug 30° C im Schatten. Die niedrigste beobachtete Tempe-
ratur betrug + 3° C. In der kalten Zeit steigt das Thermometer häufig auch mittags nicht über
10—12° C. In der heißen Zeit ist es wirklich heiß nur mittags. Die Nächte sind stets kühl. Malaria ist unbekannt. Moskitonetze werden nicht gebraucht.

Die Wasserverhältnisse sind sehr günstige. Ein starker Bach entspringt auf der Farm
in mehreren Quellen und durchfließt sie. Ein anderer starker Bach begrenzt die Farm auf einer
Strecke. Die Quellen des zuerst erwähnten Baches sind zum Teil natronhaltig.

Die Niederschlagsmenge betrug im vorigen, sehr regenreichen Jahre 1799 mm. Der Durch-
schnitt dürfte 13—1500 mm betragen. Auch in der trockenen Zeit ist etwa alle 10 Tage auf ein
Gewitterschauer zu rechnen. Nach der Regenzeit sind Nebel sehr häufig und fehlen auch, ebenso
wie starker Tau, in der Trockenzeit nicht ganz.

Die Größe der Farm beträgt 3800 ha. Der Besitzer der Farm hat außerdem noch etwa
2000 ha in Kaufpacht. Dieses Land ist von Ngongongare nur durch einen etwa 1 Stunde
breiten Streifen Waldreservat getrennt und zeigt bei einer Höhenlage von 1500—1800 m
im allgemeinen die gleichen Verhältnisse wie Ngongongare. — Der Boden der Farm ist ein
schwarzer, durchlässiger humoser Boden vulkanischen Ursprungs und sehr fruchtbar, aber
außerordentlich steinig und flach. Schon auf 20—30 cm trifft man auf Lava, die zwar halb
verwittert, aber doch hart genug ist, um das Gedeihen von tiefwurzelnden Kulturpflanzen
unmöglich zu machen. Stellenweise tritt die nackte Lava zutage. Daß dennoch Wald darauf

The feature article on the Trappe estate, published in Germany in 1913. [Dr Jobst-Ulrich Trappe]

stables and various other structures built to adequately house the livestock that were the
main focus of the farm. Mention is made of the workforce and their wages, paid in the
currency of the day, the rupee, and where requested, partly in livestock. Future plans to
start cultivating coffee on a section of the estate were also mentioned in this example of
German acumen in East Africa.

Elephant drinking from the Trappe swimming pool. [Emil Karafiat]

The Trappes and their workforce had already created a self-sustaining community of such excellence as to merit this special attention in the above-mentioned publication.

The fact that the farm was in the heart of big game country with elephants in the orchards, lion in the cattle kraals, rhino in the pasturelands, buffalo at the lakes and leopard in the dense forest perimeter, vying with monkeys in the maize fields and antelope among the vegetables was glorious confirmation every day for Margarete that her new life was not confined only to farming, much as she excelled at it. Her passion for the wilderness, for riding out into the uncontaminated freedom on her doorstep to explore and to hunt would become the hallmark of her life in Africa. News had long travelled back to Germany of this special place under the Southern Cross and of the young huntress who lived there.

The Trappes had a wonderful cement and rock swimming pool built below the house on *Momella*, in the fold of a valley with a stream running close by. All about were large trees and wild shrubs where the colobus monkeys in particular and a grand array of birdlife would fill the air with their calls and song. This was a favourite spot in the summer months when the children and other family members would gather. A fence and a small gate surrounded the rock pool, not that elephants or buffalo would take much notice. In fact, an early photograph shows a young elephant happily slurping out of the pool.

Hunting Ordinances

German East Africa did not countenance a shooting free-for-all where settlers could do as they liked with the abundant wildlife. As early as 1891, a mere six years after the German Protectorate was established, Dr Hermann von Wissmann, the noted African explorer, writer and Imperial Commissioner between 1888 and 1891, issued the first hunting regulations in the district of Moshi to the east of the Trappe farm. The fact that a veteran hunter in the grand German tradition was the force behind these initial regulations gives them credence. Von Wissmann was the antithesis of an office-bound bureaucrat when it came to hunting and game conservation in German East Africa. He embodied the finest quality of the ethical hunter, namely a thoroughgoing concern for the future of wildlife and its habitat.

As Governor of the colony between 1895 and 1896, Von Wissmann oversaw the proclamation of the first two game reserves in the colony by May 1896. The first was situated in what is today the northern section of the famed Selous Reserve and the second was in the district of Moshi, west of Kilimanjaro. They were the first proclaimed game reserves in all Africa, predating South Africa's Umfolozi, Hluhluwe and Sabi (the forerunner of the world-famous Kruger National Park) game reserves by about two years. Ethiopia's Menegasha-Suba afromontane forest, however, was the first proclaimed nature reserve on the continent, dating back to the time of Emperor Zera Yacob who died in 1468.

It is of special interest today to learn that it was Von Wissmann who first promoted the idea of an international conference to debate uniform conservation measures of East Africa's wildlife treasure. This came about after correspondence with British East African officials and with the respective colonial governments in London and Berlin. The first 'International Conference for the Preservation of the Wild Animals, Birds and Fishes of the African Continent' took placed in London in May 1900.

Representatives of all the colonial powers in Africa attended the Conference except for the British self-governing Cape Colony. As quoted in the book *Impossible Dream*, edited by Ian Parker and Stan Bleazard (Milton Brodie, Kinloss Moray: Librario Publishing Ltd., 2001), the British colonial officials stated in a memo on 9 June 1898:

> '… our laws are sufficient to protect our game, and we have hardly any game left anyway. With regard to elephants, it is feared nothing further can be done within the Colony…'

The main focus of the Conference was to restrict elephant hunting and introduce a series of ordinances to regulate hunting and the export of ivory, to create game reserves and to introduce a system of hunting licenses. The supply of firearms was also to be restricted, closed seasons were to be introduced and the hunting of female animals was to be prohibited. Although only the Germans and the British in East and Central Africa were prepared to implement these decisions, the fact remains that Margarete Trappe's new home was already a fairly regulated environment at a surprisingly early stage in Africa's conservation history.

All hunting was prohibited in the reserves created during Governor Von Wissmann's term of office. They numbered fifteen by 1911 and covered some 30 000 km² (11 583 square miles). Anyone caught poaching in these reserves could face a prison term of three months or a fine equivalent to ten times the cost of an elephant licence. Dr Rolf Baldus, the noted modern-day authority on African hunting and conservation issues, quoted Von Wissmann in the March 2008 issue of the Newsletter of the International Council for Game and Wildlife Conservation (CIC):

> 'I am planning to create hunting reserves in game rich areas in order that wildlife can find refuge there and sustain their populations. In such areas hunting of game will only be permitted with the explicit prior permission of the Imperial Government. Their establishment should serve science, in order

The hunting licence issued in July 1899 to the author C.G. Schillings to hunt elephant and black rhino. Strict conditions prevailed to protect, amongst other things, immature animals and females. [In Wildest Africa, London: Hutchinson & Co., 1907]

to conserve such game species which have already become rare in East Africa.'

The first general wildlife ordinance in the colony was proclaimed in 1896 before Von Wissmann's term of office as Governor expired. Dr Baldus quoted him in the above-mentioned CIC Newsletter as stating:

'I felt obliged to issue this Ordinance in order to conserve wildlife and to prevent many species from becoming extinct, which would happen soon if present conditions prevail… We are obliged to think also of future generations, and should secure them the chance to enjoy the pleasure of hunting African game in the future.'

This epitomizes the ethical hunter and huntress. It is astonishing to think that Von Wissmann wrote those words in 1896. He spoke of the importance of establishing the 'sustainability of the off-take' in hunting, words that could have come out of any international conference on conservation in the new millennium.

As well as being an indefatigable international traveller and explorer, Von Wissmann was also the author of five significant books. His last, In Den Wildnissen Afrikas und Asiens [In the Wilds of Africa and Asia], was published in 1901, the year Margarete's father died. This book has lavish full-page illustrations of African game animals by Wilhelm Kuhnert, the greatest wildlife artist of his day. The book was widely acclaimed and went into several editions until well after the demise of the German presence in Africa.

There is no doubt at all that Margarete knew the book because her favourite wildlife artist from her childhood was Wilhelm Kuhnert. He was a prolific, highly gifted artist who dedicated his talent to the animal world. To this day, he is known for his lion paintings. In fact, his nickname was Löwen-Kuhnert – Lion-Kuhnert. He had gone out to German East Africa in 1891 to study animals in their natural habitat, bringing back an amazing collection of drawings, paintings and sketches that earned him high praise and a gold medal in 1893. Further such expeditions to German East Africa followed in 1905-6 and in 1910-11.

Margarete certainly knew of the final Kuhnert expedition as the Trappes were already firmly established by then. That the former Imperial Commissioner and Governor had chosen Kuhnert to illustrate his last book was a natural decision – the hunter-conservationist joining forces with the wildlife artist connoisseur.

Additional decrees were proclaimed in 1898, 1900, 1903 and 1908. By 1911, all commercial hunting, especially for ivory, was outlawed in German East Africa and hunting restrictions were enforced, as many a European settler was to find out. By the time Margarete Trappe began guiding guests on big game hunts, the environment was strictly regulated.

Some of the early game ordinances of German East Africa are appended for interest. They are taken from Edward North Buxton's classic Two African Trips: with Notes and Suggestions on Big Game Preservation in Africa (London: Edward Stanford, 1902). The ordinances reveal, amongst other things, that all carnivora were exempt from game licences in the early days.

While on the subject of game ordinances and regulations, records from the German colonial era reveal that the German authorities had become disenchanted with the Boer immigrants – those of largely Dutch descent – from South Africa who had begun arriving after 1902 and the end of the calamitous Anglo-Boer War in South Africa. Facing personal ruin, a ravaged land, shattered communities, humiliation and renewed subjugation to the British, many Boers chose to leave the country, one group even going to Patagonia in South America.

Margarete knew several such families in the greater Arusha-Meru region. Records reveal that she interacted very well with them. She and her husband developed a close friendship with the Pienaar family, mentioned earlier, who farmed nearby. In a confidential report dated 25 July 1913, however, Dr Heinrich Schnee, the Governor of the colony stated the following about the Boer immigrants:

'... our experience with them in the Arusha district has shown that it is not advisable to allow them to settle in any region where game is plentiful. Nor is it wise to allow them too far from the seat of a Magistrate's office where they would be able to give rein to their poaching instincts.'

It is true that South Africa's wildlife was virtually wiped out in many regions before the end of the 19th century because of the unbridled slaughter of game by people with no tradition of hunting ethics living at a time when trade in animal products was one of the main sources of income and the environment was all but unregulated as far as wildlife was concerned.

The Germans had the resolve to enforce the game ordinances, especially after 1911 when more and more hunters and settlers started coming into the colony from other countries. While on this subject, Mrs Abel Pienaar wrote about the Boers and their experiences in German East Africa in her historic diary, *Baanbrekers in die Maalstroom* [Pioneers in the Maelstrom] (Cape Town: Nasionale Pers Beperk, 1942), published posthumously by the writer H.J. C. Pieterse who had worked closely with Abel Pienaar in sifting through his late wife's diaries.

Mrs Pienaar was full of praise for the German authorities who, although exceedingly strict, behaved very well towards the Boer community. She confirmed that as far as excessive shooting of game by the Boers was concerned "the government was rightly disappointed in the class of Afrikaner who chose hunting as a profession and who simply abandoned his farm" [page 15].

Denis D. Lyell, the noted hunter/settler and author, in his now-rare book, *Wild life in Central Africa* (London: The Field and Queen Horace Cox Ltd., ca.1913) quotes a lengthy article from a German publication of 17 December 1911, the *Naturwissenchaftliche Wochenschrift*. It refers to the warnings issued by Professor C.G. Schillings and Professor Fritz Bein concerning '... the appalling slaughter of big game which is now taking place in German East Africa, and the urgent need of prohibitive legislation in order that a remnant of the fauna may be saved.' [pages 120/121]. In this context, space is devoted to the activities of 'unprincipled whites who get far from civilisation and slaughter the game...' [page 120], the Boers in particular being taken to task. Here one is not speaking of legal hunting and adherence to strict limits governed by licences, but of unconscionable slaughter for private commercial purposes. The point is that the German authorities showed early awareness of the need to regulate hunting in the colony and that hunting ordinances were enacted and enforced, albeit not always effectively, in an early demonstration of responsibility towards wildlife and its habitat.

The Royal Hunt

Margarete had begun receiving requests to take out European visitors to hunt. The scepticism of some people in the early days about this young woman's ability to act as a professional huntress had dissipated and been replaced by growing respect as she took charge and guided her clients for up to three months on classic big game safaris. Be it on foot or on horseback, Margarete's skill at arms, consummate riding

Ernestine Zehe, known as Tante Tine, Margarete's sister. Photograph taken in Germany before she sailed out to join Margarete and the children. [Yorck-Michael Trappe]

abilities, prowess as a tracker and detailed knowledge of the game and of its environment set her visitors at ease. High-ranking and aristocratic Europeans began arriving at *Ngongongare* to hunt with Margarete as her reputation grew and as the stunning magnificence of German East Africa and its incomparable wildlife became more and more widely known.

It was at this juncture that her sister Ernestine, known as Tine, came out from Germany to spend an indefinite period of time with her sister. She would prove to be invaluable, especially with the children. The banana-leaf house had given way to a more robust corrugated iron structure that was quite soon replaced by a solid brick home with accommodation for visitors as well.

Margarete's success as a huntress guide was such that a special request came from none other than the Bavarian Royal House of Wittelsbach. Prince Leopold of Bavaria, Field-Marshal of the Imperial Army and son-in-law of the Kaiser Franz Josef of Austria, and his son Prince Konrad, requested Margarete to organize a safari with them. When the news broke, the German authorities went into a dizzy spin as they prepared for this royal safari. Official visits, amongst others, to the serum station outside Arusha, were lined up, as well as excursions to nearby plantations to share with the royals some of the early achievements in the colony.

The young huntress oversaw the organisation and kitting out of the entire safari, obtaining all hunting licences, especially for big game, stocking up on provisions, and engaging the safari retainers, from cooks to gun bearers, trackers to skinners, tent 'boys' to grooms for the horses and the all important headman to keep discipline and take

The ruins of the Trappe home, now incorporated into the Arusha National Park. [Bernd Reufels]

responsibility for pitching and striking camp as the safari progressed.

The hunting expedition, conducted mostly on horseback and covering a very extensive area, was hugely successful. The Prince, a professional military officer much-decorated for bravery, was already in his sixties when he went on safari with Margarete. Coming from European nobility and having been raised in European hunting traditions from childhood, the Prince and his son were used to the best. With Margarete, they did more than just bag trophy animals: they also learned about the natural world and about the lives and traditions of some of the tribal peoples of the region, especially the Maasai.

As recounted by Gerd von Lettow-Vorbeck in *Am Fusse des Meru*, Prince Leopold was so impressed with his safari that he discussed plans with Margarete to send her some chamois from Bavaria in order to launch a breeding programme in the high-altitude Mount Meru region.

Prince Leopold of the Bavarian Royal House of Wittelsbach, one of Margarete's early hunting clients. [Dr Jobst-Ulrich Trappe]

The Prince and his son came away enchanted with this fearless lady and the news spread even further back home in Germany. It was exceedingly rare to hear of a woman working as a professional huntress in Africa, albeit it in a part-time capacity. This alone fuelled interest.

Having the cachet of the Bavarian Royals was of inestimable value. International hunting was still very much the preserve of the European aristocracy and upper classes in the early years of the 20th century as they had the traditions from childhood, the wealth and, indeed, the leisure to be out in the wilds for three months or longer.

African safari and exploration of the late 19th century and the first three or so decades of the 20th century, however, speak of remarkable women in British East Africa in particular. There were huntresses in East and Central Africa who had also guided guests on big game hunts, who had headed ambitious museum-collecting expeditions as well as foot-safaris of exploration on their own and who had worked as transport riders, aviation pioneers and farmers, leaving valuable written accounts of their achievements. Margarete Trappe was indeed in exceptional company.

Lieutenant Colonel Paul Emil von Lettow-Vorbeck

In January 1914, almost seven years to the day that the Trappes docked in Dar es Salaam, the S.S. *Admiral* of the *Deutsch Ostafrika Linie* berthed as usual. One of its passengers stood out from the crowd. Lt-Colonel Paul Emil von Lettow-Vorbeck, a military veteran descended from the Prussian aristocracy, had been sent out to German East Africa to take command of the *Schutztruppe*. His lengthy voyage had been enlivened by the

Lt-Colonel, late General Paul Emil von Lettow-Vorbeck, Commander-in-Chief of the Schutztruppe in German East Africa during the First World War.

presence of young Karen Dinesen from Denmark, the future Baroness Bror von Blixen-Finecke, who would also establish a farm in Africa.

The new Commander had seen active service in China as part of a multinational force where he helped quell what became known as the Boxer Rebellion, an uprising against the Ch'ing Dynasty and against all foreign influence in China. Von Lettow-Vorbeck was then posted to German South-West Africa between 1904 and 1908 where the infamous slaughter of the Herero and the Nama peoples occurred. After four years commanding the 2nd Sea Battalion of the German Marines [*Kaiserliche Marine-Infanterie*], Von Lettow-Vorbeck spent a short while commanding the German colonial forces in Kamerun – today's Cameroon – before arriving in German East Africa. There, he and Margarete were destined to meet and maintain contact under highly unusual circumstances.

This battle-hardened officer immediately instituted a fresh training regime and extended it to include almost 3 000 native *askaris* who would be placed in uniform, drilled, armed, paid and deployed throughout the colony in fourteen field companies in the service of the German Empire. Von Lettow-Vorbeck travelled to the far corners of the land under often arduous conditions, visiting every military outpost. He met the Trappes when in Arusha as part of his familiarisation tour as they had become one of the most prominent and successful settler families in the region. The colonel's overriding objective was to prepare not only his forces, but the settler civilian population for the *possibility* of an eventual war with the other European colonial powers in Africa! He was a strategic thinker *par excellence*. The Colonel, in any case, was a keen and experienced hunter.

The End of the Beginning

Siegfried von Richthofen, a member of an aristocratic Silesian family, was on safari with Margarete towards the end of July 1914 when Ulrich Trappe sent an urgent note to her with one of their workers, Kisawe. He eventually reached their camp after days on foot through tough terrain inhabited by dangerous game. War had broken out in Europe. Archduke Franz Ferdinand, the heir apparent to the Austro-Hungarian throne, and his wife had been assassinated by a Bosnian nationalist in Serbia on 28 June. Exactly one month later to the day, Austria declared war on Serbia. While Russia was mobilizing, Germany had declared war on Russia and France, invading Belgium soon afterwards. Britain, the strongest financial, naval and colonial power in the world at that time, was about to enter the war as Europe teetered on the edge of a veritable conflagration. There was no way the European colonies in Africa could escape this catastrophe.

Margarete had been instructed to abort the safari and return home immediately. The stench of imminent disaster hung in the air like a rotting carcass. Soon, the Austro-Hungarians, Germans, Turks and Bulgarians – the 'Central Powers' – would be ranged against the British Empire and its slew of allies. This signalled the end of the buoyant, joyous, pioneering years at Ngongongare and Momella. Margarete, barely thirty years old, was about to enter a world war in a highly unusual capacity. Bloody conflict and suffering would engulf Europe, the malignancy of world war eventually eating into the very heart of German East Africa and cornering the Trappe family.

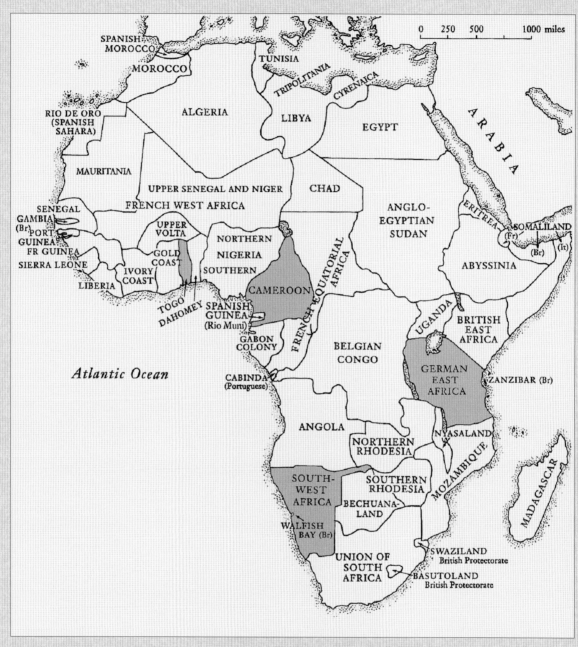

Map of Africa on the eve of the First World War, indicating the German colonies.

PART TWO

"Cry havoc and let slip the dogs"

WILLIAM SHAKESPEARE

World War

"*Die Briten haben den Krieg erklärt!*" [The British have declared war!] The sixth of August 1914. The words were like a bucket of iced water sloshed in her face, as Margarete tried to absorb the implications of the news. She had just returned from the curtailed Von Richthofen safari, exhausted and filled with an anxiety she had never experienced in her whole life. Although the war had been declared on 4 August, the news only reached Dar es Salaam on 6 August in the early evening, courtesy of the Germans' wireless transmission from Togoland in West Africa, on the Gulf of Guinea.

Margarete's immediate concern was for her children, in tandem with the welfare of the entire Trappe workforce and the estate itself. After seven years of often Draconian hard work and sacrifice, of huge physical hardship, risk-taking and personal expense, Margarete, Ulrich and everyone about them now faced a threat nobody could actually see, but which everyone felt that day. The young woman's head felt thick with tension as she unsaddled Comet and gave directions to her workers.

'The Congo Act' – the General Act of the Conference of Berlin of 26 February 1885 – dominated most conversations. This Act, signed by the leaders of Belgium, Britain, France, Germany, Italy, Japan, Portugal and the United States of America, stated that in a war situation, all colonies would be considered as belonging to a non-belligerent state, that no hostilities would be unleashed by one colony against another and that no colony would be used as a base for war operations.

Even the Governor of German East Africa, Dr Heinrich Schnee, was already pleading for neutrality, for concluding a pact with the British across the cutline in the colony of Kenya. Described by the legendary British intelligence officer, Captain Richard Meinertzhagen, as "a nice little man, weak, no character and typical of all second-rate civil servants", he was no match for Von Lettow-Vorbeck – the tall, forthright Prussian officer with excellent English and years of combat experience.

Here, it is interesting to note that Dr Schnee's wife was a New Zealander by birth. New Zealand would enter the war against Germany and her allies. One wonders how the Governor handled this domestic situation as the war clouds thickened. He did not want his civilian projects to be jeopardized by military action. Exports now exceeded imports, the colony was on a strong growth trajectory and the country was remarkably peaceful and stable after the horrors of the various rebellions over the previous couple of decades. It was known among the settlers that Dr Schnee was not a militarist. He promptly issued an order to Lt-Col. Von Lettow-Vorbeck that he not launch any hostile action of any sort. Everybody was hoping 'the Congo Act' would be respected and that the war would bypass Germany's African colonies.

The Trappe Children Moved

Margarete, a practical person to the core, was not about to wait for distant politicians to act. She and Ulrich took immediate steps to get the children off the estate with Tine and into a more protected place. Leudorf Leganga, east of Arusha, across the Makumira River and in the southern foothills of Mount Meru, was chosen. Founded in

The children – Ursula, Ulrich and Rolf – in 1914. [Yorck-Michael Trappe]

1906, the settlement was where Captain Leue, the officer who had accompanied them in 1907 on the journey to the high country and a new life, was stationed. An appreciable number of mostly 'Volga' Germans from Russia lived in or close to the post where Captain Leue gladly took in the Trappe children and their aunt. Ursula was five years old, Ulrich was nearly three and Rolf was a baby of just over one year. Tine prevented any separation anxiety in the children, but Margarete suffered very much.

In those anxious couple of days before Tine and the children left by donkey cart for Leudorf Leganga, *Schutztruppe* of the 1st Field Company, based in Arusha, called at N*gongongare*. They often did so, not only because the Trappes kept an open-door policy, but because of Margarete's veterinary skills and because many of the officers liked to hunt. The Trappes began witnessing greatly increased military activity around the estate and they wanted their children out of the way.

War Looms

Talk this time turned to the threat of war and the state of preparedness or otherwise in German East Africa. With hindsight, it is certain that those crucial days were spent briefing Margarete Trappe for personal involvement in the forthcoming war. In 1914, the colony had approximately 5 336 whites, of whom 4 104 were Germans. The rest of the settlers comprised mostly Arabs, Boers, Goanese, Greeks and Indians. The blacks numbered about 7 650 000 and were spread over a hundred or more tribes. Von Lettow-Vorbeck had already organised the colonial armed force into 14 *Feldcompanien* [Field Companies] with headquarters in Dar es Salaam. Almost 3 000 men were under arms. There was an artillery division, a signals detachment and a recruiting depot as well. The force now numbered 260 Germans and 2 472 African troops, called *askaris*.

The core of these rigorously trained black troops was drawn from some of the most belligerent tribes in the colony such as the many sub-tribes comprising the Wanyamwezi as well as the Wangoni, the Wachagga and the Wahehe. They were deployed in the 14 Field Companies under German officers. These companies were highly mobile combat units unique in all colonial Africa. There was also a sprinkling of black officers known as

Left — *Trained Askaris in wartime German East Africa. [They Fought for King and Kaiser by James Ambrose Brown, Johannesburg: Ashanti Publishing (Pty) Limited, 1991]*

Right — *Askaris being drilled by a German non-commissioned officer. [In Wildest Africa by C.G. Schillings, London: Hutchinson & Co., 1907]*

effendis as well as warrant officers, non-commissioned officers and medical officers.

The *askaris* eventually numbered somewhere between 11 000 and 15 000 troops while thousands of other tribesmen were enlisted as porters for a country where the tsetse fly reigned supreme, tracks had to be hacked out of thick bush, tropical diseases flourished and transport was often a nightmare in hellish, malarial terrain, especially during the rains. It is a matter of historical record that Von Lettow-Vorbeck earned the fierce loyalty and trust of the *askaris*, that he never evaded hardship, even when seriously ill on campaign, and that he stuck it out and stayed with his men, leading from the front to the very end of the war.

The *askaris* were equipped with Mauser *Jägerbüchse* light infantry rifles, some companies having already received the more modern Mauser Gewehr 98. The older firearms used black powder and gave off a pungent cloud of smoke when fired. This, of course, betrayed position. Every *askari* company had a minimum of two Maxim machine guns and most had at least one 37mm field gun. For active service, the *askaris* were kitted out in khaki uniforms with dark blue-grey puttees over leather boots and with leather ammunition pouches worn on a belt. The *askaris* wore *tarbush* headdresses with a white metal imperial eagle emblem on the front and the characteristic khaki neck shade cloth at the back. The eagle emblem was usually removed in combat as it afforded an easy target for enemy sniper fire.

The *askaris* underwent the standard German infantry training, mostly conducted in German, and became skilled at weapons maintenance and use. Inspections of *askaris*, barracks, equipment and uniforms were constant, rigorous and relentless. Discipline was in the grand Prussian tradition, the *askaris* also being paid twice the going rate compared with their counterparts in Kenya.

As part of a diligent strategy to foster *esprit de corps* and override tribal affiliations in favour of loyalty to the distant Kaiser, a newspaper in Kiswahili called *Kiongozi* [The Leader] was published at regular intervals to cater specifically to the world of the *askaris*. They would soon emerge as an elite fighting force with exceptional morale. In fact, as Charles Miller states in *Battle for the Bundu* on page 38 concerning Von Lettow-Vorbeck and his handling of the *askaris*:

> 'It is probable that no white commander of the era had so keen an appreci-
> ation of the African's worth not only as a fighting man but as a man.'

Before war reached German East Africa, Von Lettow-Vorbeck had already formed *Schützenkompanien* [shooting companies] comprising German settler reservists and civilians. They were all issued with *Jägerbüchse* rifles, were drilled in the Prussian manner and were ready at the shortest notice to take up arms and fight. By 1915, these shooting companies were fully integrated in the *Schutztruppe*. Von Lettow-Vorbeck had focused from the outset on defence of the colony.

The Boer Community

Among the volunteers as the war clouds thickened were Boer immigrants from South Africa. Their hatred of all things British was understandable in the wake of the protracted Anglo-Boer War in South Africa. Known by the Boers as the Second War of Independence, it had brought the Boer people death, appalling levels of suffering, dispossession and privation – and the first concentration camps in Africa, courtesy of the British Empire, where inmates, overwhelmingly women and children, died in their thousands from disease and severe malnutrition. The Boers were hoping to eventually overthrow the British Dominion Government and found an independent Boer Republic of South Africa. The thinking was to solicit German support down the line after serving under the German flag in their new home.

Piet Nieuwenhuizen, pictured with General Paul von Lettow-Vorbeck on his left. He was an early Boer émigré from South Africa and a legendary tracker and big game hunter who served as the General's right-hand man. [Baanbrekers in die Maalstroom by H.J.C. Pieterse, Cape Town: Naionale Pers Beperk, 1942]

The Boers formed the *Südafrikanischen Freiwilligen Korps* [The South African Free Corps] known in German as the *Freikorps*. As fate would have it, Von Lettow-Vorbeck's right-hand man was a Boer by the name of Piet Nieuwenhuizen, a tall, fine-looking man who was a veteran big game hunter and a brilliant tracker and reconnaissance operative. He became a German subject.

Margarete knew of the increasing tensions within the Boer community as they were to directly affect her close friends, the Pienaars, and involve her before long. Those Boers who had emigrated to Kenya had generally sided with the British in the war. In German East Africa, the Boers, for the most part, simply wanted to be left alone to establish new lives after the Anglo-Boer War horror in South Africa.

There were Boers in Kenya who became involved, amongst other things, in reconnaissance missions that spilled over into German East Africa where the sizeable Boer community came under suspicion for possible collaboration with fellow Boers from Kenya. In the Arusha region, some Boers began spreading rumours about fellow Boer communities in the district being British collaborators. The Germans were well aware of these rumours and set about a strategy of their own. They introduced martial law that entailed, amongst other stringent measures, a curfew after dark.

The Germans launched a campaign to have the Boers undertake an oath of neutrality or to openly side with Germany in the war. Many refused to do either, the fact of the matter being that they were still British subjects as carriers of South African passports. Most of the Boers wished to be left out of this war, but the Germans were taking no chances. The Boers were to be interned at a camp in Kondoa-Irangi, south-west of Arusha.

Come mid-December 1914, the Pienaars joined the rest of the Boer community in having to vacate their farm, abandon everything on it and go into an internment camp for an unknown period of time. This involved arduous treks by oxwagon, elderly relatives and newborn babies also having to make the journey through dangerous country. Two mounted German officers accompanied the Pienaar trek. The officers were courteous, as were their colleagues who took over their duties after a certain stage of the trek.

L-R Mrs Abel Pienaar, her husban, the child minder and their seven surviving children in front of their farmstead Broedersrus, close to the Trappe estate. [Baanbrekers in die Maalstroom by H.J.C. Pieterse, Cape Town: Naionale Pers Beperk, 1942]

Ulrich Trappe did everything possible, as did Margarete, to persuade the German authorities to allow the Pienaar family to remain on their farm, but to no avail. The family was escorted to the camp near the Ufiomi River, south of Babati on the road to Kondoa-Irangi. There was already a sizeable Boer community there. Many subsequently chose to become German subjects while others remained neutral. Given the circumstances, the Germans behaved very correctly towards the uprooted Boer community. They compensated the Boers in hard cash for any trek oxen or cattle that died during the move and they also paid out for any wagons and oxen commandeered for the war effort. The Boers were assisted with extra tribal labourers to build new homesteads and to cultivate small agricultural plots.

When the Trappes heard that the Pienaars had lost their daughter to malaria, Ulrich Trappe contacted the German authorities afresh. He assured the Germans that he would stand guarantor for the good behaviour of Abel Pienaar and that he and Margarete wanted the entire Pienaar family to come and live on the Trappe estate as their guests for as long as the war lasted. When all seemed hopeless, the Germans authorised the Pienaar family to travel back to the Trappe estate where they were to remain for the foreseeable future. They would be close to their farm *Broedersrus*, next to *Ngongongare*. Their farm had been named after their two sons who had died of malaria soon after the family arrived in the Mount Meru region in 1907. Given the circumstances and the tragedy of having lost three children since arriving in German East Africa, the Pienaar family was being offered a way out and a degree of hope for the immediate future by accepting the Trappe offer.

The Countdown

Von Lettow-Vorbeck, as part of his strategic planning, even succeeded in establishing an Arab Volunteer Corps. It did not last long, but the point was that the German Commander was investing all his energy and military acumen in placing the colony in a state of drilled readiness to engage in war if forced to do so. Dr Schnee's serious reservations about the Boers and their poaching activities were now overtaken by much more ominous issues. The Boers had been interned *en masse* anyway.

Ordained as well as lay missionaries from Germany also volunteered as soldiers or as medical orderlies. Some of the mission stations in the Pare Mountains, forming part of the border with Kenya, were ordered to turn their facilities into military garrisons. Military records reveal that Von Lettow-Vorbeck had arranged for about one hundred Pare tribesmen to serve as soldiers, equipped with bows and arrows! The point is this; these tribal peoples knew the terrain and could report unusual activity to the Germans. The Germans had already concentrated troops in the Moshi area, close to the Trappes, and sizeable food depots had long been established at all the military stations in the colony.

Ulrich Trappe joined the *Schutztruppe* and left the estate before the Pienaar family could get there. Margarete was now solely responsible for the farm. The children and their aunt had arrived at Leudorf Leganga, leaving a strangely silent farmhouse and a workforce perturbed at the changes and wondering what the *Wazungu* were up to this time.

The Maasai in their reserve only a few kilometres away saw a fresh opportunity to engage in their passion – cattle rustling. This cattle-centered people sensed a potential power vacuum as the whites became increasingly distracted by talk of war. Margarete and her workers were pushed to new extremes of vigilance as attempts were made to break into the cattle kraals at night. Margarete would spend whole nights awake at the kraals, armed and ready to fire in order to protect not only her livelihood, but that of dozens of other people, tribal people, who relied on her, who trusted her and who would show their loyalty time and time again as the colony was drawn closer and closer into open conflict. The atmosphere was becoming oddly heavy, like the calm before a typical thunderstorm in sub-Saharan Africa began unleashing its fury from horizon to horizon.

British East Africa Prepares

Margarete was aware by then that across the cutline, in Kenya Colony, the settlers were in the grip of 'war fever'. They began congregating at one another's farms and in Nairobi to discuss how best to defend their interests and the colony. Lord Delamere, the founding father of Kenya colony, had organized a unit to patrol the extensive and unguarded border with German East Africa. Settlers flocked to this unit, among them Baron Bror Von Blixen-Finecke. His wife, Karen, who was just eight months younger than Margarete, was already the object of suspicion and pro-German mutterings because of her known friendship with Von Lettow-Vorbeck. She and the German Commander-in-Chief had travelled out to East Africa on the same boat. In fact, Karen had been in the process of selecting and preparing to send ten Abyssinian brood mares across the border to the German commander when Britain declared war on Germany. She and Von Lettow-Vorbeck had even had tentative plans to go on safari together the very month war was declared.

Karen was to play a key role in ensuring that supplies by oxwagon reached Delamere's men on the cutline. She led several such supply runs by herself, hunting for the pot on the way, standing guard against marauding lion by night, even whipping lion off her oxen with a stock whip in a particularly frightening incident when she had no rifle handy. The young Dane also headed an urgent mission to the far south of the colony, close to the cutline, to shut down a safari camp and bring back the food supplies when the clients grew nervous at being so close to German territory. During all those missions, Karen carried a signed photograph of Von Lettow-Vorbeck in case she was captured by a German patrol. The situation was becoming more foreboding and it was not made any easier by the Maasai, who straddled the border with German East Africa. They were now increasingly visible in full war regalia as they stalked the countryside and let rip with their war cries. Something was up.

The British settlers were not nearly as well organized as were their German counterparts next door. Both sides were unprepared for offensive operations, true, but the Germans already had their *Schutztruppe* and *askaris* deployed and well positioned for defensive operations. The King's African Rifles in Kenya were engaged in operations against Somalis on the border with Italian Somaliland, far to the north, leaving Kenya totally vulnerable to German aggression. The Germans under Von Lettow-Vorbeck had already prepared observation posts on the cutline in the bracing Usambara and Pare Mountains.

These barriers had very few passes, but the best of them was one Margarete knew – a breach at the northern extremity of the Pare Mountains, leading into the foothills of Mount Kilimanjaro. Just across from this gap was the British settlement of Taveta. The Germans had a forward base right there to keep the British under surveillance and to gather intelligence as the countdown to war in the colonies began.

Hostilities Begin

Just days after the Trappe children were sent away to Leudorf Leganga, Britain began hostilities in East Africa. As events will show, Margarete was to be drawn into the war like no other woman in the colony or anywhere else in East Africa, including Karen von Blixen-Finecke in Kenya. An overview of the war in East Africa is essential for clearer understanding of Margarete's highly unusual life.

On 8 August 1914, two British cruisers steamed into range, off Dar es Salaam, one of the cruisers shelling the port and destroying wireless communications with Berlin. Governor Schnee crumbled in the face of this attack and signed a 'truce'. Days later, the British also destroyed the wireless communications at the port of Tanga in the north. Governor Schnee sanctioned another farcical 'truce'.

Von Lettow-Vorbeck, already enraged at the Dar es Salaam attack, ignored previous orders to the contrary from Governor Schnee and seized the initiative. In a lightning raid, his men overran and occupied the highly strategic settlement of Taveta, across the cutline, on 15 August 1914, just 40kms (almost 25 miles) from Moshi. Von Lettow-

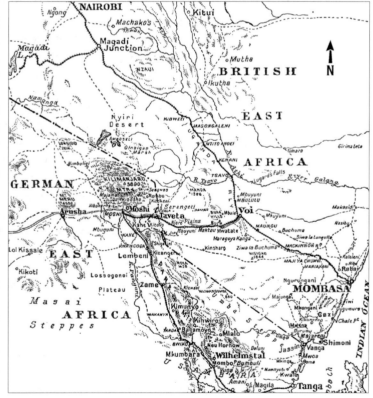

Map of early military operations in German East Africa

Vorbeck became the only German commander in the entire First World War ever to actually occupy British territory. Governor Schnee was apoplectic, stating in a signal that '... All arms are needed to protect the defenceless white population from possible native uprisings. I forbid their use in unnecessary provocation of the enemy.' Von Lettow-

Vorbeck ignored the little man. Margarete would have been derisive of any talk of the 'defenceless white population' bit.

The Germans then launched a whole series of military engagements against the British, beginning with raids against the Uganda Railway to destroy communications and infra-structure, rolling stock and lives. Lines were blown up, trains derailed, bridges destroyed and telegraph lines, which were often tapped successfully for information, were cut. From the start, Von Lettow-Vorbeck realised that the German East African theatre of operations would be a mere addendum to the war in Europe and that the colony's best chance of survival lay in guerrilla warfare – highly mobile, flexible, hit-and-run tactics where direct confrontation was avoided. As supply lines from Germany were impossibly lengthy and as the British Navy dominated the sea lanes, this was all the more reason to try to avoid conventional warfare.

The idea was to tie down an increasing number of British and colonial forces and utilise the difficult terrain and often deadly climate in the process. The overriding aim was that of diverting allied forces away from the European theatre and buying time so that an eventual settlement would be reached in Europe concerning the African colonies. As for Dr Schnee, now known widely as 'a liberal pacifist and a weakling', to quote a prominent German settler, he could not counter his military commander's ruthless resolve that would eventually take the fight to the border regions with the Belgian Congo, Northern Rhodesia, Nyasaland, Portuguese East Africa and Uganda, an area the size of France and Germany combined. Von Lettow-Vorbeck would never be bayed into a decisive confrontation at any stage of the war in East Africa. His unconventional warfare credo was simple: do not risk having to surrender; fight and retire to a prepared position after inflicting as much damage as possible; and prolong the campaign by forcing the enemy to disperse forces over a wider and wider area.

News reached the Trappes and fellow settlers of Von Lettow-Vorbeck's finest moment in the early stages of the war in East Africa. On 3 November 1914, the British attempted a highly ambitious amphibious assault at Tanga. They were planning to land at Tanga and push up to Moshi in one grand military operation, and be joined by more British forces from Voi, just east of Taveta. The plan was to converge on Taveta and 'thrash the German before Christmas', to quote General Aitken, the British commanding officer of Indian Expeditionary Force 'B'. The General also boasted that 'the Indian Army will make short work of a lot of niggers'. The talk was of a quick end to the war in East Africa.

The British did not heed Meinertzhagen's intelligence warnings to reconsider: the German-trained *askaris* – the bulk of the German colonial forces – would be fighting on home soil; they knew the terrain, had the crucial psychological advantage of the territo-rial imperative to defend that home soil, were battle-hardened, exceptionally well trained and well disciplined, exceedingly well-led, their morale was of the best and, in classic guerrilla mode, they would pick the time and place to engage the invaders. The *askaris* also did not exhibit the potentially fatal divisions seen in the Indian ranks – signif-icant caste, religious and dietary differences.

Meinertzhagen warned Aitken that it would be military suicide to discount German fighting abilities on land and at sea. It would be deadly to underestimate the intelli-gence-gathering capacity of the enemy. It was advisable to delay the Tanga assault. Aitken did not listen and proceeded to commit major, rudimentary tactical mistakes as dawn broke and the landing proceeded. Although outnumbered eight to one, Von Lettow-Vorbeck's forces crushed the British and their ineffective Indian Army troops, killing 795 men for the loss of 15 Germans and 54 *askaris*. Large supplies of arms, includ-ing enough modern rifles to equip three companies, 16 machine guns, and 600 000 rounds of ammunition, were seized in the process by mostly *askari* forces who had no machine guns or artillery.

It was one of the most disgraceful routs of British forces in the war in East Africa. The Kaiser promptly promoted Von Lettow-Vorbeck to the rank of General and, on 4 November 1916, conferred on him the highest decoration for bravery, the *Pour le Mérite*. Commonly known as the *Blue Max*, the decoration is in the shape of a blue Maltese cross with four golden eagles. When the *Schutztruppe* and their redoubtable *askaris* returned to Moshi by train, they were overwhelmed by the welcome organised by the settlers: food, flowers and song swamped the troops upon arrival. Produce from *Momella*'s fruit, vegetable and flower gardens most certainly found its way to the Moshi station. The *esprit de corps* in the community and the camaraderie between German and *askari* after the Tanga victory were tangible and Margarete Trappe was right there to witness it.

As for the British-led forces, troop morale plummeted, heat and ensuing thirst provoking panic, inter alia, among the gibbering 13th Rajputs as the British withdrew in disgraced defeat on 5 November 1914. A critical juncture had been reached. While the Kaiser himself lauded the forces, and morale on the ground in German East Africa was at a new high, General Aitken was withdrawn and a search launched to find a commander able to match Von Lettow-Vorbeck.

The British forces and their allies, unlike the Germans and their formidable *askaris*, had little idea of the hellhole in which they would be fighting. Edward Paice, in his book *Tip and Run* (London: Weidenfeld & Nicholson, 2007) on page 9, put it very accurately when he wrote:

> 'Imagine a country three times the size of Germany, mostly covered in dense bush, with no roads and only two railways and either sweltering under a tropical sun or swept by torrential rain which makes the friable soil impassable to wheeled traffic; a country with occasional wide and swampy areas interspersed with arid areas where water is often more precious than gold; in which man rots with malaria and suffers torments from insect pests, in which animals die wholesale from the ravages of the tsetse fly; where crocodiles and lions seize unwary porters, giraffe destroy telegraph lines, elephants damage tracks, hippopotami attack boats, rhinoceroses charge troops on the march and bees put whole battalions to flight. Such was German East Africa in 1914-18.'

Margarete Enters the War

By the time the news of the Tanga victory had reached the highlands, Margarete had decided to bring her sister and children home from Leudorf Leganga. Despite military activities across the border in Kenya and on the coast, the situation in the high country was calm and she felt confident that the British would be kept at bay. In fact, on 4 November, in the middle of the Tanga fiasco, there had been an attempted British assault on Longido, 80km (almost 50 miles) northwest of Arusha, on the road to the Kenyan border. The Germans succeeded in stampeding the mules with the water casks, forcing the British to retreat because they had run out of water in a notoriously arid region.

The children came home not only to the intense relief and joy of their mother, but also to the delight of Karimbe, the young child minder. He was soon entertaining the Trappe brood with wonderful tales from his culture as Christmas drew closer. When darkness fell, story time began, as was the custom in the tribal homesteads. Margarete would hear Karimbe beguiling her children with tales passed down for generations in the finest of oral tradition. The children's laughter and squeals of delight lit up the night as they heard how the giraffe developed such a long neck, why hare and baboon tried to trick mighty elephant and the reasons why the hyena was so feared. The cadence and richness of the Meru language mirrored the vivid tales of that culture, conveying lessons to the young on behaviour and explanations for natural phenomena, couched in the imagery of the natural world that was home to the Trappe children from birth.

As for Margarete, she was in a heightened state of readiness, based on information reaching her via the officers stationed in *Momella*. This war, despite the heady victories in Tanga and Longido, was not going to be a brief affair.

Another setback for the British forces occurred not ten weeks later at Jassin on 17 January 1915. This was inland, just over the border with Kenya and north of Tanga. Von Lettow-Vorbeck's men overwhelmed the Indian troops who surrendered anyway as they had expended all their ammunition and had run out of water. The whole idea was to nip in the military bud any British plans to attempt a fresh assault on Tanga from the north. The news was spreading that German East Africa was not going to succumb any time soon and that serious loss of life was in the offing.

The German commander, however, also suffered several losses in the early months of the war. This persuaded him even further that the war in German East Africa had to be conducted along guerrilla warfare lines – avoiding direct engagements and indulging in lightning raids into enemy territory to strike at key installations such as forts and means of communication and infrastructure such as roads, railways and bridges.

Margarete had long made arrangements with the *Schutztruppe* to bring any ailing military horses to her estate where they were stabled, fed and cared for. The animals were usually cured of the conditions that had sent them to Margarete in the first place. Apart from skin infections, the main problem was leg injuries from the rough volcanic ground and tough thorn scrub country. The mounts usually responded well to complete rest. The equivalent of this care today would be the mechanical fine-tuning of armoured personnel carriers!

Margarete was personally involved in the returning of any healed animals to their military posts, using a variety of routes to avoid possible British patrols and ambushes. She also participated in clandestine missions on horseback through the mountain pass in the northern Pare Mountains, opposite Taveta in Kenya. While there is no written record of these missions, it became known after the war ended that Margarete had helped bring over horses 'acquired' on the other side and that she was able to deliver them to the Germans in the Arusha/Moshi region and elsewhere without being detected by any British patrols. In fact, the 8th Shooting Company acquired fresh mounts via this method. Certainly, Margarete's powers of observation would have been invaluable under such circumstances concerning British troop concentrations and movements and, in particular, the critical 'national asset', the Uganda Railway.

After the first military hidings meted out to the British and their less than adequate Indian Army troops, Von Lettow-Vorbeck spent the rest of 1915 on a concerted campaign to increase his troop strength and their training. This also involved 'on-the-job' training that saw small 'sticks' of Germans and *askaris* crossing the border and sabotaging the Uganda Railway at regular intervals. Trains were blown up, mines laid, freight trains attacked and oxwagon supply runs ambushed. By February 1916, the forces reached their maximum strength and stood at almost 3 000 Europeans and about 11 300 askaris and the crucially important carriers – the real heroes in that entire theatre of war on both

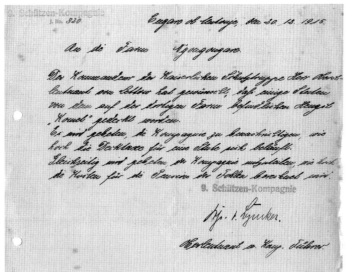

Left — *Askari women on one of the extensive safaris in German East Africa undertaken by the author C.G. Schillings. [With Flashlight and Rifle, London: Hutchinson & Co., 1906]*

sides. The *askaris* were also permitted to have their womenfolk accompany them throughout the war, to the end. They were known as the *Askarifrauen* – the askari women.

This interaction with the troops and their officers stationed in the Arusha region brought news of the escalating war in German East Africa and afforded face-to-face briefings with Margarete as well as the opportunity to refine arrangements for provisioning the troops on a regular basis with food from *Ngongongare* and *Momella*. This included eggs, milk, butter, cheese, venison courtesy of Margarete's favourite Mauser rifle, fish and beef as well as fresh vegetables. Margarete was even approached to make available her magnificent stallion, Comet, for stud purposes with a mare at the 9th Shooting Company.

Right — *A formal request by the 9th Shooting Company to have the use of Margarete's stallion, Comet, for stud purposes. [Dr Jobst-Ulrich Trappe]*

During this period, Margarete not only had to contend with the usual array of problems, both human and animal, but also with a particularly horrifying episode involving her children. This incident, well remembered in the family and recounted to Gerd von Lettow-Vorbeck many years later, confronted Margarete the moment she had returned from a hunt for supplies. Her sister came rushing out to her in a state of near-hysteria. The children were very seriously ill. They had drunk milk brought in by a Maasai called Kironga who was not the usual 'milk boy' assigned the task.

Quicker than water evaporating on sun-scorched earth, Margarete raced into the house and prepared a strong emetic solution, made from the roots of the *Harrisonia abyssinica* tree and used by the Maasai. Margarete forced her children to drink the fluid. They vomited for a frighteningly long time before finally showing the first signs of recovery. That same day one of Margarete's headmen came down with the exact same symptoms of dreadful nausea and stomach cramps. He, too, had taken milk from the same milk container brought in by Kironga. Margarete dosed the headman straight away with the same brew and saved his life.

She then summoned Kironga and asked him to deliver a letter to the *Stabsarzt* – the military doctor – in Arusha, making no accusations and giving nothing away. The Maasai, suspecting nothing, headed for Arusha and delivered the letter. He was promptly arrested. When eventually released, Margarete threatened him with the direst of personal consequences if he ever set foot on her estate again in his life. He never did.

This most terrifying of experiences merely sharpened Margarete's vigilance and increased her resolve to outwit and outpace any threat to her, her family, her workforce or the estate and all it contained. The Maasai were renowned for their warlike history and their reputation for independence and dominance over others. This petite woman from northern Europe was forced to stand her ground with increasing urgency.

Fighting Escalates

The British tried to enforce a blockade of the lengthy German East African coastline, but this was never entirely successful. German vessels managed to run the blockade on a number of occasions. One such foray during April 1915 resulted in the Germans gaining sufficient Mauser 98 rifles to rearm their troops with the more modern weapon. A fair amount of undamaged ammunition was also recovered from the ship in question. When this news reached the high country, Margarete and the settlers in general felt more secure in their prospects of overcoming the British in German East Africa.

The German cruiser SMS Königsberg in East African waters.
(Photo – German *Bundesarchiv*.)

The ultramodern S.M.S. Königsberg light cruiser in Dar-es-Salaam harbour. Known in Swahili as the Manowari na Bomba Tatu (the man-of-war with three pipes).

The Hunting of the SMS Königsberg

The ultra modern light cruiser SMS *Königsberg* of the Imperial German Navy was a huge threat to British shipping. With a top speed of 24 knots, it was faster than any ship in the British Navy. The cruiser was equipped with two 450mm torpedo tubes, ten 105mm and ten 37mm quick-loading guns. Interestingly enough, the *Königsberg* also had on board as freight two 88mm quick-loading guns that could be fitted to a German trading vessel to transform it into an auxiliary cruiser. These two 88mm guns and some 400 rounds of ammunition were handed over to the *Schutztruppe* in 1914 in Dar es Salaam, before the outbreak of hostilities, as the return of the *Königsberg* was not envisaged at that stage. It had come out to the colony 'to show the flag' during a major exposition to celebrate the completion of the railway from Dar es Salaam to Kigoma on Lake Tanganyika over 1300kms (over 800 miles) away and to help boost the German naval presence on the

Indian Ocean littoral. War was declared while the *Königsberg* was in Dar es Salaam.

With a firing range of about 16 kms (10 miles), the *Königsberg* was also stocked to last for a 24-month cruise. The 322-man crew's oath of allegiance included the words 'to be strong before the enemy … to remain faithful through battle and all trials until death …' And so it was. When war broke out, it was the only German warship in the Indian Ocean, ordered to conduct *Kreuzerkrieg* – hit-and-run interceptions to capture supplies. This posed considerable danger to the British not only off the East African Coast but also to supply routes to Kenya, Zanzibar and India, via the Suez Canal chokepoint and Aden in Yemen during the latter part of 1914 and into 1915.

Just three months into the war, the cruiser sought refuge in the steaming, mangrove maze of the Rufiji River Delta, south of Dar es Salaam, opposite Mafia Island, to undergo maintenance work on her engines and to resupply with coal and food. Unbeknown to the British, the Germans had already surveyed the many-channelled delta and knew exactly which channel was able to take the draught of the *Königsberg*.

The deadly German cruiser got word on 19 September of a British cruiser in Zanzibar harbour. She sailed out of her mangrove hideout, straight into Zanzibar's main harbour and promptly set the cruiser ablaze, killing 31 crew members, wounding a further 55 before sailing out of range, destroying another British vessel that was supposed to be on 'guard duty' outside the harbour entrance. Survivors jumped into the shark-infested waters and that was that. Boiler problems forced the *Königsberg* to seek fresh refuge in the Rufiji Delta.

Pieter Pretorius, Chief Scout for the Allied Forces under General Jan Smuts, who helped seal the fate of the cruiser SMS Königsberg on 11 July 1915.

The British eventually succeeded in detecting and blockading the cruiser, finally scuttling her on 11 July 1915, but not before it had effectively tied up twenty Allied ships, almost a dozen Allied aircraft, an unknown amount of coal reserves and manpower, killing and injuring dozens of seamen and destroying their ships. Captain Max Loof signalled Berlin that 'the *Königsberg* is destroyed but not conquered.'

The person who discovered the exact position of the *Königsberg* and the state of its combat readiness was Pieter Pretorius, the legendary Boer big game hunter and bush craft wizard from South Africa. He was the chief reconnaissance operative or 'scout' of the Allied forces. Margarete, like any fellow hunter, would have understood his value as hunters tend to develop detailed knowledge of terrain and how to survive in the harshest of climes. Pretorius knew the malarial complexities of the Rufiji Delta intimately well, having lived, explored and hunted in the region. He knew all about the tides and currents, the depth of certain channels and any natural obstacles such as dangerous sandbars.

He was an intelligence operative made in heaven for the British and it was he who located the cruiser, giving accurate information that resulted in its eventual demise. With 33 Germans killed, the remaining crew members of the *Königsberg* managed to escape and join Von Lettow-Vorbeck, having salvaged all ten of the field howitzers and about 1 500 shells for them as well as any other useful equipment. Gun carriages were then made at workshops in Dar es Salaam, transforming the naval guns into field artillery pieces that were hauled about the colony with immense difficulty. Those massive weapons were of inestimable value to the Germans for the rest of the war in German East Africa. They

The dinner gong made from ivory and two shell casings from the Königsberg that was presented to General Smuts during the First World War by his officers.
[Tom Fassaert]

aided in holding off a variety of Allied offensives and ensured comparative tranquility in the colony for the rest of 1915. Margarete and the rest of the German settlers felt they had new breathing space. The *Königsberg* saga, however, signalled a turning point in the East African theatre.

The loss of the SMS *Königsberg* was followed by ominous news in January 1916 that the British had enlisted the help of a huge South African force under the brilliant, battle-hardened General Jan Christian Smuts, later Field Marshall Smuts. He assumed command of all the forces in East Africa that included, in addition to the British and the Belgians, troops from the Gold Coast, forces from three other west African colonies, Nigerians, Portuguese, Rhodesians, the crack King's African Rifles from Kenya, Kashmiris, Baluchis and Pathans and, finally, the men of the 25th Royal Fusiliers.

The Fusiliers represented the most astounding conglomeration of men ever to assemble anywhere, let alone on a battlefield. They included ex-convicts, American cowboys, a millionaire, ex-French Foreign Legion soldiers, Russian exiles from Siberia, circus artists, gun-runners, remittance men, an Arctic explorer, a Scottish lighthouse keeper, opera singers, academics, a former Buckingham Palace footman, hunters and military adventurers. One of their members was the by then renowned Africa pioneer, naturalist, hunter-explorer and author, Frederick Courteney Selous. The value of this veteran hunter with his advanced bushcraft skills and knowledge of local conditions was of automatic interest to any military commander and intelligence unit.

By March 1916, Von Lettow-Vorbeck's forces were facing tens of thousands of troops, a slew of Generals and Brigadiers, modern armament that would eventually include aircraft, regular supplies of ammunition, transport vehicles, thousands of transport animals, even more carriers and the prospect of even more troops. The fact that Smuts and his fellow Boers, numbering no more than 30 000 men, had tied up over half a million British Imperial forces in the first true guerrilla warfare campaign in all Africa during the Anglo-Boer War of 1899-1902 was not lost on the British. Smuts was perhaps the only man to cope with Von Lettow-Vorbeck in East Africa.

The Noose Tightens

The 9th Shooting Company under First Lieutenant Van Lyncker had been sent to Momella as intelligence reports were received of allied forces intentions to push towards the Meru region. The Portuguese had entered the war on 9 March 1916, guarding the southern front on the Rovuma River; the Belgians were activated in the north-western section of German East Africa and a British force was to operate in the southwestern region of the colony.

The most important battle plans were being formulated in British East Africa to repel the Germans out of Taveta in British East Africa. The overriding strategy was, firstly, to deprive the Germans and their redoubtable *askaris* of any escape route and, secondly, not only to invade German-held territory, but to effectively occupy it and prevent any German forces from splitting up into smaller units, bombshelling in classic guerrilla warfare fashion, to continue the war in a multiplicity of localities. Pressure was also mounting around Kilimanjaro as the Allied forces pushed ahead with plans to try to encircle and annihilate the German forces.

Margarete, now fully committed to supplying the 9th Shooting Company with provisions and to assisting it with its horses, was resolute: she would go further afield, if needs be, to resupply the German forces. She even offered Comet to Von Lettow-Vorbeck

at one stage. He declined, clearly knowing what an unthinkable sacrifice this would have been, but the Commander warned her early on never to allow the stallion to fall into enemy hands or, indeed, her huge herd of cattle and her other horses. Margarete kept an iron grip on the estate and remained ever vigilant for renewed antagonism of the kind that nearly killed her three children.

The first sign of a serious change in the air came from Major Fischer, the officer commanding the Meru sector. He had come in early March 1916 to order Margarete to drive all her cattle – over one thousand head – and horses off the estate and into a large, fortified laager some distance south of Arusha where they would be lumped with other cattle and horses. The war – at first confined to the coast – was now moving inland and heading for the high country. Von Lettow-Vorbeck had avoided encirclement and had moved south of Kahe, close to the Pare Mountains in a region of swamps, rivers, thick forest and dense bush.

Margarete refused any notion of having her prize cattle herds and brood mares, some in foal, mixed up with other livestock. She refused to budge from the estate. Von Lettow-Vorbeck himself had to send orders to his subordinates to leave her alone, especially when she gave her word that no enemy force would ever impound her cattle and horses. "She keeps her word!" was the reply from Von Lettow-Vorbeck. He knew because Margarete had already carried out missions for him! In any case, Margarete had no intention of stopping the supply of food to 'her' Company. This meant knowing the terrain and being able to move after dark, when need be. She also had no intention of ceasing the care provided the military horses.

The Königsberg gun that now stands at the western entrance of The Union Buildings in South Africa. [Tom Fassaert]

Ulrich Trappe – Missing in Action

Ulrich Trappe was missing. Margarete had known for a while that there was tension and a lack of trust between her husband and his officer commanding. This fact propelled her on Comet to the military post where he was stationed. She braced the commander and discovered that no search party had gone out to look for her missing husband.

Margarete exploded, announcing that she would launch the search herself right then. The hapless commander crumbled in the face of her rage when he tried to forbid this. The troops, watching the drama, were astounded at this young woman's toughness and offered to join her in the search. The shaken commander contacted Von Lettow-Vorbeck in his dilemma, but the supreme commander slapped him back into line and told him to mobilise his entire company and get cracking

The official notification to Margarete, dated 21 August 1915, that her husband had been lightly wounded in action. He was captured by the British Forces. [Dr Jobst-Ulrich Trappe]

immediately. He did – and he joined a growing list of people, from Maasai warriors to inept civil servants, who came to regret crossing Margarete Trappe.

It was established that Ulrich had been lightly wounded, was in a stable condition, but that he had been captured by the British and that he was to be evacuated as a prisoner-of-war. What Margarete did not yet know was that her husband was about to be shipped out to India for the duration of the conflict and that it would be years before she would see him again.

Back at the estate, Margarete was watching the horizons around Kilimanjaro with a new intensity. She was waiting instinctively for the day when she would start seeing red dust rising from the Kilimanjaro plains. The first sign of thousands of troops on the march – enemy troops, accompanied by hordes of chanting black porters, mule trains and spans of oxen drawing supply wagons, ready to fight to the end. Margarete, armed with the most powerful ammunition of all, the ammunition of no alternative, was preparing for a fight that would last well beyond this 'Great War'.

She succeeded in having a letter delivered to the Pienaar family who were still making their way by oxwagon from the Ufiomi River. She begged them to make all due haste as she needed them to help her run the farm and manage matters now that her husband had been captured. Margarete spoke of things becoming too much for her. On 14 September 1915, the Pienaars reached N*gongongare* where Margarete was overjoyed to see her friends again.

Margarete and the Boers

With strong and willing hands to help, Margarete was able to better concentrate on her activities concerning the 9th Shooting Company stationed nearby. She had

A request from the German military, dated 20 September 1915, addressed to Margarete for butter supplies. [Dr Jobst-Ulrich Trappe]

been supplying dairy and other food products to the troops as well as providing expert care for the military horses. She had also been sharing her knowledge with the Company concerning local conditions in order to gather information about British troop movements and potential threats in the immediate region. Margarete would be absent for short periods in connection with reconnaissance work. Everybody at N*gongongare* knew better than to ask what she had been doing or where she had been.

The Pienaars fitted in well and were a source of strong support. Margarete tried her best to persuade the Pienaars to become German subjects, but they refused. Here, it is interesting to note what Mrs Pienaar wrote about Margarete in her diary. While emphasizing her profound gratitude towards the Trappes, the Boer lady expressed her consternation at the fact that

Ngongongare was entirely fenced! As stated in *Baanbrekers in die Maalstroom*:

> 'The huge farm is fenced because Trappe is afraid that cattle diseases can be
> brought over its borders and, without a permit, nobody can penetrate the
> farm through the always-locked farm gates.'

Mrs Pienaar spoke of the profusion of wildlife on *Ngongongare* that included black rhino and hippo, but she also spoke of feeling trapped 'in a huge camp' whose boundaries were guarded. No casual movement in and out of the property was allowed, Mrs Pienaar writing:

> 'For me, a lover of freedom and space without borders, such a thing is a
> bitter experience, the thought alone that oppressive restrictions curb my
> movements.'

The Germans were on high alert in the region because of spoor picked up, indicating enemy reconnaissance. The Boers were automatically suspect and this meant that Abel Pienaar in particular had to restrict even further his movements off the farm when he would usually accompany Margarete to visit other farms in the district.

The tensions of wartime and the loss of personal freedom and space are reflected in Mrs Pienaar's words when she wrote about sharing living space with Margarete. She remained infinitely grateful for the hospitality and kindness, but wrote:

> '... there is a deep chasm between her and me... she is a typical German
> woman; we, on the other hand are Afrikaners, or rather Boers. We differ in
> traditions, however much we may try to agree and feel. We are not *one*. Not
> *one* in terms of language and habits and outlook on life. Despite a friendship
> of years' standing and mutual affection and respect, despite mutual grati-
> tude, there is a spirit of reserve. We feel foreign towards each other... the
> Germans are proud and rigid and inflexible. They are disciplined and every-
> thing bears the stamp of strict formality. Now, this overwhelming spirit of
> militarism is seeping into everything and hangs like a dark cloud over one's
> comings and goings. This is alien to the Boer. It scares me. Our spirit is free
> and flexible. The Boer's character is vivid and much more predisposed to
> new impressions ...'

Mrs Pienaar also spoke of Margarete's Draconian discipline towards the workforce, but defended her, saying that she could not overlook misdemeanors or slacken her stance 'because of the huge and demanding farm Mrs Trappe, like any other pioneer, must act very strictly. Weakness cannot be tolerated.' As Mrs Pienaar wrote:

> 'She was strict, terribly strict, but just. She paid her workforce well and regu-
> larly but if they bungled, the lashes were quick in coming. As far as her
> orders and rules were concerned, I feel she was very hard.'

Mrs Pienaar, like most of the Boer community, was increasingly anxious about the future as the war dragged on. The arrival of Boers with General Smuts also meant that Boer would be fighting against Boer in the East African theatre and this caused Mrs Pienaar intense anxiety.

In November 1915, Abel Pienaar reported to Margarete that there were rumours of a British spy patrol having slipped over the border from Kenya and that it had penetrated the Meru district. German soldiers and some *askaris* were called in and a search launched. Margarete joined the *askaris* in the tracking, but nothing was found. What did arise the next day was yet another rumour that Boers were involved with the British in this latest espionage scare. Margarete was full of concern for her Boer guests, especially when she learned that Abel Pienaar was a suspect. She pleaded with the Pienaars to become German subjects, but Abel Pienaar reiterated his innocence of any espionage charges on behalf of the British and refused to change nationality. Margarete then warned that the Germans were now speaking of shooting dead anyone believed to be a spy. Back came the reply: "They can do as they see fit. I shall remain what I am; I am innocent."

Two days later, the Germans informed Abel Pienaar that a thorough investigation had proved he was innocent and that the charge had its origins in the bad faith of fellow Boers!

Time to get out

Just as Margarete was about to deliver fresh supplies of venison to the 9th Shooting Company she was informed on 10 March 1916 to get off the estate as fast as possible with her cattle and horses and head away from the Kilimanjaro plains. She was briefed that General Smuts had taken Longido in the northwest and that he and his forces were heading for Moshi. The intention was to surround Von Lettow-Vorbeck and force him into a decisive confrontation. Margarete knew that the German commander would retreat in the face of overwhelming force, in classic guerrilla warfare mode.

Smuts would try again and again to entrap the German commander and draw him into the eye of the storm in the crucially important highlands. This never happened. The wily German had withdrawn south of Moshi to Kahe, close to the Usambara Railway, well positioned on two croc-infested rivers where one of the *Königsberg* guns and several maxims were primed and ready. Von Lettow-Vorbeck was drawing the Allies into a trap as Margarete was given the briefest of time to round up help and drive out her huge cattle herd and stud of horses to a safer region.

By the time the British arrived in Kahe, they had suffered heavy casualties, hunger and thirst. The Germans had vanished overnight, disabling the *Königsberg* gun and laying waste to anything else of use that they could not take with them. This scorched earth policy would be resorted to again and again as one of the tactics to thwart and delay Allied attacks.

Smuts was taken aback at Von Lettow-Vorbeck's military prowess; he was stunned by the fighting qualities and bush skills of the *askaris* and he had begun to discover the huge threat posed by the country itself – the climate and diseases such as malaria, blackwater fever, guinea worm, jigger fleas, tick fever, typhoid and amoebic dysentery that would decimate his army. Extreme exhaustion and severe malnutrition were further curses that scythed through the troops. Horses, mules, donkeys and oxen succumbed in their thousands to tsetse fly, attracting predators, especially lion, that sometimes turned man-eater when coming across scores of sick and dying humans. Easy meat.

Smuts also made acquaintance with the most formidable foe of the lot, the torment of the heavy rains that usually began in March and that would last for a relentless two months. It would prove to be the worst rainy season in living memory at the time. This was a reality that 'surpassed the worst I had read or heard,' to quote Smuts. Mildew, damp, rust, sodden clothing, wet food, mud, swollen rivers and impassable terrain took on a whole new dimension in the Allies' vocabulary.

Here, Margarete had the advantage. She knew and respected the tribal peoples, spoke fluent Kiswahili and never viewed them as 'a lot of niggers'. They were part of her life and helped her and her family survive. She had lived in the country under often tough conditions for seven solid years before this foreign-incubated war and she knew all about tropical diseases and the rains. She was inured to the climatic hardships. Most of all, she had everything to lose and, therefore, the most powerful motivation to clear out and stay ahead of the Allied forces with her cattle and horses.

In a matter of hours, Margarete had to take leave of her sister, children and the Pienaars in the midst of this latest crisis. Mrs Pienaar wrote:

'She was always a courageous woman, very courageous – I can even say hard, for a woman – but she became distressed when she had to say goodbye to us, her sister, and bitterest of all, her children. Believe me, her faithful old natives were in tears.'

Margarete, after hugging Rolf, turned to Mrs Pienaar and said: "Look after him well because he is my darling."

The 9th Shooting Company had already withdrawn from *Momella* as Margarete summoned her headman and workforce to select people to help her herd the cattle off the property and take the entire stud of horses with them. The rest of the workforce, under Abel Pienaar and his family, would remain to look after the estate as best they could until *Yeyo* returned. As she gave orders to prepare to clear out the kraals and stables, stunned herders and stable hands complied, trying to fathom this latest *Wazungu* madness.

It was a surreal experience: in a handwritten letter by Margarete shared with the author, the feisty pioneer described to relatives how a thousand head of cattle were rounded up out of the pastures and out of the kraals, several cows heavy with calf. Dozens of horses were taken from paddocks and stables and driven ahead, controlled by a handful of mounted 'horse boys', Margarete on Comet moving in and out of the masses of livestock, giving directions. The air filled with the bellows, snorts, whinnies and lowings of animals in varying stages of unease as this doleful procession headed east towards Moshi before turning south. Margarete did not look back as she moved along the track leading away from the estate. To look back was to risk being paralysed with distress.

She rode ahead, seeking back ways and cross-country paths to minimize detection. Every high point and opening was used to try to spot distant dust clouds and other signs of enemy movement. It was a constant fight to keep the cattle more or less together and to round up strays and get them back into the main body of cattle. The first forced march was hardly over before the first calf was born. No sooner had the cow licked the calf clean before the little creature was hoisted onto the pommel of a saddle and the march continued. Several other calves would be born before that fearful experience was over. Streams on the way mercifully slaked the thirst of animal and human alike.

Before night fell like a stone, rudimentary enclosures of thorn and scrub were erected to try to contain the animals and protect them from carnivores as Margarete shared guard duty in relays throughout the night. Fires could not be lit for obvious reasons. Hyena arpeggios, counterpointed by the staccato calls of lion and interspersed by the scavenger musings of black-backed jackal – usually so comforting to Margarete – now carried ominously on the crisp air that night so long ago.

The following day saw a couple of calves drown when the cattle missed the ford over a river. Margarete moved about on Comet, barking orders until all the cattle had been accounted for before galloping back to the horses and cracking down on the workers for letting the horses wander off. Margarete had to spend hours after dark in not quite so familiar terrain rounding up the last of her horses. It was beginning to feel like a march of the damned.

During the afternoon of the third day, as the moving mass of livestock and the few human herders pushed ahead, Margarete caught sight of two mounted *Schutztruppe*. It was like seeing a mirage of an oasis in a desert such was the relief after the intense stress. Comet was given his head and Margarete caught up with the Germans who instantly recognized her and passed on a message from Von Lettow-Vorbeck. The riders were from the 9th Shooting Company. The Germans had scored another victory over the enemy to the east, but the British had taken over Arusha on 20 March 1916.

The Trappe livestock was moved to the Company's laager where Margarete joined the forces. It was at this stage that she rendered further services to the war effort. She also managed to move additional horses and some cattle through a section of the Pare Mountains to a German base without being detected by the allied patrols. Her knowledge of terrain was the key factor.

There are all sorts of apocryphal, even nonsensical stories about Margarete Trappe from that time, one being that she flew an aircraft against the enemy. Margarete was never a pilot. She was a bush-hardened operative who knew how to obtain information and co-operation from the tribal peoples. She had supplied the *Schutztruppe* with a wide range of foodstuffs and had provided advanced care for their horses. She had also carried out personal reconnaissance missions for at least two years to glean information for the *Schutztruppe* about enemy force disposition and concentration. Margarete knew the region and interacted well with the tribal peoples, from the simplest tribal woman to the chiefs.

It would be over three months before Margarete would see her children again and return home. In that time, the Allies had finally penetrated the Kilimanjaro region and had occupied it. In fact, just days after Margarete's dramatic departure, a worker reported to Abel Pienaar that the N*geresa* [Waingereza] had arrived! Mrs Pienaar's diary describes that day:

> "'N*geresa*, N*geresa*,'" he shouted. English, English. How many English?... "Au, Bwana, like grass, so many!" How many wagons? "Au, like stones, so many stones!..."'

Von Lettow-Vorbeck never remained in an area where he risked being forced into a conventional fight and where he knew he could not repulse the enemy and hold the land. He understood guerrilla warfare tactics to perfection. Orders finally came from him to Margarete to leave the company as British war propaganda was already churning out stories of the Germans using women in German East Africa in active combat.

A document made available to the author by one of Margarete's grandsons, reveals that the British Commander-in-Chief had formally contacted Von Lettow-Vorbeck. The document complains about 'a German woman', the British Chief then warning Von Lettow-Vorbeck that the British were aware of the use he was making of a woman who was participating in this war and that she was 'perpetrating inhumanities'. Obviously, the 'inhumanities' part was nonsense, but what was abundantly clear was that Margarete now had to cease her clandestine activities and go home, but not before completing one last mission. She was to leave with Comet, a mare and two foals as well as three of her 'boys' by rail for Mombo, a good 216kms (just over 133 miles) southeast of Moshi. There, she was to head into the Usambara Mountains, near Wilhelmsthal and lie low.

Valuable insight was provided by Maximilian von Rogister, who had been at *Momella* in the early 1950s and who had hunted with Margarete's second son, Rolf. The year preceding his safari, Von Rogister had spent quality time in London with General Von Lettow-Vorbeck and with a British officer by the name of Isherwood who had fought in the German East African campaign against Von Lettow-Vorbeck.

The three men had lunch at the British officer's London club and it was there that Von Rogister was 'regaled' by *both* men concerning Margarete's 'amazing adventures'. The fact that *both* men spoke of Margarete confirmed how aware the British military had become of her. They, like the Germans, knew that she was 'venerated and feared' by the tribal peoples because of the way in which she would disappear and then, like a supernatural entity, suddenly reappear on horseback, unscathed, mission accomplished, whatever it may have been.

General Von Lettow-Vorbeck and his British host could relax and speak of once strictly classified missions because the campaign in German East Africa had ended almost forty years previously and there was no longer any danger in mentioning details concerning Margarete Trappe and how she had resupplied German forces and undertaken reconnaissance work. The 'war to end all wars' had long since been overtaken, anyway, by the subsequent world war and its fallout.

The General described how the Germans had already been forced to retreat away from the high country into the interior, but that Margarete had managed to deliver 'two large transports of cattle and provisions' to the General and his men. One of these transports concerned the Trappe estate cattle and horses, already mentioned.

The final operation saw Margarete taking over complete command of a mission to bring 'a large convoy of horses' through British lines. A group of German farmers had failed to get through the British lines and were pretty well surrounded by the enemy, exhausted and fearful of capture. Margarete made use of a British deserter and, in classic psychological warfare mode, she used him to help spread disinformation back to the British about the actual route that this convoy of horses would be taking to get past the British lines.

The mission took place in the thickly forested region of the West Usambara Mountains. Under cover of darkness and via passes and tracks over the mountains that the British did not know at all, but that Margarete had clearly reconnoitered previously, she and her tough tribal workers from *Momella* managed to deliver every single one of the horses to safety, right under the noses of British patrols and intelligence scouts. It was straight after this extraordinary accomplishment that General Von Lettow-Vorbeck ordered Margarete to then ride into Wilhelmsthal and give herself up.

The General knew that his highly mobile guerrilla war would take him further and further away from the high country and from Margarete's home. She could not remain with the troops. They were deliberately moving southwards and forcing the British and their allies to follow them, dispersing the enemy's troops and, hopefully, diluting the fighting strength, at least for a time. In any case, as Margarete wrote in a letter to a relative in Germany years afterwards, General Von Lettow-Vorbeck felt that if Margarete had remained any longer with his forces, things could have gone badly for the other German women in the country, implying some sort of revenge such as internment or worse.

It was now becoming clearer that German East Africa was falling little by little into enemy hands. Margarete surveyed her position: the cattle and horses were off the estate, but what now? How would she, her immediate family and her whole workforce survive under enemy occupation? Ulrich Trappe was long gone. She was alone as never before.

The Occupation Years

Margarete and Comet emerged from their bush hideout and rode into the beautiful hill station of Wilhelmsthal, now occupied by the British and their allies. The effect of this young woman on her black stallion, boldly riding into the heart of the settlement can but be imagined. The Allies knew about her and had heard and maybe even added to stories about her transport supply activities with Von Lettow-Vorbeck and the *askaris*.

Wilhelmsthal was filled with about 500 German women and children – the families of men serving in the *Schutztruppe*, and missionaries who had been forced to abandon their stations in the bush. The settlement had seen no strife at all and was quiet. General Smuts ordered it to be placed under the command of an officer, a subaltern and 25 mounted men. The German population was depressed at the retreat of their forces, however calculated, and at the growing number of Allied troops in the colony.

Proof of suspicion about Margarete's activities came when she was brought before a British officer who proceeded to interrogate her about what she knew of *Schutztruppe* movements. Margarete knew a great deal. She knew the troops were heading south, away from the Pangani River and into the centre of the country through arid, sandy terrain where rearguard actions would be launched against the Allies to try to disperse their forces and weaken their clout. Margarete shot back a reply that the *Schutztruppe* would never have divulged their plans to a mere woman! This doubtless found resonance with the male mentality of the time because the line of questioning was dropped forthwith. Women are said to make good intelligence agents because they are often underestimated. Men relax their guard in their company and ask the sort of questions that often indicate what they do not yet know!

Now the pot was on the boil. The British officer then changed tack and accused Margarete of supplying the German forces with large cattle herds and many horses – as in the major mission she had recently completed without the British having been able to catch her. The feisty lady barked back that she was merely doing her duty, as she wrote in yet another letter to her family in Germany long afterwards. She told her inquisitors that she now had nothing left, that she wanted to return to her children and farm. She also undertook not to act against the British in the future.

This was deemed not good enough. The British interrogator wanted to intern her in a prisoner-of-war camp. He was immediately overruled by a General Lane who then started taking an unhealthy interest in Comet. Margarete warned anyone within earshot that she would shoot her horse dead right there, right then in front of the General and his men rather than see it fall into British hands. She had given her word on this score to Von Lettow-Vorbeck and, as the assembled officers could see, Margarete was armed. She kept Comet and was told she could also keep any other horses she so chose.

The British then ordered Margarete to hand over her Mauser rifle and sidearm as well as all ammunition. While emptying her pockets, out came a few rupee coins that had been shot through the middle – by her in a very recent impromptu shooting contest with German troops. That did it for General Lane. He ordered that she keep her firearms and that his officers take the rupees as souvenirs and be sure to tell their families back home of this German woman's skill at arms. Clearly, Margarete's reputation – embellished or not – and her cold-eyed resolve in a wartime situation had somewhat puzzled and impressed the enemy soldiers. She was to be given an escort back to *Ngongongare* and *Momella*.

Homeward Bound

Margarete arrived back in Moshi with several of her workforce who had been with her throughout. Her military escort took her to the military *boma* or headquarters where the German Imperial flag no longer flew. It was early July 1916, the coolest time of the year, but nothing as to the chill of the news awaiting her. General Smuts had ordered her internment in a camp. Overwhelmed by images of the previous nine years and more in the colony and by all that it had cost her personally to invest in a new life there, she erupted at the British officers present and told them to tell General Smuts she would not be separated any longer from her children and that she was leaving! She gave her word not to engage in any activities contrary to British interests. She then prepared to walk out, snubbing an order from the supreme commander of the Allied forces in East Africa.

The dismayed officer in charge scurried about, battling to contact General Smuts for advice in the face of this female tornado. Back came the reply from General

Margarete on Comet. [Dr Jobst-Ulrich Trappe]

Smuts: let Mrs Trappe go home. Her word is indeed her bond, but she is to report to the British in Arusha at regular intervals. This was like being on some sort of parole.

The light was fading and the air cold by the time Margarete and her workers were near *Ngongongare*. She had left Comet with a Boer friend in the vicinity who was doubtless taken aback at the sight of the strained and worn out woman. She and her workers then went on foot for the last section of track.

It was dark and lion were very vocal. The men did not want to move another inch, but Margarete drove them forward, no doubt talking loudly and making a noise in an attempt to scare off the carnivores as she pressed on to the farmhouse where her children and sister had returned in the meantime. The Pienaars had tried to hold the fort under difficult and dangerous circumstances. They were allowed to return to their own farm by the next month. It is curious to note that Gerd von Lettow-Vorbeck did not mention the Pienaar family at all in his book *Am Fusse des Meru*.

Mrs Pienaar's diary speaks of her husband having 'a few thousand Rupees' of Margarete's money in safekeeping. He had buried it during her absence and had dug it up and handed it back to her, together with 'some cattle, small livestock, poultry and other belongings.' The reunion with Tine and the children, after months of separation, a news blackout and the arrival in strength of enemy forces, was overpowering and it was bitter sweet. Most of Margarete's original workforce, singly and in small groups, started to reappear, having somehow heard of Margarete's return via the usually infallible and still mysterious African bush telegraph system. They were relieved to see her and she would find out why in the morning.

At first light, Margarete saw how her farm – once one of the most celebrated in the colony – had degenerated into a shambles of neglect. Almost ten years of sacrifice and ceaseless hard work lay in near-ruin before her. The Maasai had simply moved in *en masse* with their cattle. Here, it is perhaps interesting to note that Margarete was never overwhelmed by this warrior people. She never tolerated any kind of challenge to her authority. The Pienaars, as farm managers in her absence, were clearly viewed in a different light and were not respected. They were certainly not feared. Margarete, for all her consistent decency towards the tribal peoples, especially in times of illness, *was* feared because she never hesitated to call in her headman to deal immediately with any kind of insubordination or threat to her authority. Punishment was very harsh, but always fair because everyone knew exactly where the line was drawn with Margarete. They also knew that nobody ever dared step over that line a second time.

The orchards, flower and vegetable gardens were choked with weeds, the kraals empty, of course, the fences broken and the cattle dipping structures in disrepair. The poultry runs were now home to meagre numbers of birds, doubtless having been raided for protein in the intervening months. Everywhere signs of decay, stagnation and abandonment assaulted her senses. All kinds of farming equipment had yet to be inspected, if much of it was still there, that is. The houses were ramshackle in that peculiar way with all dwellings when they are not inhabited or properly maintained for long periods. Margarete would have to start over with her workers. She would start with the Maasai.

A People Apart

The Maasai were expecting a confrontation with *Yeyo* who was back on her farm. This warrior nation believed that their god, *Engai*, had singled them out as his most favoured people and had given them all the cattle in the universe to be theirs by divine right. Not believing in any life after death, the Maasai attached special importance to the here and now and that meant cattle. Their rich oral history, passed down through the generations around the tribal cattle-dung fires, was replete with colourful legends and spoke of a time when all animals and humans lived in harmony and in a state of equality, understanding each other to perfection. The natural world was inextricably interwoven with Maasai history as stories were bequeathed from one generation to the next, explaining the inexplicable, teaching codes of behaviour and conserving the striking Maasai culture in the face of an increasing European presence.

The Leipzig Mission had established a presence in Moshi in 1893 and had been trying ever since to make religious inroads into this fiercely independent people. The missionaries had even established the first orthography of the Maa language by 1912, but had made little progress in the conversion business as they intruded into the lives of tribal peoples and their ancient ways. By May 1916, however, the entire region where the Leipzig mission was active in the northeast of the colony – Margarete's territory – had been overrun by allied forces.

Margarete was alone as she rode out to the Maasai Reserve to confront the chief, his fully fledged warriors, the *Olmurrani*, and his advisors with their staffs of office. These were heavy wooden clubs or *rungus* made of olive wood that had been blackened after being buried in the wet black soil in which cotton was grown. The chief, of course, was accompanied by the most senior witchdoctor or *laibon* with his fearsome reputation for casting spells and sniffing out wrongdoers.

The chief and his subjects knew, of course, that the 'woman with many cattle' was not coming in peace and that she would not leave until she had concluded a deal to accommodate her wishes. They also knew that she knew about their culture and respected it always, but that she also had her culture and was an indomitable fighter when she was wronged or angered. Margarete knew the dictum in the Maasai culture about 'keeping your eyes closed and your mouth shut', in other words, minding one's own business, but she was never prepared to tolerate theft, insubordination, shoddy work or trespassing onto her property. And if it came to protecting her cattle and other livestock in the face of Maasai misbehaviour, as in this instance, Margarete would face down anyone, even the feared *laibon*. She knew about the curse the Maasai most dreaded: "May God give you a palm of leather!" This incorporated the Maasai's worst fear, namely of losing all his cattle and of being forced to do manual labour like tilling the soil and developing calloused hands. *Yeyo* had also surely come to speak about their cattle on her land.

As Margarete dismounted from Comet at the entrance to the *manyatta* or village and its numerous clusters of large structures with their cattle-dung walls, she was greeted by the chief's men with a gourd of a fermented drink made out of honey instead of the customary offering of milk. The Maasai knew that many *Wazungu* preferred this drink to milk.

She was ushered into the presence of the chief. After the ritual greetings, one of which would have been 'How are your cattle?', the now tougher than ever woman proceeded to speak in terms her host understood: his cattle were on her lands; they had moved there in her absence, but now she was back and in charge once more. If the chief wanted his subjects to graze some of their cattle on designated areas of her lands, they could do so by renting the right via a system of barter with livestock while she began to rebuild her own herds. Failure to come to an arrangement would result in a series of fines involving goats and oxen.

Everyone knew Margarete Trappe kept her word. Everyone also knew she was habitually armed, fearless, a deadly shot and ready to enforce any agreement reached. To conclude the proceedings, Margarete came away with over 200 goats to provide meat, milk and cheese. She also came away with a few dozen oxen to start tilling soil once more and to inspan for transport purposes. The Maasai and Margarete had reached their own *entente cordiale* as the *Wazungu* war moved well away and into the centre of the country.

Bartering kick-started the Trappe estate into renewed life. The workers and their families were once more in a structured environment where they knew their needs would also be taken into consideration. Margarete reported at regular intervals to the British military authorities in Arusha as she pursued a murderous routine of relentless toil from sunrise to sunset. Her sister, Tine, was of inestimable value with the children who, mercifully, adapted in a flash to the reappearance of their mother. As for Tine, she suffered a personal tragedy before war's end when her fiancé was killed in action in France. She never married, devoting herself instead to her sister's family to the end of her life.

Professional Poacher

Life, of course, could not run on bartering alone. Margarete needed cash to have any chance at all of re-establishing the estate and of retaining her loyal workforce without whom she could not have survived. Everything and everyone depended on her. The only way to survive was to start poaching animals for hides, ivory and rhino horn and to start liaising with certain Indian traders in Arusha who would pass on the poached products to middlemen and make over money at regular intervals.

It is easy for today's reader, going on one century after the fact, to express distaste for this decision. It is also easy for anyone to understand the desperation of a mother with three children, a sister and dozens of workers to house, feed and care for in an atmosphere of rising uncertainty and in a time of war. Margarete's first duty was to sustain her own life and the lives of those who depended on her. The country was awash with game, the AK-47 had not yet been invented and Africa was not yet the scene of unbridled slaughter by militias, guerrilla forces and out-of-control international poaching syndicates equipped with helicopters and machine-guns. This was one woman's battle to stay alive with her family and workforce in time of war.

The war had put a stop to all conventional hunting, certainly to the occasional professional hunting with notables from Europe. There is no doubt that this boosted the already robust game populations. Margarete, long known as a disciplined and ethical

Elephant [Marlies and Jörg Gabriel]

huntress, followed certain self-imposed rules in the field that she continued to respect during the poaching period. It distressed her greatly that matters had come to such a pass, that she had to resort to poaching and middlemen in order to generate an income, hold the family and the property together and feed dozens of mouths in the process. Only those who have endured such a trauma can fully understand the moral anguish.

Margarete did not use tree platforms as shooting brakes; she never shot at waterholes; she never shot females, if she could help it; she always followed up a wounded animal and she never squeezed the trigger unless she was sure of her target and of a clean kill. A firm credo was the selection, whenever possible, of mature male animals, preferably past breeding prime. Margarete rarely hunted on the estate itself, preferring to leave for any of a multiplicity of destinations in the region.

As was her habit in general, Margarete travelled light in that she never took along more than three of her workers and she lived off the veld entirely for all food and water needs. After years of apprenticeship in the wilds, she could identify edible wild fruits, berries and roots and, if in doubt, she would try to see if monkeys ate the item in question. If so, humans could do so with safety. She knew how to filter water, build campfires that burned all night and how to make a hollow in the ground in which to sleep, wrapped in a blanket under the stars. She determined the length of any hunting expedition or, as was now the case, poaching foray.

Margarete used a highly disciplined pack of dogs to hunt lion that were now more prolific than ever. They had reached plague-like proportions in the Mount Meru region during the war years. Lion killed cattle. They also killed and ate people, given half the chance. Dogs were particularly useful in thick bush, in high grass or where termite mounds hindered the field of vision. In one incident, Margarete and a helper had put out bait for lion and then spent the entire night in an open area, lying in grass, waiting for the creature to show up. It did indeed and Margarete shot, killing in cleanly, but not before experiencing a hangfire.

In fact, the scarcity of ammunition and the constant risk of dud ammunition added to the tension during the poaching years. She sold the skin of this 'cattle-killer' to a British officer who was followed by his brother officers, all wanting similar souvenirs to take back to Britain. They even gave Margarete ammunition for the purpose as it was in increasingly short supply. She concentrated after that on 'cattle-killers'. It was financially worthwhile and it was legal. One wonders how many daring stories of lion hunting accompanied the officers back home. The tribal peoples also prized lion fat as it was believed to cure all manner of physical ills. This placed a monetary value on the fat, naturally.

A particularly distressing incident took place involving lion. Margarete had ridden out with her pack of hunting dogs on a lion hunt. The pack was led by her favourite, 'Tell', a German pointer. She had shot a zebra for bait and had observed a lion and lioness at dawn the next day, moving off, sway-bellied and satiated. The dogs were let loose. The lioness escaped, but the extravagantly-maned lion was bayed. Tell led the charge, but was severely injured when it caught a swipe of the lion's paw. Margarete shot the lion dead and rushed over to her favourite hunting dog to try and save it. It was too badly injured and she had to shoot it to end its suffering.

Margarete described to Gerd von Lettow-Vorbeck many years later how she lay down beside her dead dog and wept with anguish and remorse. Such was the effect of that terrible day that Margarete was never able to use a shotgun again. Wingshooting meant shotguns and shotguns meant Tell because he was her retriever companion on such excursions for duck, francolin and guinea-fowl. After his death under such awful circumstances, Margarete was permanently traumatised. There is no record of what happened to the lion skin from that particular hunt, but Margarete had to be practical. This was about survival and to survive one had to have a cash flow.

Another fine arrangement was concluded with the Maasai – by now back in line and obeying the new rules. They used buffalo skins for their shields. Margarete would oblige, in return for Zebu cattle and other livestock. There were some exceptionally dangerous occasions involving wild animals, as recounted to Gerd von Lettow-Vorbeck and as shared with family members down the years. One such incident occurred when Margarete wounded a buffalo and then had to follow it up. Her three helpers climbed trees to try to catch sight of the animal, but to no avail. She had to go in alone through thick bush before locating the buffalo, shoulder-shot and stone dead. Raw luck.

Hippo was also on the poaching menu. The flesh, fat and hide served a multiplicity of uses in the tribal cultures and the Europeans also prized the hide for whips and the fat for candles and soap. Margarete once shot a female hippo quite unwittingly. Her workers then took fright and refused to go into the lake to secure lianas around the carcass in order to drag it to the bank. Undaunted, Margarete waded in and did the job herself, having a very lucky escape from a bull hippo in the process. A new story eventually began to circulate that Margarete 'rode hippos'.

Hippo can be exceedingly dangerous when out of their watery world and on land. Once, Margarete found herself between the water and two hippos. They were in the process of moving from one pool to another over a neck of land. One of the creatures continued on its way while the other charged her from a perilously short distance. She just had time to shoulder her rifle before dropping the bull a handful of metres from her. Margarete referred to this particular incident as one of the most horrific of her years in the bush although it was over in seconds.

Speaking of hunting dogs, there are dogs and dogs, of course. Lord Horatio Kitchener,

*Leopard
[Marlies and Jörg
Gabriel]*

he of *Your Country Needs You* fame on the recruiting posters for the First World War and of Anglo-Boer War concentration camp and scorched earth infamy, visited the Trappe estate before the outbreak of the war. News travelled in a flash to the immigrant Boer community in the immediate region for whom Kitchener was the incarnation of the devil himself. What was he doing on the Trappe estate? Surely this friend of the Boers was not about to entertain this Anglo-Boer War villain!

It turned out that the hated Lord was looking for a good new home for his pointer, Rover. Margarete's name automatically came up among the British, hence the visit. Margarete took in the dog. It was natural to suppose that it would be useful in the hunting field. Not so. Rover was a cowardly creature, especially in the face of big cats. If he charged ahead in the field, it was a sure sign there was no game. During a rhino hunt, poor old Rover raced back and sought refuge behind Margarete as the rhino charged and Margarete dropped it with one shot. Her helpers had also sought refuge – up a couple of trees! Rover became a house dog after a few such experiments in the field. There is no record to prove that he braced even a house mouse in his domestic duties.

In between poaching to fill the pantry and maintaining constant vigilance concerning potential cattle rustlers, Margarete had other dramas such as the time she came back to *Momella* to total pandemonium. Several of her dogs had been bitten by a puff adder. Remembering a curious story told her by one of the English lady settlers, Margarete quickly made a strong solution of salt and water and then squirted it into the eyes of all the dogs concerned. They recovered! Sometimes, when Margarete told this story, she was met by polite, quizzical smiles that said: 'The old girl must be daft if she thinks we believe this one!'

She had to treat several members of her workforce over the years for snakebite and had lost small livestock such as lambs and goats to pythons. Margarete's Maasai workers shared with her their legend concerning snakes. They believed that when humans die, their souls die with them and that is that. The Maasai believed that there was no after-life for humans or cattle. Unless, of course, one is speaking of a 'medicine man', a witchdoctor or a rich person.

Such people were not left outside for the hyenas or for the wild animals to devour. They were buried. Once the body had rotted, the soul turned into a snake that then slithered away into the kraal of the dead person's children. Because of this belief, entrenched when the Germans first established a presence in East Africa in the 1880s, many Maasai clans had what they called sacred snakes that were venerated and never killed. If a snake came into a hut, the custom was to pour some milk onto the floor for it to lick before it left of its own accord. The 'medicine men' were also rumoured to keep snakes in their medicine bags.

Margarete specialised in rhino and elephant during that distressing period in her life as rhino horn and ivory brought in the best revenue. Some of the horns were fashioned into walking sticks while others, as was to be expected, were sent on their way. This also meant the coast and shipment to India for use in oriental medicine with its still-pervasive beliefs in the aphrodisiacal properties of rhino horn, among many other uses. The sea links between India and East Africa are centuries' old, as is the use of rhino horn in the Unani medical tradition, as practised by Muslims.

As for elephant, the tusks had to be chopped out and hidden in great secrecy. In fact, Margarete used to take along only one of her workers when poaching elephant. She would assist in the physically strenuous work of burying the tusks so that the rest of the flesh would rot and fall away, making it easier to clean up the tusks and move them later on, after dark and with exceeding caution, to the Indian middlemen in Arusha.

Margarete also sought elephant at 4 000m on the slopes of Mount Meru in exceedingly cold conditions. The dense undergrowth and forest compounded the challenge of tracking and shooting. Once, an elephant Margarete had shot and was sure had died, suddenly stirred. Before things could turn ugly, she shot again, averting a potential catastrophe of death and scandal in the middle of the British occupation, her husband already on the other side of the world as a prisoner-of-war.

Nothing was wasted on these clandestine elephant expeditions. Margarete ensured that the women and children were given meat to dry for a steady source of rations. She also made sure the young men were at the back of the queue as the women and children were more vulnerable.

The beliefs of the tribal peoples permeated Margarete's daily life and she grew to respect and live with such beliefs. She learned, for example, that the young Wameru men would not touch elephant meat because of a legend involving an ancestral chief. He had to leave the family kraal for a while and had instructed his other children to make sure that they fed his favourite daughter well and thoroughly in her hut in his absence. Plumpness, even obesity, in many African cultures is associated with wealth, as proved in the supposedly outlawed custom of *gavage* or force-feeding of young girls in Mauritania that continues in the new millennium.

The daughter was duly fed until she reached elephantine proportions. Her hut burst and, according to the legend, out came a female elephant with breasts in the front part of the body. Young Wameru warriors ever after refuse to touch elephant meat as they refuse to eat from a female animal.

As money came in from the poaching activities, the farm started to recover. All Margarete's original workforce had returned to *Ngongongare* and *Momella*. The vegetable gardens were weeded and replanted and the cattle kraals started to fill with healthy, hardy Zebu cattle, and the nucleus of a new dairy herd had been acquired. While her

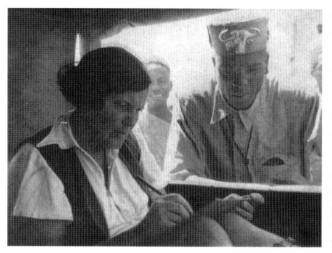

Margarete perusing reports as Honorary Game Warden under the British authorities. [Dr Jobst-Ulrich Trappe]

once impressive stud of brood mares was still a dream, Margarete's stables were once more home to new animals and there was a sense of fresh purpose and hope in the air. Goats and sheep were acquired little by little.

The children all learned to ride as toddlers and were raised with a wondrous variety of wild animal pets such as zebra foals, buffalo calf orphans, antelope and even wild dog puppies. Ulrich and Rolf accompanied their mother on horseback as young children to go out and participate in hunts for plains game and to start learning the ways of wildlife. They were taught firearms safety and proficiency while very young. The boys and their elder sister were raised without fear and amid such stupendous natural beauty and wildlife abundance that they were automatically shielded from the adult world of war games. They tended to speak only the Meru language with one another and were raised on the stories, myths and legends of two cultures from birth.

As the cattle kraals filled, carnivore activity increased. One moonlit night, in between poaching, Margarete and her Maasai herdsmen lay in wait at the cattle kraals after several losses to lion and leopard. Clouds moved over the face of the moon, turning the night into a threatening, Stygian darkness. The night wore on and the cattle started becoming restless, a potential sign of trouble on the perimeter. As the clouds leaked away from the bright face of the moon, Margarete and the Maasai made out a dark shape on the far side of the cattle kraal. It moved. It moved again. The lithe form of a marauding leopard punctured the gloom on the thorn enclosure and Margarete let fly with her firearm. The shape twisted, flipped backwards and disappeared. Was the leopard dead or wounded? Margarete and her helper remained frozen, straining to hear above the cacophony of the cattle. Eventual calm returned. The bright moon grew anaemic, giving way to the dawn skies of a new day. Stiff and chilled, both humans made their way around the kraal's edge, still ready for trouble. The leopard was found close to the kraal, dead.

The British, who were now in strength in the Meru/Kilimanjaro region, eventually became aware of Margarete's poaching activities, but they never succeeded in catching her in the act. She had the absolute loyalty of her workforce, ranged over a vast area to poach and exercised the countertracking skills of a Special Forces commando in evading detection.

Honorary Game Warden

The estate was now out of debt and doing well enough for Margarete to cease all poaching. She actually reported this to the British authorities in Arusha during one of her mandatory visits. The British were not stupid: they knew that a proficient poacher had intimate knowledge of all the subterfuges of the calling and that former poachers made excellent game wardens. The British offered Margarete the position of honorary game ranger to help them curb poaching, report on problem animals causing crop damage and to put down any injured game. In the process, the occupiers hoped to learn a trick or two from this woman whose courage they had come to admire, begrudgingly or otherwise. As for Margarete, it was a job made in heaven and one she took very seriously from the outset.

She was given flare pistols as one of the job perks to scare elephant away from her crops. One night, she and her herdsmen declared a mini-war against crop-raiding elephant. One bull had to be shot in the process. It was a persistent, foul-tempered crop raider, greatly feared by the workers. On coming up to the body of the bull, Margarete discovered that it had the remains of a third tusk. It had suffered from a massive boil at the lip where the tusk had broken off, probably in a fight with another bull. The resultant pain explained the bull's terrible temper and probably its predilection for easy feeding off crops instead of stripping bark off trees and wandering far to find other vegetation. Now the workforce could feed off the carcass. Nothing would be wasted in a world where everything ate something.

A False Dawn

The German forces were now in the far south, in the vicinity of the central railway line near Morogoro, west of Dar es Salaam. They had evaded Smuts and his men and had retreated even further south into the Uluguru Hills via a track only the Germans and their *askaris* knew. Fighting ensued and the Germans withdrew ever southwards, sabotaging what they could as they moved towards the Rufiji River. The second rainy season – known as the *vuli* – descended in all its ferocity that November of 1916, putting paid to any further pursuit by the Allies. The British had occupied Dar es Salaam on 4 September where they established their new base by early December. But the war dragged on. Margarete would study every scrap of information for some sign of an end to the hostilities and to the ceaseless uncertainty.

There was no doubt that the Allies were gaining and retaining ground. There was also no doubt that Von Lettow-Vorbeck and his forces were evading capture and effectively tying up sections of an eventual force of almost 300 000 men. General Smuts even sent a letter to his German counterpart, asking him to kindly surrender. Von Lettow-Vorbeck politely refused and the war continued.

Margarete, in the meantime, had established a very workable relationship with the British occupying force. Her reputation as an amateur veterinary surgeon spread after the German vets had left. The British consulted her about their horses, especially when the dreaded African horse sickness broke out. She was able to save not only her own horses, but those of the British. As for treating and containing cattle diseases, Margarete had acquired an impressive amount of unorthodox knowledge over the years from the Maasai in particular and she passed on what she knew.

Margarete had regular contact with the British as honorary game warden, reporting to them at frequent intervals. Naturally, some of the British officers approached Margarete to take them hunting when they had some spare time. This afforded her important opportunities to share with these officers not only her knowledge, but her passion for her farm and her hopes for the future after the end of this war, as end it surely would.

As in the pre-war years, Margarete was frequently called upon in times of need or outright crisis among the tribal peoples. One such time remained in her mind for long afterwards because of the strange concomitance of events. Among the stories shared with the author concerning the Boer community, was one concerning missing oxen. A Boer family in the vicinity had gone off for a short while, leaving their two sons in charge of their meagre possessions and their most valuable asset – the trek oxen. The oxen simply vanished one night and the frantic young men came over to *Ngongongare* in a state of panic and fear. What would they tell their parents? Margarete immediately suspected the Maasai and saddled up Comet to go over to the Maasai chief once more and have a little chat about the missing cattle. She was the arch shuttle diplomat, choosing her words with care, interacting adroitly with Boer and Maasai alike.

The obese chief, glorying in the name *Oldonyo*, meaning The Mountain, received *Yeyo* with all due ceremonial decorum, flanked by his warriors. Margarete, astute and unafraid, appealed to the chief to assist her in locating the lost oxen in order to avert trouble for the two young men with their parents when they returned. She mentioned that she could well assist the chief and his people with some special favour in return. Her fame as a healer of man and beast was entrenched among the Maasai and there is little doubt the chief thought along those lines when it came to favours. Had she not helped him when his womenfolk kept losing their newborns?

The oxen reappeared as mysteriously as they had vanished and Margarete was quick to convey the combined gratitude of all concerned, reiterating her willingness to assist the chief and his subjects in any way she could in times of trouble.

Trouble came very quickly when a Maasai arrived at night on Margarete's doorstep, pleading for her help to save a fellow tribesman who had been severely mauled by a leopard. Grabbing her medical kit, Margarete mounted Comet and left with two Maasai warriors to lead the way in the darkness over rocky terrain to the spot where she found the seriously injured man. Water was boiled and Margarete proceeded to disinfect and stitch the gaping wounds on the man's leg and arm. His injuries were well bandaged and she may or may not have given him a stiff shot of morphine in the process. No bones were broken, but the danger of blood poisoning caused by the microbe filth on the leopard's fangs and claws was the real worry now.

The next day, Margarete visited the Maasai at the same spot. He was distinctly improved and, with time, made a full recovery, bearing massive scars. The young Maasai's father was none other than *Oldonyo*, the Maasai chief who had arranged for the 'missing oxen' to return home.

When this story reached the ears of the British, as it surely would, the new military doctor in Arusha informed Margarete in writing of his displeasure at her 'helping the natives.' She wrote back a stiff reposte, reminding the British doctor that nobody would order her to refuse help to anyone who asked her for assistance. She also reminded the good doctor that 'We live in Africa' and all that this implied – interaction with the African peoples into whose land they had moved. The record does not speak of any reminder to the doctor of the Hippocratic Oath all medical doctors must swear. The said doctor was transferred and his replacement, a Major Brown, had great regard for Margarete, giving her bandages and other medical supplies. He was also a keen hunter!

The Germans and their *askaris* forced the Allies to follow them ever southwards. The climax of the entire war took place in the far southeastern corner of the colony at a place called Mahiwa. There, in October 1917, Von Lettow-Vorbeck and his men engaged in a ferocious battle amid swamps and mountains during which the Germans inflicted the most savage losses of the whole war on their adversaries who lost 2 700 out of 4 900 men. This resulted in Von Lettow-Vorbeck's being awarded oak leaves to his *Blue Max* decoration of 4 November 1916. The Germans, however, also suffered their worst losses of the war when 95 men were killed out of a total of 1 599. The losses for Von Lettow-Vorbeck were far more serious than they were for the Allied forces, given his very modest number of men under arms.

This battle propelled Von Lettow-Vorbeck and his forces by 26 November over the

Rovuma River near its confluence with the Lugenda River and into Portuguese East Africa. They routed the Portuguese and seized appreciable quantities of arms, ammunition and food supplies before pushing even further south to within 40km (25 miles) of Quelimane on the coast and raiding other supply dumps before looping back into German East Africa a solid ten months later in September 1918.

On 4 January 1917, an event occurred that was to finally bring much wider general awareness of the war in East Africa. Frederick Courteney Selous, D.S.O., was killed in action at a place called BehoBeho, just north of the Rufiji River, in what is today the Selous Game Reserve. He had been leading his men in very heavy fighting when he was felled by a bullet to the head. The news spread around the world and, suddenly, this addendum to the war in Europe was no longer the same backwater conflict. The Germans were well aware of this legendary character and there was a general sentiment of admiration for his remarkable life and courage and regret at his death at 66 years of age on active duty.

On 2 November 1918, Von Lettow-Vorbeck and his forces swung west into Northern Rhodesia, seizing and holding the settlement of Kasama, south of Lake Tanganyika, on 9 November. Despite mounting losses and the impossibility of winning this war and retaining the colony, Von Lettow-Vorbeck never remotely entertained any thought of surrender. He had already rejected out of hand a second request by the Allied Forces to surrender. In fact, the General was even personally reconnoitering the Chambeshi River south-west of Kasama that flowed into Lake Bangweulu, hugging the border with the Belgian Congo. He was planning to cross into the Congo to attack railways and mines in Katanga province before heading for the Portuguese colony of Angola! So much for surrender talk!

Margarete could tell something was up the second week of November 1918. The relationship with the British had been somewhat schizophrenic, but correct, even quite cordial. She knew by then that the war in Europe was lost, but she could not have foreseen the sudden change in attitude among the British in Arusha. As she toiled from sunrise to moonrise to re-establish the farm, co-operating expertly as honorary game warden, rebuilding the basic fabric of her family's life and the lives of all in her employ, never knowing exactly when or how the war would end, the wind shifted. On 11 November the armistice came into force in Europe. The hitherto workable relationship with the British authorities changed and Margarete's acutely developed sixth sense knew that fresh anguish was in the offing.

Forced Removal

Margarete and her family learned that the armistice came into effect at the eleventh hour on 11 November 1918 in France. It brought to an end a war that saw over ten million people die and more than twice that number injured and mutilated. The war had devastated town and countryside on a hitherto unknown scale in human affairs and words such as trench warfare, mustard gas and Ypres entered the lexicon of horror. Europe was subsequently plunged into a social trauma so vast and so terrible that the seeds of the Second World War were already being incubated in the hothouses of defeat, bitterness, unparalleled suffering, economic meltdown, hatred and despair, engulfing nation after nation for years after the armistice. The allies lost about 20 000 soldiers in East Africa and almost 45 000 recruited labourers, an estimated 650 000 tribal people also dying in a country where plunder had laid waste the land and devastated village after village as the war progressed.

General Von Lettow-Vorbeck was only informed of the armistice on 13 November, on the banks of the Chambeshi River, when he received a message from General Van Deventer, who had succeeded General Smuts. The German, after scrupulous verification of the news, obeyed British orders on 14 November to march with his entire force to Abercorn, north of Kasama and on the banks of Lake Tanganyika. There he ordered his men to lay down their arms and he *disbanded* his undefeated army. Technically speaking, he did not surrender. He then placed himself at the disposal of the British Army commander, General Edwards.

Governor Schnee and 154 German officers, non-commissioned officers and other ranks, the remaining 1 156 *askaris* and the unsung heroes of the entire war on both sides, namely 1 598 porters, were present. This was the only German force to remain undefeated in the entire war and the only German force to have invaded and occupied British territory, however briefly, on two occasions in that war. In recognition of the exceptional endurance and courage of Von Lettow-Vorbeck and of his force, the British allowed him and his officers to retain their personal weapons 'for the present in consideration of the gallant fight you have made …'

All this was to no avail now. Margarete and the rest of the German settlers knew worse was to follow. There would be no peace for them. They were Germans and they had lost the war. That week, British army officers arrived at *Ngongongare* and told Margarete that she was to hand over all her horses. She refused, of course. No sooner had the officers left than Margarete and Comet, as well as several other top class horses in her stables, accompanied by highly trusted workers, left the property. Hours later, she returned without her stallion or the other horses. Comet, in particular, was one animal she would never relinquish.

Each night, with all the remembered skills of someone who had participated in unconventional warfare operations, Margarete would slip out and go to Comet and the other horses and the groom in a hidden location. This went on for weeks and, inevitably, the British were finally alerted to her activities after dark. They even sent a tribesman to seek work with her. Margarete immediately suspected a 'third force' attempt at placing her under surveillance. She sent the tribesman back to Arusha with a stiffly worded note for the British District Officer.

Silence ensued and her nightly excursions to see Comet and company continued. Margarete eventually brought the horses home. She then rode over on Comet to see the District Officer. He was asked to take a long hard look at the horse – the 'German' she was suspected of having hidden.

The cat-and-mouse atmosphere of uncertainty and fear gathered momentum. Germany had collapsed; the Kaiser had abdicated and fled to The Netherlands and Imperial Germany was no more. A Republic had been declared and the streets of Berlin and other German cities had been taken over by 'revolutionists', as The New York Times of 11 November 1918 termed them. Germany was forced to accept total responsibility for the war.

The soon-to-be-renamed German East Africa experienced a savage drought in the wake of the armistice, a drought that was compounded by the widespread scorched earth policies experienced during the war. Famine ensued and diseases and deaths escalated. Margarete and all on her estate were able to survive because it was a well-watered region, but nobody at all escaped the hell of the Spanish influenza pandemic that descended on East Africa before the end of 1918.

Margarete enforced rigid quarantine conditions. Everybody, however, children included, came down with the disease. Among the products Margarete utilised were teas made of eucalyptus leaves and turpentine oil in milk. The Maasai taught *Yeyo* to make a daily drink out of the crushed bark of the *cassia* tree and a cup of ox blood or milk. The brew tasted like liquid cayenne pepper. Another Maasai remedy for fever was derived from the bark of the *Acacia albida* that was boiled and the liquid then drunk. This caused vomiting that somehow reduced the fever. Whatever the explanation, nobody died on the Trappe estate.

Hunting for the pot continued as Margarete waited for the axe to fall. She also took Major Brown, the military doctor, out for a final hunt during which he bagged a splendid bull elephant before returning to Britain. It was a stressful time – taking leave of a British officer who openly respected and liked her and who had tried his best to see that she was treated reasonably after the showdown involving his predecessor. Major Brown gave Margarete a gift of new hunting shoes – a luxury after the privations of the war years.

During this strange, tense time in her life, Margarete was suddenly summoned in all urgency by the Pienaar family to come over to their farm as fast as she could as Abel Pienaar had been mauled by a lion and was in a very bad way. It was December 1918. Margarete saddled up Comet, grabbed her medical kit and rode over to the Pienaar farm, taking four hours over really dangerous terrain before she reached the farm.

Abel Pienaar had been tracking a cattle-killer with his pack of dogs and had managed to get off a shot that skimmed the cat's chest. Before he could reload, the lion grabbed his shoulder and the rifle went flying. In the ensuing battle, the lion bit into Pienaar's left arm as several dogs rocketed out of the undergrowth and attacked the animal. The lion let go and turned its attention to the dogs. Pienaar, according to his wife's diary, was able to pick up the rifle with his right hand, reload it and shoot the lion dead.

After emergency treatment with permanganate of potash, Margarete arranged for Abel Pienaar to be taken to the hospital in Arusha where he spent ten days, surviving blood poisoning. His arm was saved, but it was mutilated. As Mrs Pienaar wrote of Margarete:

'Where does one find such people nowadays?'

Just a couple of weeks after that drama came news of an uprising in Berlin in January 1919. It involved the communists who had been inspired by the Bolsheviks and their October 1917 revolution in Russia. This German revolution was crushed by the new Weimar Republic, but the atmosphere of hatred, bitterness and defeat continued as the social boil festered across the country. The Germans abroad watched and waited for the terms of the peace treaty and the inevitable retribution that would follow.

The Treaty of Versailles and Deportation

On 28 June 1919, the Treaty of Versailles was signed. It was the death knell for Germany. German East Africa came under the League of Nations as a Mandated Territory and the British became the mandated power to govern Tanganyika, as the country was now known. Ruanda and Urundi were given to Belgium and a tiny section of territory in the far south, the Kionga Triangle at the mouth of the Rovuma River that formed the border with Portuguese East Africa, was given to Portugal. Germany had lost all her colonies in Africa and was now facing punitive war reparations and assorted measures that would bring fresh misery in unimaginable doses to an already shattered country.

In mid-1920, the order Margarete and all the German settlers had been dreading finally came through: all German nationals were to leave Tanganyika by September that year, missionaries included – well over 4 000 people. A British officer, deportation order in hand, called on Margarete, informing her that she and her family would be allowed to take personal clothing and effects and absolutely nothing else from what had been their home since 1907. They would not be allowed to sell anything. All property, moveable and immovable, had been confiscated by the British. Some 600 head of cattle, fifty horses and about 300 head of sheep and goats, acquired with such hardship after 1916, had to be forfeited.

While trying to digest the implications of this order, Margarete contacted a friend in Kenya who agreed to take Comet and his groom immediately. She had been prepared to shoot the animal if there had been no other way of keeping this remarkable horse out of British military hands in Arusha. The day broke and Comet left. It is all but impossible to imagine the rage and the grief this parting occasioned in Margarete.

Within four weeks, and before she and her family were forced off the land and out of the country, Comet was dead. Despite excellent and compassionate care by someone she knew and trusted, the animal died. It is reasonable to suppose that the stallion simply lost the will to continue without his mistress, refusing to eat and losing condition rapidly. The animal pined to death. This was confirmed in 2006 in Tanzania by David Read, one of the great personalities of East Africa. A published author, admired for his book, *Barefoot over the Serengeti* (1979), a brilliant linguist and an acknowledged expert on several tribal cultures of East Africa, he knew Margarete and he knew about Comet. Elephants separated from their *mahouts* and many a dog separated from a loving owner have lost the will to live and have died. History is replete with examples of human beings who lose the will to live after a traumatic experience.

The impact of Comet's death on Margarete was acute. Life as she and her family had known it had also perished. There was no escaping the forced repatriation to a country now facing appalling levels of poverty, unemployment, political turmoil and deprivation. The workers were stunned at this latest development. Such was the consternation at the thought of *Yeyo* being forced once more to leave that she was urged to see a diviner, a tribal soothsayer. Always sensitive to the customs and beliefs of the tribal peoples among whom she had lived for what now seemed a lifetime, Margarete agreed. The Wameru diviner was brought up to *Ngongongare* where he performed a lengthy ritual with fire, incantations and the sacrifice of two goats under an African moon.

The wizened diviner, in a trance-like state and speaking the language of the Wameru, informed Margarete through his interpreter that she would indeed be forced to go away for quite a long time, but that she would without any doubt at all return to this same place. Margarete never discounted the intuition of people still living closely with the natural world. She had experienced sufficient examples of extraordinary events with the tribal peoples not to discard the reality of extrasensory perceptions.

Exit

The oxwagons were loaded and the animals inspanned for the journey to Moshi and the rail trip down to Tanga and then on to Dar es Salaam. There, they and all the other Germans would be held in an internment camp behind barbed wire in sweltering, malarial heat, to await the steamer for Germany. Ursula, now eleven years old, Ulrich, going on nine and Rolf just seven, knew this was an unusual trip. They had far too many clothes with them and their mother and aunt were too upset for this to be a normal journey. Even the family pets, including Cäsar the German mastiff, and Kibo the fox terrier, now left behind, seemed to sense the devastation of spirit. The livestock, the contents of

Margarete and her prized stallion, Comet, shortly before she was forced to send the animal over the border to friends in Kenya where he pined to death within four weeks. [Emil Karafiat]

the houses and other structures and everything else that comprised N*gongongare* and M*omella* were now at the mercy of unknown people, as were the workers. They had all gathered to bid farewell to this woman from a far country who had done them no harm.

British officers on horseback flanked the oxwagons, like guards escorting captives to prison, as they creaked along the path eastwards, passing mini-lakes and lush vegetation, leaving Mount Meru and the forests behind and heading towards the Kilimanjaro foothills, going down bush tracks and through open spaces where giraffe and buffalo watched in silence as the humans disappeared from sight. Memories of joyous days, weeks and even months afield, hunting big game and living boldly, were anchored in the soil of this magnificent country. Margarete's three children had been born here. The emotional umbilical cord simply could not be severed.

Margarete had refused an offer by the officers to ride one of their horses. To do so would have been a strange kind of betrayal of the memory of her stallion, so recently dead because of events that had been beyond her personal control. The young woman could not bring herself to look back at the disappearing vista of her home in Africa and of the mute groups of tribal people there who had become part of her new life. Everything was now in reverse as numbness set in, the natural anaesthetic when humans are overwhelmed with sorrow and trepidation.

Ursula and her brothers Rolf and Ulrich in Sagan, Silesia after the Trappe family was deported back to Germany in 1920. [Yorck-Michael Trappe]

PART THREE

"Freedom is a system based on courage"

CHARLES PÉGUY

The Hunt for Freedom

The Trappe family returned to Sagan in Silesia as winter began to descend on a defeated, traumatised society. It was late October 1920. Severe inflation accompanied political chaos and strikes in a country facing crippling war debts, the collapse of industry and an ever growing army of the unemployed, the sick, the mutilated and the destitute. Two million Germans had died in the war and five million had been injured. The scale of the horror was appalling.

Ulrich Trappe had survived and had also returned to Sagan, once the scene of his mili-

tary pride and now the shabby stage of an anguished, uprooted family who could not have escaped the sense of alienation inherent in such prolonged upheavals of normal life. The previous March, just two months after the failed communist revolt in Berlin, General Von Lettow-Vorbeck and his *Schutztruppe* were accorded a victory parade through the Brandenburg Gate in Berlin as Germany's only undefeated military commander and force. Even his former enemies in the field admired and respected him. As Edwin Hoyt wrote in his book *The Germans Who Never Lost* (London: Leslie Frewin, 1968), Von Lettow-Vorbeck had masterminded 'the greatest guerrilla operation in history, and the most successful.' This, however, in no way eased the crisis for the Trappes.

After 13 often tough but purposeful years in the sun and space of her African home, Margarete felt asphyxiated by the bleak surroundings. She could see no future for herself or for her family in post-war Germany where a pall of despair clung to the nation's psyche as surely as a shroud clings to a corpse. There is very little on record of the five or so years the Trappe children and Tine lived with Margarete's mother in Sagan. Too much had happened. Everyone bore scars, so much so that Margarete knew that she had to find a way out, a way back to Africa. Ulrich Trappe, in order to enhance his already considerable practical experience, undertook intensive training in agriculture in Leipzig from November 1920 until October 1923 as part of the plan to return to Africa.

General Von Lettow-Vorbeck enters Berlin during a victory parade held in his honour as the only undefeated German military commander and force during the entire First World War.

This lay through a family connection. A prominent South African family of German origin by the name of Malcomess was related to the Trappes. The Malcomess family had its roots in the state of Hesse where they had factories as well as a large estate in Lomnitz, near Hirschberg in Silesia. Fritz Malcomess had married Hanne Zehe whose grandfather, Moritz Zehe, was the brother of Margarete's grandfather, Carl Friederich Traugott Zehe.

Fritz and Hanna Malcomess had a son called Friederich Karl, known to his friends and family as B*ubi*. He developed a very fine farm called Wolseley Estate in the Eastern Cape in South Africa, between the port city of East London and King William's Town. The large property was devoted to cattle and sheep ranching and was home to one of the most spectacular private gardens in the entire country, spread over 25 hectares. It was known as the Kirstenbosch of the Eastern Cape, a reference to the world-renowned, strictly indigenous National Botanical Gardens in Cape Town.

It was decided that Margarete would go out alone to South Africa while Ulrich pursued his studies in Leipzig. This would also afford the children more stability as they would see their father on a regular basis during yet another time of stress and separation. The plan was for Margarete to acquire a South African passport as rapidly as possible, thereby becoming a British dominion subject in order to facilitate the return to Tanganyika, now a British mandated territory. The real fight would then begin to reclaim the confiscated Trappe properties.

So it was that Margarete set sail alone for a region steeped in conflict where stupendous mountains and valleys, rivers and streams, forests and bush, grass-covered downlands and shifting coastal dunes had witnessed times of great tragedy and bloodshed during the 19th century. The British had occupied the Cape for the second time in 1806. As the century progressed, clashes between British forces and the martial amaXhosa tribe grew in number and intensity in the Eastern Cape region, near the Great Kei River. Military garrisons were developed in the region as the fighting intensified.

In 1837, there was an influx of German soldier-settlers when the British German Legion was disbanded after they had fought with the British in the Sixth Frontier War against the amaXhosa. Another similar disbandment and settling of German soldiers took place in 1857 after the Seventh Frontier War. The ninth and last such war ended in 1878. A further 2 000 German men, women and children had already arrived in 1858 and 1859 in East London, at the mouth of the Buffalo River, to expand the German settler community. Today, place names such as Berlin, Braunschweig, Frankfort, Hamburg and Stutterheim speak of this German legacy.

Senator Friederich Karl Malcomess was a noted member of the South African Parliament and a personal friend of Field Marshal Jan Smuts. The Senator was also a prominent businessman and farmer of note, who extended an invitation to Margarete and Ulrich to come out to Wolseley Estate as farm managers and set in motion the process to obtain South African naturalisation. The Trappe children and their Aunt Tine, however, would have to remain behind in Germany until such time as their parents had been able to re-establish themselves in Tanganyika.

Before making this momentous decision, Margarete had managed to contact General Von Lettow-Vorbeck who advised her to accept the Malcomess invitation and try to become a British subject as this was now the only way for her to try to recuperate some if not all of her properties in Tanganyika. From 1922 until early 1925, Margarete lived and worked on the Malcomess estate. As soon as Ulrich completed his agricultural studies in Leipzig, he sailed out to join Margarete on Wolseley Estate.

This was a lifeline that helped the couple remain hopeful, but the price of fresh separation from her children was very high for Margarete in particular. Although the surroundings were beautiful and the family invitation heartfelt, this could never be anything but a stopgap, a stage in the Trappes' struggle to return to the one place in the world they had never wanted to leave under any circumstances. South Africa was already far too populated and developed anyway and could not remotely compete with the sheer size of the wilderness areas, the stunning magnificence of the Mount Meru and Mount Kilimanjaro region, and the seemingly limitless profusion of game animals in East Africa. South Africa, at that time, had been largely shot out after a history of relentless slaughter. It could never be home or even begin to replace the personal and deep emotional bonds with East Africa.

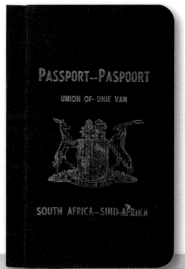

Margarete's South African passport, first issued in 1925, that enabled her as a British Dominion Subject to return to Tanganyika. [Yorck-Michael Trappe]

Around this time Margarete not only inherited a sum of money from her paternal grandfather, but she also finally obtained her South African passport. Fate seemed to be taking a more benign interest for a change. The money was deposited in a Swiss bank and the right of disposal entrusted to a South African 'friend of the family' in Arusha with instructions to buy back *Ngongongare* while the Trappes made ready to sail for Dar es Salaam. The South African, however, in a show of spectacular bad faith and fraud, embezzled Margarete's inheritance and purchased land for himself in Tanganyika. He was never brought to book and his name remains shrouded in ignominious silence. Given Margarete's indomitable, fiery character, it is unknown why she did not pursue this person legally. The chances are that he had simply disappeared by the time she and Ulrich had returned to Tanganyika.

Repeated disasters simply made Margarete more resilient. Once in Dar es Salaam, Margarete and Ulrich called on esteemed old friends of theirs in Dar es Salaam, the Michalakis family. Michael Michalakis had bought *Momella* and a General Boyd Moss of the British armed forces had bought *Ngongongare*. Purchasing property expropriated during wartime somehow carried a taint: it was akin to purchasing stolen goods. Facts were facts, however, and a solution had to be found. On hearing the plight of a woman he had always greatly admired and had probably not expected to see again after the world war disaster, Michalakis offered to give her back *Momella* straight away and let her repay him as and when she could in the coming years. Such magnanimity was uncommon and it gave the Trappes hope which, in turn, gave fresh purpose to their lives.

Ulrich and Margarete returned to Arusha in early 1925 via the same route they had travelled some 18 years previously. The train, of course, now ran all the way up to Moshi from Tanga and the first motor vehicles had started appearing in Arusha in the early 1920s, facilitating travel. The Trappes felt a rush of excitement on reaching the scenic little town once more after years of absence, especially in the case of Ulrich Trappe.

Margarete, in particular, noted how much the little pioneer settlement with its graceful casuarina trees and their clusters of pink flowers had changed since her arrival in 1907. A spot on the map that began life in 1886 around the German fort or *boma*, Arusha had started out with one glorified boarding house masquerading as a 'hotel' and a clutch of rustic shops owned by Germans, South Africans, Indians and 'exotics' such as Greeks and Sikhs, selling anything from rhino horn to bedding. They also served the burgeoning farming community in this almost malaria-free Eden with its rich volcanic soil, lakes, rain forests and spectacular mountains.

Arusha had since grown and become an increasingly important outfitting and transit point for big game hunting safaris. It lay roughly halfway between Cape Town and Cairo on the Great North Road. Where Margarete used to do her 'shopping' in the early days at the modest little stores on one street without ever dismounting from Comet, a sprinkling of cars and a few lorries now shared space and there were so many more people of all races living in and around Arusha. Clipped upper class English accents and American drawls mingled with Boer, Greek and Indian varieties of the same language. It was energizing and it filled Margarete with hope for a new life once more.

Starting Over

The bush telegraph had lost none of its efficacy. After meeting up with some old acquaintances in Arusha from the pre-war days who were unfailingly cordial, as was the British Governor, the Trappes headed for *Momella*. The news of her return had already reached the Maasai Reserve, spreading to the surrounding Wameru and Waarusha communities. *Yeyo, Mama* had come home! After almost five years.

The powerful nostalgia of seeing once more the familiar landmarks of her old home surged through Margarete. One former worker after another filtered out of the bush in noisy jubilation at the return of *Yeyo* and her man. The child-minder and many of the cattle herders, grooms, house servants, gardeners and night watchmen who had helped build a memorable estate out of pristine bush had heard the news in relays and all had come back to see for themselves. Even the omnipresent Colobus monkeys in the nearby forests seemed to put on a special display of raucous welcome that day, competing with the showy turacos and orange-breasted starlings. Swallows, in from Europe for the summer, performed victory fly-pasts in the bright morning air of that wonderful day, flocks of wild pigeons and red-headed weaverbirds joining in as the sweet song of black-helmeted shrikes provided the music. The heady aroma of home after exile filled Margarete's lungs like a shot of pure oxygen.

The Trappe couple started all over again living in one tent, using another to store food and other possessions, and organizing a kitchen in the open. With their limited means, the couple could only actually employ a skeleton staff to rebuild their lives. They were overwhelmed, however, by the number of former employees who asked to be allowed to come back and live on the property and work for free in return for this accommodation and basic necessities from the land. They would help replant and tend the vegetable gardens and care for the livestock that would be acquired a little at a time as the Trappes sought to reclaim their lost lives. The couple had hope. They were together again, in good health and still had useful years ahead of them. After all, was not the last world war the war to end all wars?

One of the tribesmen astonished Margarete when he produced her side arm and gave it back to her, still in working order. Dogs soon roamed the property again. Margarete later began breeding greyhounds and then German shepherds. The loyalty of her work-force and relentless hard work seven days a week helped Margarete and Ulrich come to terms with the acutely painful loss of N*gongongare* and to value the fact that they at least had *Momella*.

New Life Again

Margarete fell pregnant that same year with her fourth child, symbolising a new life in every way. She had acquired a few horses and continued to work and ride right up to the last few days of her pregnancy. In fact, on the day of confinement, she had undertaken a strenuous walk in the foothills of Mount Meru, accompanied by a nursing sister from the nearby mission station. Most of the German missionaries had been allowed back into Tanganyika from 1925 onwards and Margarete had reconnected with several of them.

A daughter, Rosie, was born at nightfall on 16 January 1926 in a tent in the shadow of Mount Meru. A sizeable herd of elephants had been in the vicinity all day, stripping bark, breaking branches and delighting in succulent leaves as they rumbling their secret elephant language to one another. They remained fairly static all day, as if they were awaiting an important event. As the little baby girl gave her first lusty cries, a herd of elephant had gathered and began trumpeting for an extended period of time, their calls carrying for quite a distance on the night air. It was as if the elephants were celebrating this new life as one of their own, welcoming back the baby's mother. Elephants are known to trumpet when a calf is born.

Research findings readily available in the new millennium reveal that elephants have extraordinary intelligence; they are able to recall significant events in their lives, known as 'episodic memory'; they experience grief and a whole range of other complex emotions, including stress disorders, and they are also known to have intention in their actions, revealing a level of self-awareness hitherto only guessed at. The elephants that gathered around that tent the day Rosie was born knew exactly what they were doing and they clearly knew who Margarete Trappe was.

People got to hear about this extraordinary event and spoke of it often down the years. It had a tremendous impact on Margarete. She had always felt a particular bond with elephant, by far her favourite animal. In the old days she had been more than tolerant of these massive creatures breaking into the orchards and gardens, gorging in the banana plantations and feeding like potentates at an oriental banquet. After Rosie's birth and the highly unusual reaction of the elephants, Margarete would not countenance any harsh methods to chase them off *Momella*. Now, they had veritable *carte blanche*! Margarete also decided not to allow any further hunting of elephant on *Momella*.

It was not easy caring for a newborn baby in a tent in the bush. Once, a plague of rats had to be dealt with in order to keep them away from Rosie. Records indicate that they had come up to East Africa in the horse feed that had accompanied the horses and

The Trappe house on Momella. [Dr Jobst-Ulrich Trappe]

troops from South Africa during the war. Another common threat in the African bush was the vicious *siafu* ants. They left nothing in their wake and their bite was extremely painful. Legs of tables and chairs were placed in containers of oil while ash or grease was used to form other barriers. A Kiswahili riddle describes this menace: My necklace is long but cannot go round the neck! *Useja wangu mrefu lakini hautiliki shingoni!*

Reunion

By July 1926, the Trappes had built a modest little house and *Momella* was now beginning to produce vegetables, cereals, some beef and dairy products on a small scale. The baby was flourishing as news came in that Margarete's sister, Tine, and the three other Trappe children were on their way by steamer to Dar es Salaam.

A track leading up to the Trappe house on Momella. [Dr Jobst-Ulrich Trappe]

Margarete and Ulrich were reunited with their family at the station in Moshi after almost six very long, emotionally enervating years. A new baby had to be introduced to the other children and everyone had to readjust to living under one roof again. The preamble to this new life together could only have happened in Africa: just a few days previously, a lion had attacked and partially eaten a tribal woman not far from *Momella*. It was still on the loose as the Trappes made their way on foot in darkness down a track to the house. Nobody had thought it would take so long to return home so nobody had thought to bring along lanterns. The lion population had reached alarming proportions in the region since the outbreak of the war. This could be ascribed, amongst other things, to the super abundance of meat provided by the carcasses of thousands of

dead pack animals that had been used in the war, the disruption of normal farming activities and little to no control of lion populations on and near farms that had been abandoned.

Left — Rosie and one of the many pets on Momella. [Emil Karafiat]

Margarete and Ulrich strode in front and Tine brought up the rear, all of them singing German songs to celebrate, as the children thought, but in fact to scare off any loitering man-eating lion or lioness. *Momella* was ignited once more with the excited chatter and laughter of children, the night alive with sounds that did not exist in Germany and that lay dormant in the memories of the Trappe brood, now finally home. Little Rosie and her minder were waiting for the rest of the family.

Right — Ulrich with an orphaned baby elephant on Momella. [Dr Jobst-Ulrich Trappe]

From the next morning, at dawn, the family resumed life in the wilds. Margarete made the time to involve her family in all aspects of the natural world. They were soon riding again and *Momella* played host once more to all kinds of orphaned wild animals. Monkeys and wild dog, cheetah and zebra, a black rhino calf, eagles and even a baby vulture all inhabited this magical menagerie where the children were taught how to care for the animals and birds as they learned about their ways. Bushbuck and reedbuck, duiker and Thomson's gazelle, lion and leopard cubs, serval and jackal also found their way into the Trappe domain. In the early days at *Ngongongare* Margarete had a very special little springhare as a pet, reminding the reader strongly of the close association

Margarete with a lion cub and one of her dogs on Momella. [Emil Karafiat]

between Karen Dinesen, the Baroness Von Blixen-Finecke, in Kenya and her buck that used to follow her about the house like a puppy.

The children accompanied their mother on horseback into the bush and were involved in hunting very early on. In fact, both Ulrich and Rolf had successfully hunted dangerous game such as leopard, black rhino and lion before their sixteenth birthdays. Ulrich also had an uncanny ability to imitate animal cries and calls. All the children learned about ethics from their mother who taught them their first lessons about conservation of the land and respect for its tribal peoples. The children resumed speaking the language of the Wameru tribe as if there had been no break. There is a delightful story in this regard, shared with the author by Dr Jobst-Ulrich Trappe. When the three Trappe children went to school in Sagan, they communicated with one another only in that language. This resulted in the school authorities prohibiting the Trappe brood from using this unknown tongue when at school.

From the early days, Margarete was welcomed into the heart of the tribal cultures where she lived and worked. The better the peoples came to know her, the more accessible their villages and their lives and the more readily they trusted her. She was an honoured guest on an unknown number of occasions at Maasai *ngomas* for example, the mass tribal song and dance festivities, where she would witness firsthand the glorious spectacle of warriors in celebration. Hundreds of young men, arms and legs decorated with wire embellishments, necks festooned with beaded ornaments, stretched earlobes filled with trinkets, heads sporting elaborate headdresses, converged on the open spaces at their *manyattas*. As one they would raise their voices in rhythmic waves, roaring choruses to the lead voice chant, hands clapping, the night air reverberating as perspiring bodies, daubed in red earth, glistened in the light of large campfires.

As the sung story progressed, the voices of Maasai women joined in, perfectly counterpointed against their men's deep tones. Roast sheep on a spit and honey beer in calabashes was on the menu as the Maasai sang and enacted their oral history in the presence of 'the lady with many cattle'. In fact, during one such occasion, Margarete was invited by the young warriors to join them in their dance ritual that involved vertical jumps on the spot. This was an unprecedented gesture towards the *Wazungu* and a woman at that. She was not seen as an alien, but as a benefactor, a friend of the people whose goodwill and healing powers regarding humans and animals alike had engendered genuine trust.

Margarete's life as a huntress was inextricably associated with her life as a pioneer farmer. The land and its wildlife fed the people, by-products such as hides and horns being part of tribal identity. The Wameru, for example, were particularly fond of giraffe hides as they favoured these for their shields. Margarete never shot giraffe as she did not regard it as a game animal. She would, of course, assist any safari client who had a licence for a giraffe. The Maasai, on the other hand, favoured buffalo hides. These were the sort of items that formed part of the barter trade that was a feature of life at *Momella* from the earliest days. By engaging in this exchange, goodwill was engendered and sustained between Margarete and the tribal peoples of the region. Everything had value for someone somewhere along the line of co-existence in the African wilderness.

The circle seemed complete: nobody was fighting anyone anymore, the tribal peoples were like an extended family and *Momella* was becoming more self-sufficient. There was healthy structure to the children's lives and life now looked more hopeful than it had been since the outbreak of the First World War over twelve years previously. The children were tutored at home on *Momella* by a very strict German teacher. This led to their reaching *Abitur* level, being the equivalent of A Levels in Britain needed for university entrance. It was out of the question for financial reasons, however, for the children to return to Germany to sit for the final *Abitur* examinations.

The Hunt Resumes

Margarete was known for keeping her word. She was profoundly aware of the extraordinary generosity shown by Michael Michalakis in enabling her to go back to *Momella* and started paying him in installments as and when she could. Her overriding concern now was to repay that debt at fast as she could. Margarete shouldered the strain, faced the problems and sought solutions as the family sought equilibrium after turmoil.

An early example of these post-war years illustrates this to perfection. While in South Africa, the Trappes had met a 'baron'. This nameless person could well have been a German. Ulrich had invited him to come up to Tanganyika to hunt. The worthy gentleman duly arrived and, as Gerd von Lettow-Vorbeck revealed in *Am Fusse des Meru*, Ulrich informed him: "My wife will take you hunting." The 'baron' was taken aback at a 'mere woman' being his professional guide. He would learn, quickly.

Margarete had had only two months to be with her children again, and Rosie was still tiny. Her husband seemed to have simply taken it for granted that she would go out and earn the money with this 'baron' from South Africa and be prepared to stay away from home for three solid months on a classic big game safari. Such was the financial situation that Margarete had little choice. Her husband was certainly not a novice hunter, but it is significant that he did not offer to conduct the lengthy safari in place of his wife so that she could be with the children. This sort of situation may have already started infecting their relationship. The pressure on Margarete simply never let up.

By that time, Margarete had acquired a Ford lorry that helped safari logistics. She, the 'baron' and a small crew of safari staff, together with all the permits and other essentials for living in the bush for the next three months, duly left for the Mahenge district in the far south. It was situated in the Mbarika Mountains, just west of today's Selous Game Reserve and the Rufiji River.

Margarete's reputation had not been forgotten. With the certitude of hindsight, over half a century after her death, it can be stated that Margarete Trappe was as good as any of the finest and most knowledgeable hunters in East Africa at that time and for decades afterwards. This was stated unequivocally in 2006 by Arusha-based author David Read who had known Margarete. She had not been a dilettante huntress, doing a bush 'grand tour' in East Africa in order to grace the social columns back home. She had had to learn and refine the skills early on in order to survive and feed many mouths. Ulrich Trappe knew his wife was a sure bet for a successful big game hunting safari.

The hunting party traversed the Maasai Steppe country south of Arusha, with its arid *miombo* woodland and the ever-present tsetse fly. Baobab trees, some young and others gigantic with age, grew out of the parched land like misshapen beings, arms outstretched in supplication. The party skirted the slopes of the Irangi hill country, proceeding ever southwards, past the Rubeho Mountains and into the densely forested Udzungwa Mountains with their waterfalls, lakes and swamps. The heat and humidity rose the closer the party came to Ifakara with its floodplains where the malarial mosquito reigned with particular impunity.

The track narrowed as it led into the spectacular Kilombero Valley and the Mahenge region where elephant and sable shared this wonderland with large herds of waterbuck and buffalo and more modest concentrations of eland and smaller antelope. Margarete had also long since discovered that the chances were always better than average in the Kilombero region of finding sometimes spectacularly well maned lion. This was a favoured haunt of the legendary Jim Sutherland, the Scottish elephant hunter, who pursued big ivory in German East Africa from about 1902 until the outbreak of the First World War. One wonders how many times he and Margarete came close to crossing spoor in the early days in the Mahenge wilderness, he with his Westley Richards double-barrelled .577 and she with her Model 98 bolt-action Mauser.

The Kilombero River roiled with crocodile amid huge pods of hippo, making any crossing very risky. As for the rocky fastnesses of the Mbarika Mountains to the south, they hid unknown numbers of leopard while lion had right of way in that wildest of country. This was the jumping off point for the 'baron's' safari.

A Client from Hell

Margarete always ascertained a client's shooting abilities before going anywhere near game. Rifles, in any case, had to be sighted in. The 'baron' was a mediocre shot. That was not the most pressing problem. The man's character was the concern. After coming down with malaria and then being pulled through thanks to Margarete's close attention and skill, the gentleman threw a tantrum when two of the trackers fell ill. He snapped at his professional huntress that he could not tolerate being around sick people. Maybe he meant sick black people.

That did it. Margarete told him to go on alone while she tended to her staff and accompanied them to a mission station for more advanced care. Naturally, the boorish 'baron' would not have been able to survive in those wild, genuinely dangerous surroundings where he would have been lost in a flash and would have died of exposure, thirst or another attack of malaria, if a wild animal had not polished him off beforehand. Man-eating lions, in fact, had been active in the region at the time of the safari, having killed seven tribesmen before an eighth escaped to raise the alarm. The three-metre high grass was also treacherous as elephant and buffalo could be concealed at a few paces. Margarete had to put down a young bull elephant with mediocre tusks after it charged out of such grass and dropped a mere five metres [about 16 feet] or so from the huntress.

With both trackers now in the care of the mission and with two replacements to continue, the safari from hell proceeded. Tension escalated as the client wounded animals, placing an increasing burden on Margarete to follow up and put down the wounded game. The client would not listen to instructions to get up as close as possible before shooting. Instead, he expected his professional huntress to fill out his quota, having discovered that she was a consummate shot and indefatigable on the trail. Margarete declined as this jinxed safari progressed.

There was a close call with lion in the sooty heart of night when several of the cats came right up to the campfire, their pug marks brazenly implanted in the earth as the safari party lay sleeping nearby. Margarete's ever sharpened sixth sense jolted her out of deep sleep, in time to see a couple of the felines clearly take fright and slip back into the ink of night on the perimeter. The huntress always had her rifle right next to her as she knew that she could never relax her vigilance in the bush.

The strain of the safari worsened with a flash flood and a forced crossing of a river full of crocodile. Stifling heat followed as the party tracked a huge elephant. Margarete came down so badly with 'relapsing fever', as tickbite fever was termed, that her eyesight was seriously affected for a while, causing actual loss of vision for a short period. The party had to return to Arusha where the 'baron' bilked and disappeared. Margarete, out of pocket, out of almost three months' precious time and saddled with skins and trophies that would never be paid for, recovered her eyesight and her general health as she returned home to a crisis to cap them all.

A Parting of the Ways

After months in the bush with the loutish 'baron' who also turned out to be a thief, Margarete returned to *Momella* to find it in a state of quite severe neglect. It had not been managed properly and debts were beginning to soar. A poorly supervised workforce obviously was one of the problems. Tine, thankfully, had looked after the children with complete devotion. Margarete knew she would have to mortgage the property to the hilt, even sell off a part of it to survive. There was a family to support, a farm and livestock to maintain and a workforce to care for. Margarete also knew that the marriage had to end. She had been confronted by an intolerable situation on the domestic front alone and, true to her fiery character, she decided to draw a line through her marriage and get out.

The law being what it was at the time, Margarete and Ulrich were obliged to return to Germany in 1928 to file for divorce. The emotional and financial upheavals since 1916, Ulrich's wartime imprisonment in India, confiscation of property, deportation back to a shattered Germany and a sense of humiliation and defeat, and further stress-filled, lengthy separations would have tested any marriage. The couple's resultant alienation was such that even the presence of four children – one of whom was still a toddler – could not hold the marriage together any longer. Margarete's temperament and accomplishments may have overshadowed her husband from the start. She did not have an easygoing, acquiescent nature and had a strong steak of intolerance for mediocrity. Her tenacity and multiplicity of skills, however, would now help her survive and earn a living like no other woman of her time or for long afterwards.

Margarete on board ship for Germany, December 1928. [Emil Karafiat]

M. Trappe – Professional Huntress

After her return from Germany in 1928 and the granting of the divorce, Margarete tasted a new kind of freedom. Whereas her status as a divorced woman would have made life more uncomfortable in the strictures of European society at that time, back in Africa, she would know a fresh self-realisation where she would call the shots – literally.

As the world moved towards financial catastrophe the following year, the 44-year-old huntress moved into another mode in order to free herself of fresh debt and seek new horizons. Count Heinrich Rantzau-Oppendorf, a good friend, great hunter, splendid shot and connoisseur of the natural world in the finest of hunting traditions, encouraged Margarete to go commercial and become a full-time professional guide for big game hunting safaris. Most of her clientèle would come from Europe and, indeed, from some of the great families of European society. The period between the two World Wars, as it turned out, would be the first 'golden age' for big game hunting safaris in East Africa, closely followed by a second, although different period after the Second World War.

There had been considerable excitement around Arusha in mid-November 1928 as Margarete made preparations to turn professional. The Prince of Wales was in town, at the start of an ambitious safari. The whole settlement was in festive mood as a mass Maasai *ngoma* and a military parade by the Kenyan King's African Rifles electrified the atmosphere. Two of the great names in professional hunting – Denys Finch Hatton and Baron Bror von Blixen-Finecke – were also in town with the Prince. The New Arusha Hotel had been opened and the Prince attended a dinner-dance such as the colony had not seen in all its short life.

The owner of the hotel was an American millionaire banker and dedicated big game hunter, Kenyon Painter of Ohio. Everyone, including Margarete, knew Painter, a veteran of over thirty African safaris. He had invested significantly in Tanganyika after the First World War, where he developed a fine coffee plantation and other massive real estate holdings outside Arusha. He also funded the building of the first post office in the settlement and had built a church as well as a hospital.

This personal friend of President Theodore Roosevelt came on his first hunting safari in German East Africa in 1902 where he hunted a monster black rhino on the western slopes of Mount Meru – fairly close to Margarete's estate. More than one hundred years later, the trophy is still the top-ranking animal in *Rowland Ward's Records of Big Game* and is unlikely in the extreme ever to be surpassed, given the critically endangered status of the black rhino in the new millennium. In the wake of a major financial scandal back home, Painter left East Africa after 1935, never to return, and became a complete recluse until his death in 1940 in Ohio.

Margarete was now entering a field where professional hunters had long dominated, as had their male hunting clients, and where full-time professional huntress guides were unknown.

The Huntress in Colonial Africa

A brief look at the lives of some exceptional women in Africa is useful for a clearer perspective of Margarete Trappe's unique role as a full-time professional huntress at that time.

The unforgettable Florence Baker rewrote history as far back as 1861 when, as Florence Szàsz, she became the first white woman to penetrate what is today southern Sudan. There, over several years, she explored, fought slavery and hunted to survive, side by side with the redoubtable Samuel Baker, her future husband.

In this context, the name Katherine Petherick is recalled. She was the wife of the British Consul to Khartoum, John Petherick, a contemporary of Samuel and Florence Baker and of the explorers Richard Burton, James Grant and John Hanning Speke. Katherine was a splendid shot who shared her husband's hunting, travel and exploration adventures, in what became Sudan. She was also directly involved in writing two books with her husband, published in 1861 and 1869 respectively. They were *Egypt, the Soudan and Central Africa, with explorations from Khartoum on the White Nile to regions of the equator being sketches from sixteen years' travel* and *Travels in Central Africa*.

The largely anonymous Boer women of 18th and 19th century South Africa accompanied their menfolk in oxwagons through unknown and often very dangerous country far from anything that passed for civilisation in those days. They could ride, shoot and hunt with the best of the men, often having to cope alone for months on end in isolated camps while their men went off in search of ivory and other animal products for sale and barter. They also bore and raised generations of children in the wilds in the process. Their approximate counterparts could be found in other parts of colonial Africa, the difference being that the Boer women's descendants are still in Africa in the new millennium, having dissolved all ties with Europe after over three centuries in Africa and now speaking Afrikaans, a language that evolved in Africa.

Mary Henrietta Kingsley, a Victorian spinster and no 'shooting lady', broke all moulds and rewrote the history books in the 1890s. She undertook two major exploration expeditions alone to the French Congo in 1893 and 1895 through utterly remote, wild country. During those forays into largely unchartered territories, she observed and recorded, amongst other things, the culture and hunting traditions of the Fang tribe. Two substantial books as well as numerous articles followed, as did extensive public lectures. Mary Kingsley died in 1900 in Cape Town from enteric fever. She had been nursing Boer prisoners of war during the Anglo-Boer War. She was only 38 years old.

Dr May French-Sheldon, a medical doctor from a wealthy Pennsylvanian family, was an accomplished huntress who led her own private foot safari in East Africa in 1891. Although not a hunting safari as such, she shot for the pot throughout her expedition. Starting out from Mombasa, Dr French-Sheldon proceeded up into the Kilimanjaro foothills and back to the coast via German East Africa through exceedingly primitive and dangerous country. Her book, *Sultan to Sultan*, published in 1892, is a great collectible today.

Not to be outdone, Cecily and Agnes Herbert, cousins from England, indulged in a five-month big game hunting expedition in British Somaliland in 1905. They were alone with their Somali retinue throughout and they had the time of their already adventurous lives, publishing *Two Dianas in Somaliland* in 1908.

A Mrs Walsh and her second husband were among the earliest pioneers in British East Africa. They were veteran transport riders between Mombasa and Uganda, almost 600 miles (965.5kms) inland, before the turn of the 20th century and the advent of the Uganda Railway that would link Mombasa with Lake Victoria by December 1901. Uganda had become part of the British East African Protectorate in 1894. Mrs Walsh was a fiery tempered Irish redhead who was nicknamed B*ibi Kiboko* – Madam Whip – by the Kiswahili speakers. She is believed to have been the only white woman transport rider in British East Africa at the time and for some years afterwards, plying this route with her donkey wagons to convey supplies on behalf of the colonial government to the shores of Lake Victoria. All transport riders had to be handy with a rifle and wise in the ways of the African bush merely to survive. Mrs Walsh was no exception, also packing a pearl-handled revolver for good measure.

Cara Gurney Buxton, a member of a distinguished British Quaker family from Norwich, hunted from southern Sudan to the shores of Lake Victoria in Uganda in 1910 after having travelled from Cairo down the White Nile. She settled in Kenya where she established a farm and hunted big game. An early example of a 'liberated woman', Cara travelled into Abyssinia, German East Africa, the Belgian Congo and far-flung Nyasaland and South Africa on solo expeditions, in between training teams of oxen for other pioneer farmers back in Kenya where she farmed alone to the end of her life in 1936.

Just four years after Cara Buxton arrived in Kenya, Karen Dinesen, the Baroness von Blixen-Finecke of Denmark, disembarked in Mombasa in January 1914. Within seven months of her arrival, she would be leading oxwagon supply runs from north of Nairobi down to the border with German East Africa during the First World War, hunting and wingshooting to feed her caravan. She also went on many hunting safaris with her husband, Bror, and hunted with several other notable Kenyan personalities of the day such as Frank Greswolde-Williams, Charles Bulpett, Baron Erik von Otter and, most importantly, the Honourable Denys Finch Hatton. Her book *Out of Africa*, published in 1938, is an icon in world literature. It helped communicate to generations of readers the wild and uncontaminated beauty of Africa at that time, the magnetic allure of her special places and the ways in which they inspired one of the great literary talents of the last century.

Vera, Lady Broughton, first wife of Sir John Henry Delves Broughton, was described as a 'mighty huntress and adventuress' in the celebrated book *White Mischief* by James Fox. She was reputed to have hunted many elephant in British East Africa between 1919 and 1927. The beautiful Diane Caldwell, Sir John's second wife at the time he was implicated in a murder that rocked the colony for decades afterwards, was another splendid huntress, but also a denizen of the debauched 'Happy Valley' crowd in the Aberdare Mountains.

Many women from the aristocratic and royal families of Europe hunted in Africa before the First World War and, indeed, before the outbreak of the Second World War in 1939. The British Royal family and Princess Hélène of France, the Duchess of Aosta, are prime examples, the latter writing extensively of her African expeditions. After the First World War, several highly accomplished women made Kenya their home where they hunted as a routine part of their pioneering new lives in Africa, carving out farms and raising families in many cases.

Elizabeth Cross, the mother-in-law of Tony Dyer, the last President of the East African Professional Hunters' Association, was a woman of extraordinary courage who came out to Kenya under the Soldier Settlement Scheme after the First World War. She, too, began farming on her own northeast of Nairobi and became a highly proficient huntress and transport rider.

Another memorable Kenyan huntress-pioneer was Kathleen Seth-Smith. She undertook many classic big game safaris on foot in the 1920s, surviving a terrible goring by a black rhino to pass on her formidable knowledge of African wildlife and hunting to her son Tony Seth-Smith, one of the great 'names' in the annals of African hunting.

Rose Cartwright, a devoted friend of Karen von Blixen-Finecke was also an extraordinary young huntress. She had learned to ride, fish and hunt during her childhood in England. In Kenya, she refined her hunting skills on dangerous game to such a degree that she was hired by the legendary Bror von Blixen-Finecke and by the fastidious Denys Finch Hatton in the early 1930s as an assistant professional huntress for a number of safaris.

The exquisite Vivienne de Wattville of Switzerland led a major museum-collecting expedition alone in Kenya, Uganda and Sudan from July 1923 until April 1924 for the Berne Museum after her father died early on the expedition as a result of a lion mauling. She wrote two exceptional books about her life in Africa.

The equally astounding Delia Akeley from America, first wife of Carl Akeley, the father of modern taxidermy, hunted dangerous game and many other species from late 1905 to early 1907 in Kenya for The Field Columbian Museum in Chicago, and in 1909 for the American Museum of Natural History in New York. She subsequently led a year-long collecting expedition alone and mostly on foot from October 1924 to September 1925 right across Africa. Starting out from Mombasa on the east coast of Kenya, Delia reached the mouth of the Congo River in the west many kilograms lighter when she was already 50 years old. Her book, *Jungle Portraits*, published in 1930, reflects some of her extraordinary life.

Beryl Markham, unforgettable aviation pioneer and *femme fatale* of the early African safari industry, came to Kenya as a toddler in 1904 where she was raised among the Kipsigi and Nandi peoples in the stunning Rongai Valley after being abandoned by her mother. She learned to hunt warthog with bow and arrow and developed great bush skills among the tribal peoples while still a child. She grew up to become the first person in 1933 to scout for and evaluate elephant from the air as a pilot and then to relay the information to Bror von Blixen-Finecke and Denys Finch Hatton on the ground. She was hired soon afterwards in this capacity for an extensive safari with the famed Vanderbilt family, meeting Ernest Hemingway in the process. More such safari assignments followed, as did her controversial book, *West with the Night*, published in 1942.

Celia Salmon, the South African-born wife of the revered Captain Roy Dugdale "Samaki" Salmon, the Chief Game Ranger of Uganda in the 1930s, became such a proficient huntress of dangerous game, especially concerning elephant, that she sometimes replaced her husband as a professional guide when his duties kept him from the field.

The Americans Osa and Martin Johnson astounded the world with their hunting and filming accomplishments in Kenya, Uganda, Tanganyika, the Belgian Congo and Sudan from 1921 to 1936. Their literary output was also prolific.

There were huntresses in the first three decades of the last century who came out to Africa on big game hunting or museum expeditions and who wrote of their experiences. Marguerite Roby hunting elephant in the Belgian Congo in 1910, Diana Strickland on a full-bag big-game expedition in the same country in 1923/4, Gabrielle Vassal hunting in French Equatorial Africa in the early 1920s, Mary Hastings Bradley accompanying the Akeley mountain gorilla expedition in 1921 in the Belgian Congo and in Ruanda-Urundi, and Gretchen Cron hunting in Tanganyika between 1925 and 1930 are foremost examples of such huntress-writers.

Not one of these notable women, however, became full-time professional huntresses as the only viable means to earn a living, support a family and maintain a large property, often against intimidating odds. This in no way detracts from the remarkable lives these women led in Africa. The foregoing, however, places in greater relief Margarete Trappe's accomplishments from 1928 onwards and facilitates better understanding of the 'road less travelled' that she followed to the end of her days in Africa. Certainly, she was the first of her kind in all East Africa.

The Early Days

Count Rantzau became Margarete's first safari client when she became a full-time professional huntress. As each season passed, Margarete's reputation consolidated and grew by word of mouth in European society. The Count would return to hunt with her almost every year and was her most enduring client. He was also the epitome of the gentleman hunter and the antithesis of the ego-inebriated killer/collector chasing trophies by fair means or foul, whichever works first. Ernest Hemingway referred to such people as 'shootists', not hunters.

The Count and Margarete would often interrupt the safari for a couple of days or so simply to observe game and soak up lessons from the natural world. An example of this came when they were on safari in the Singida area, to the far southwest of Arusha, amid beautiful country west of the Irangi Hills. The couple were on the southern flank of the Great Rift Valley, in country strewn with giant boulders and granite outcrops, near the Mwaru River. It was full moon and the safari party was camped near a waterhole surrounded by glorious umbrella thorn trees. A blind had been built in such a thorn tree so that Margarete and the Count could watch game at the waterhole.

Lion, rhino, elephant and willowy giraffe were among the many animals that appeared at dawn, at dusk and sometimes in the brightest moonlight. One night, elephant came up to the tree where the blind had been cleverly camouflaged and began to pull at the branches! It was unnerving – and thrilling. They had not been detected and, fortunately for posterity and this story, the elephant soon wandered off.

This incident reminded Margarete of another occasion involving elephant that remained unique in all her decades in the African bush and that she referred to down the years. It was at just such a waterhole where she observed a herd of elephant actually preventing a cow from coming down to slake its thirst in terrible heat. The animal was plainly sick and the herd did not want it to wander into the water to drink and cool off and then not be able to exit, subsequently dying and contaminating the only waterhole for miles around.

It was distressing scenes such as these that underscored the value Margarete placed on frequent careful observation of game animals as an integral part of the hunting experience. Her clients did not simply go out and shoot a list of animals as if it were a foray into a butcher's shop to buy meat. Margarete obliged her clients to observe and learn, to watch and wait and to respect their quarries in the process. She was known never to bow to an impatient client's wishes. Margarete had endured too much by that time to tolerate anyone who tried to challenge her authority in the bush.

Close observation of big game and the shared wisdom of her senior trackers taught Margarete many things. She learned, for example, about body space and what a wild animal would tolerate before going into 'fight or flight' mode as it began to feel threatened by human encroachment into its zone. She and Count Rantzau experienced this with lion on more than one occasion. They would spot lion in the distance during a break in actual hunting and they would approach the animal on foot. There was a definite radius outside of which the lion did not feel an immediate threat. Its yellow-brown eyes staring, unblinking, it watched, taut-framed and ready for the moment when the humans would approach the fringes of the forbidden zone. The moment Margarete and Rantzau stopped dead, the lion relaxed. As soon as they resumed their slow and cautious walk, the animal bunched up and then hunkered into classic attack mode, its head lowered, in line with its tawny body, near invisible in the yellow grasses. Just one injudicious move could provoke a charge and the distinct risk of a mauling and probable death. Being in the lion's domain and having to think and move with particular caution in order to survive had a vibrancy all of its own for Margarete and her guests. The tension was a shot of pure adrenalin to the brain and a rapid education in never relaxing one's guard in the wilds.

Although Margarete acquired the Ford lorry that facilitated displacement between certain hunting areas, her safaris, either lengthy big game excursions or much shorter expeditions, still entailed a great deal of walking and the utilisation of porters as in the very early days in East Africa. This strenuous effort and close contact with the earth and with the peoples of that world enabled the visiting hunter and huntress to see, absorb and understand with greater clarity the different cultures and habitats of that time.

As with any first class safari operation, Margarete maintained a hands-on approach with every aspect, from engaging and training appropriate staff to ensuring the client's comfort and safety in the field and the correct handling of trophies. Margarete could do it all: in addition to an encyclopaedic knowledge of the natural world, she knew the appropriate regions, could track with the best, identify trophy animals, shoot like a veteran, skin and field dress any animal and maintain discipline throughout. Her ability to handle injuries and disease and to interact effectively and fearlessly with all peoples was a particular advantage.

She continued to be a fire-brand in the face of shoddy work or injustice, but she was fair to the core and never bore grudges. The fact that the Maasai respected her said it all. They had tried their luck in attempting to rustle her cattle, invade her pasture lands with their cattle in her absence and intimidate her in the very early days but this diminutive 'woman with many cattle' was impervious to their wiles, witchcraft and trickery.

Margarete, third from left, in camp during a big game hunting safari. [Dr Jobst-Ulrich Trappe]

Firearms safety was drilled into her gun bearers and clients alike. Early on in her professional career, Margarete experienced a potentially lethal incident with firearms that she never forgot and that she never allowed anyone else to forget. She, a gun bearer and a tracker were out on one of her lone hunts after elephant in the foothills of Mount Kilimanjaro . The team was scouting the western foothills with their lush grasslands and abundant acacia tree thickets flourishing in the dark, rich volcanic soil. The region was well watered, another factor that provided abundant food and cover for game animals. It was an elephant haven and already known by then for some spectacular ivory. The Arab slaving and ivory caravans, of course, had long frequented the Kilimanjaro region.

One of the gun bearers had been carrying Margarete's double-barrelled rifle as the group struggled to remain downwind from a promising herd of elephant. Margarete was finally satisfied with their position and reached out to take the rifle. She had spotted a splendid old bull and wished to approach it as closely as she dared and on her own while both trackers stayed back.

The gun bearer whispered to her to be careful as the rifle was already cocked! Margarete went utterly berserk and the elephant took off amid the rage of Swahili invectives spewing from the huntress like a modern-day flame thrower, engulfing the hapless gun bearer. The 'Fierce Match' [*kiberiti kali*] had been struck and there was no extinguishing her ire until Margarete had burnt her anger into his eardrums, the poor devil being reduced to a cowering wreck. He had flouted the most basic of safety drills she had instilled in any safari staff who would be handling firearms at any stage. It is not known if the gun bearer in question was ever allowed to handle firearms again after that day.

From that incident onwards, Margarete became even more stringent in her vigilance of gun bearers and, indeed, of any casual hunting companion or paying client. It did not matter how experienced they were. Familiarity with firearms could lead to unwitting negligence and the cutting of safety corners. Nobody was ever to cock a firearm and then proceed to struggle through thick bush and over rocky terrain or climb onto an oxwagon or, much later on, into a lorry and merrily bump along, a round up the spout and a ghastly tragedy in the making. The gun bearer was truly roasted, Margarete was satisfied, despite the aborted elephant hunt, and the party returned home.

The Road Less Travelled

Kilimanjaro and Mount Meru in the moonlight: clients arriving to hunt with Margarete Trappe were always awed by the sheer expanse of her world and the ethereal magnificence of Kilimanjaro in the east during full moon – a hunter's moon. *Momella*, with towering Mount Meru as its backdrop, was situated on a plain overlooking a series of low

Margarete and some of her askaris on Momella during the 1930s.
[Emil Karafiat]

hills and lakes. Margarete and her visitors would sit outside on the verandah to enjoy the view as jackal yapped in celebration of another day in paradise. Sometimes the muffled notes of lion drifted in on the twilight air. The last of the herons and other waterbirds such as ibis and pelicans made for Lake Kusare, close to Mount Meru where dead swamp acacias rose from the waters, providing secure roosting places. Fireflies punctuated the gathering gloom as wide-winged moths flirted with the lamps and cicadas thrummed. This was another world, one which could now be reached a little more easily. In 1931, an air service was inaugurated from Britain to South Africa, via Nairobi, amongst other places. The flight lasted nine days from start to finish. Margarete and her sons were well practiced in driving over the border into Kenya to meet their clients for the start of a sojourn in another world.

As clients settled in and began to adjust to the atmosphere, talk often turned to superstitions and other beliefs belonging to that world. Margarete was a source of sometimes incredible stories concerning the surrounding tribal cultures and their interaction with wildlife. The Wameru, for example, told Margarete many years previously of a giant, ape-like creature they called *Loldaika* that walked upright, like a human being, and that inhabited the *Momella* region. Many claimed to have known somebody who had seen this animal, but it remained mythical, ever-present and ready to intervene in human affairs – a tribal bogeyman, a tropical *yeti*!

African hunting literature is replete with examples of mythical creatures whose origins are shrouded in legend. Joseph Hughes, author of the great collectible, *Eighteen Years on Lake Bangweulu* (London, The Field, circa 1933), would have had much to share with Margarete about the 'huge prehistoric animal' (page 146) called a *Chipekwe* that the local tribesmen swore inhabited the waters of Lake Bangweulu in what was then Northern Rhodesia. Hughes made his living in the region as a hunter and trader before the First World War. He, like Margarete, did not deride local beliefs despite the lack of any proof that the *Chipekwe* existed.

All cultures have mythical entities in their belief systems that are referred to as part of the human struggle to understand the mystery of life itself. Margarete recalled one of her earliest experiences in this regard that shook her to the core. One night, she heard a prolonged and terrible noise that resembled someone being throttled. When she spoke of this to the Wameru, they told her she had heard the *Gurumico*, a devilish entity that looked like a pitch-black dog, but that moved like a cat. The Maasai also believed in this creature and feared it just as much as did the Wameru. Margarete was never able to figure out what had made the noise.

She, in turn, was viewed as possessing her own 'magic' because of the way in which she had helped sick and injured tribal people from the earliest days. She had made a sustained effort to learn about the cultures, legends and assorted beliefs of the indigenous people. Her experience had taught her that the older and more entrenched the belief, the greater the likelihood that it had some foundation in fact. She discovered this with the Maasai and their taboo on drinking milk and eating meat on the same day. The Maasai believed that this was an insult to the cattle and that the milk of the cows would dry up as a result. The Jews, through the millennia of their history, have observed the same dietary law about separating meat and milk products. Today, modern dieticians advise against accumulating too much protein in a short space of time, thereby vindicating this ancient practice on medical grounds.

Many were the nights that Margarete was an invited guest in Maasai *manyattas* where she would sit by the fire and listen to the legends and other stories passed down through the ages in the finest of oral traditions. In this way she tuned in to their world as best she could, fostering sound relations and cultivating sources of support and information as a professional huntress and pioneer farmer. Margarete held a special admiration for the Maasai who, in her experience, did not exhibit the same dreadful cruelty towards animals as did the Wameru. Of course, no Wameru or anyone else, for that matter, dared mistreat any animal anywhere near Margarete Trappe because they knew that she would descend on them with such ferocity that they would rue their actions and remember the lesson forever afterwards. She enforced her standards, regardless of consequences. Such resoluteness in a woman no doubt antagonised some people.

Margarete would revel especially in any opportunity to share a campfire with the grizzled old tribal elephant hunters as they exchanged stories and shared superstitions and tips to bring luck in the field or to avoid disaster. One such elephant hunter advised Margarete that whenever she struggled to find or catch up with a really decent elephant, she should try to find some of its warm droppings. The next step was to take a pinch of the elephant dung and place it in the turn-up of her shorts. The elephant would now be 'tethered' and she would then be able to find it and shoot it.

Another tip from the tribal peoples concerned the crested eagle. When out tracking whatever animal, one should try to seek out such an eagle and observe the direction in which its head was cocked or where its eyes were staring. By following that direction, fresh spoor would be found and a successful hunt would ensue. Margarete actually

Margarete, professional huntress, in camp with a client during the 1930s. [Emil Karafiat]

admitted to having followed this advice with success.

She had a personal superstition about a member of the finch family with a very distinctive four-tone call. Whenever she heard it, she knew there would be trouble of some sort. Whether this was merely a self-fulfilling prophesy is beside the point: on more than one occasion Margarete had been charged by a wounded animal or experienced some mini-disaster after hearing the finch's warning cry. Another bird that was feared as being a harbinger of bad luck was the eagle owl. Margarete was asked on a number of occasions over the years to shoot this bird whenever it made its appearance. She always refused, maintaining the delicate balance between respect for other people's beliefs and her own ethics.

Margarete noticed that whenever her trackers came across the honeyguide and were led to hives, they always made sure never to harvest all the honey and, above all, never to remove the honeycomb. This was seen as showing respect for the little bird in this symbiotic relationship in the wild. Thousands of miles southwest of the country, in what is today the Republic of Namibia, the Ju/Wasi Bushmen were practising this very tradition in the dying days of the 20th century.

Belief in omens was all-pervasive in Margarete's home in Africa. Many of the tribal people believed that if a wild dog was seen at the outset of a hunt, it would be successful, whereas the spotting of a giraffe promised the opposite. *Momella* had robust populations of giraffe and Margarete's reputation for successful safaris became a byword so maybe this belief did not hold true for *Momella* and the immediate neighbourhood!

It was years before Margarete ever shared any stories about actual events she had witnessed and that were linked to superstitions because they were so extraordinary, so outlandish. Among the stories shared with the author was one concerning a hippo hunt. Before Margarete's team could recover the carcass, crocodiles had swarmed onto the animal, ripping out chunks of flesh. Suddenly, one of her porters told her of a great 'wizard' nearby who could help chase off the crocodiles so that the hippo could be brought to land.

Margarete, feeling she had nothing to lose and never being one to deride any tribal beliefs, agreed. Along came the said 'wizard', a very old man. As Margarete watched, he went right up to the edge of the river bank, pulled out bunches of grass and then proceeded to mutter some sort of incantation over the tufts of grass as he turned to face each point of the compass. When he finished this ritual, the crocodiles ceased instantaneously to gorge and dispersed in all directions. The 'wizard' then waded into the water, followed by Margarete's team, and they dragged the hippo to the bank with the aid of lianas. No crocodiles in sight, no fear and no rational explanation!

The huntress had also witnessed how some Maasai men 'called' hippo out of the water whenever they so wished. She once heard a group of Maasai break into a repetitive drone as they ordered a pod of hippo in a river to come out onto the bank. Before Margarete could even start thinking about what was happening before her eyes, out came two hippo, making straight for the trees that the Maasai had climbed and from where they had continued to 'call' the hippo. They did not seem belligerent and did not take the remotest interest in Margarete who had sought refuge on a steep part of the bank. She knew the fearsome reputation of hippo out of water and near humans. Amazed at this 'show', she asked the Maasai how this worked and was told that hippo also belonged to their tribe, as did cattle, and that they would listen when 'called'.

This particular incident made a marked impression on Margarete, so much so that she tried to imitate the Maasai for a bet! She was with a film crew when a bet was placed – a bottle of whiskey – if she could 'call' hippo over to the bank. Margarete imitated the Maasai as closely as she could, droning the words over and over again as she faced the hippo in midstream. Some hippo did come up to the river bank, although they did not leave the water. A bottle of whiskey exchanged hands and yet another story started circulating about the 'woman with many cattle' who healed the sick and also talked to hippo!

Margarete undertook some of her most memorable safaris down on the Rufiji River in the southeast, where lagoons and swamps jostled with islets and side channels in the riverine forests on the country's mightiest river. Here too, she learned about a strange custom involving hippos and humans and one that other hunters had witnessed and recorded. She noticed how the tribesmen on a significant stretch of the river always carried a rooster in their dugout canoes. According to legend, the hippo recruited the rooster as an early warning system to avoid being hunted on land by humans. At night, hippos routinely leave the safety of the water and seek succulent vegetation nearby and, according to the legend, to strip the tribal maize fields. The first crow of the rooster was a warning to the hippos to prepare to return to the safety of the river before dawn broke; the second crow was a more urgent reminder to finish up and leave; the third crow was an ultimatum to get back into the water with all due speed. The legend maintains that since that pact between rooster and hippo, all humans on the water are safe if they have a rooster on board!

Speaking of rivers, while out elephant hunting at one stage, Margarete came to a river notorious for crocodiles. One of her porters suddenly stripped off his clothes, except for his 'magic' necklace, and waded into the river, swimming towards the mass of crocodiles that simply scattered as the man neared them. Margarete was so flabbergasted at yet another incident involving crocodiles that she did not even tell Count Rantzau for a very long time as she feared being ridiculed.

Man-eating Lions and Werelions

Throughout the 1930s and thereafter, there have been many cases of man-eating lions in Tanganyika. Whenever Margarete departed on safari, especially with guests, she exercised caution and never became complacent because of the prevalence of lion. She and her son Rolf had both been called out on a number of occasions, individually and together, to assist in tracking down and killing man-eaters in Maasai country and much farther afield. It was one thing for the Maasai, for example, to seize the initiative and purposefully seek out a lion for their culturally related rituals to mark passage into manhood; it was quite another when marauding lions engulfed whole communities in terror as children and adults were seized, killed and devoured.

Lion would not only lie in wait for their human prey out in the bush; they would also invade village compounds and make short shrift of flimsy hut walls and roofs and their terrified occupants. Margarete found that such attacks tended to take place after dark and at dawn. She had seen adults and children, men and women fall victim. Sometimes she had come across a near-intact corpse that had only been disembowelled. In other instances, most of the body had been devoured, a heap of blood-caked bones now all

that was left to bear mute testimony to lion that had been undisturbed in its feasting.

Margarete and her client Herr Langen and a brace of lion. His inscription on the back of the photograph reads: 'Dear Mrs Trappe, A photograph for you in grateful memory. The journey will soon be over and one will be back again in Europe. Weidmannsheil! Yours, Langen. [Emil Karafiat]

More than once Margarete had been called out to a village where lion seemed to have had the village under observation for a while before striking. More than one victim had been attacked in near-identical circumstances. They had either been seated at dusk on the outskirts of the compound or they had left the thorn-enclosed village at dawn to go to relieve themselves in the nearby scrub. Some victims had indeed been attacked in daylight as they worked their fields or as they moved through dense vegetation to go to a neighbouring village. Women routinely fetching water from rivers were also easy targets.

During these special assignments to track down and eliminate man-eating lions, Margarete was aware of the powerful superstitions linked to such events. She concentrated on finding the killer and kept out of tribal politics. The trouble often started with cattle being seized and killed as well as other small creatures before the lion in question changed course and started seeking out human prey such as youngsters herding cattle. Once the culprit was tracked and killed, it was sometimes found that the lion in question was in failing health or that it had an injury or dental problems that impeded hunting efficacy. Man-eating was easier. Other factors were availability of human flesh through the tribal custom of the Maasai, for example, of leaving their dead out in the open for scavengers, a decline in natural prey through drought and heavy poaching, and human encroachment into habitat through agricultural and livestock activities. The seasons also played a role: when there was plenty of water, the lion's natural prey scattered over wider areas and was not so concentrated, hence making the hunt for this natural prey a more arduous affair. As Frank Puxley wrote on page 53 in his book *In African Game Tracks: Wanderings with a Rifle through Eastern Africa* (London: H. F. & G. Witherby, 1929), when speaking of scarcity of natural prey:

> '... since lions have to live – or at least such is their opinion – they have to substitute one diet for another. Man, white or black, is easier to secure than the more elusive buck; and while not so tasty, perhaps has to serve at a pinch.'

Was man-eating purely opportunistic or was it mainly propelled by other factors? Margarete could never be sure, but she felt that plain hunger was usually the overriding motivation. As Guy Coheleach, the world-renowned wildlife artist, recalls on page 126 in his book *The African Lion as Man-eater* (Panther Press, 2003) when quoting Frederick Courteney Selous: 'A hungry lion is a true devil and fears nothing in this world.' Selous also regarded the lion as the most dangerous of the big five to hunt.

Margarete was not always able to track down the killer. Man-eaters would often simply snack on the corpse and then leave quite quickly, never to return to the same spot. Rain would also obliterate drag marks and immediate spoor, and dense terrain as well as very poor visibility were some of the other challenges Margarete and her helpers had to face. Research has shown that man-eating can become learned behaviour and that this behaviour can be transmitted to the offspring and to their offspring as well – three generations! This became evident from the early 1930s until well after the Second World War in the southwestern corner of Tanganyika, around the village of Njombe. It lies northeast of Lake Nyasa where the celebrated game warden and professional hunter, George Rushby, faced a veritable plague of man-eating.

Between 1 500 and 2 000 tribal people were killed by lion before Rushby was able to dispatch the entire pride in the district by 1946, whereupon the man-eating ceased, proving that the astronomical number of victims could not possibly have been the work of a couple of rogue lion. It was a family business.

News reached the northern highlands of Rushby's ordeal which was compounded by potent tribal superstitions, something Margarete had experienced firsthand. People feared that their enemies were changing into lions, attacking them and then changing back into their human form. The people around Njombe referred to these 'werelions' as *Wabojo* and no outsider, be he missionary or big game hunter, could shake this belief. What was worse, relatives of victims refused to speak of their loss or report it to game wardens for fear of becoming the next victim. Fear abated only when the man-eating stopped after Rushby had wiped out the entire pride. Chiefs were often believed to possess these transmutable powers and the ordinary tribal subjects lived in fear of this manifestation.

Tanzania has the largest lion population in all Africa and a distressingly well-documented history of man-eating that continues to this day. As closely detailed by Dr Rolf Baldus in a major study of Tanzania's lion population in the new millennium, about 70 people on average are killed every year by lion in that country. Man-eating lions, to give only one example, killed and ate thirty-five men, women and children and injured ten others between August 2002 and April 2004, not far from Dar es Salaam. The list goes on.

The Name Grows

Already well-known and respected as a professional huntress, Margarete's reputation grew in Europe via a very select clientèle. Her intuition while tracking and her ability to sense danger grew in tandem with her name. She never panicked, no matter how bad the situation, and her energy levels never slackened.

While camp was being set up, she would take the client out in order to sight in the rifles, ascertain the client's shooting abilities and, in the process, bring bushbuck and other plains game meat back to camp. There, Margarete went into overdrive, supervising her staff and not turning in for the night until late. She was the first person up before dawn to take stock of provisions for what were usually lengthy foot safaris from the base camp and to issue orders for the comfort of the client and the general running of the safari.

In order to function as a full-time professional huntress, Margarete had to be away from *Momella* and her children for many weeks, even a couple of months at a time. This was nothing new. Her sons, Ulrich and Rolf, began accompanying her as assistant hunters in their late teens. They displayed all the qualities of marksmanship, tracking

Left — *A handwritten letter by Margarete to relatives in Germany, dated 2 December 1938, in which she describes in the first paragraph Ulrich's talent for taming animals. [Gabriële Löhrl]*

Right — *Ulrich with his tame cheetah hunting companion. [Yorck-Michael Trappe]*

skills, knowledge of wildlife and habitat and ability to relate to the tribal peoples that distinguished their mother. Ursula, the first-born, married during this period and left to live with her husband on a sisal plantation that he managed in the Lindi region of southeastern Tanganyika. The youngest child, Rosie, was in the excellent care of Aunt Tine when she came home from school in Arusha. Margarete's workforce, who looked after the growing cattle herds and the horses as well as the horticultural side of things, was a key part of this support system in those tough years after the divorce and before all the debts were liquidated.

Speaking of her sons and little Rosie, the author was privileged to be given access to personal correspondence between Margarete and relatives in Germany concerning her children. In a letter dated 2 December 1938, for example, she wrote:

> 'Rolf has inherited hunting from me. He is a passionate hunter ... Ulrich is not as keen a hunter but he has a talent for taming animals. He has a tame cheetah ... always taking the cheetah with him when he goes out hunting. It runs like a dog behind him.'

In another letter dated 19 April 1939, Margarete speaks of her daughter Rosie, saying:

> 'She really loves to ride and wants to go hunting later on and shoot as I do.
> She is such a lovable little thing and we adore each other.'

One of Margarete's finest trackers was Zaidi. He had spent enough time in the field on dangerous game hunts with Margarete to have total faith in her judgment and good nerves. He was put to the test during a particularly terrifying experience with a wounded elephant on one of Margarete's solo safaris. He and the 'lady boss' had been out in thick thorn bush and hilly country on the spoor of a herd of five bulls. Margarete had managed to crawl through thorny undergrowth and get up very close to the elephant, spotting the bull with the best ivory. The wind remained favourable and Margarete squeezed her 9.3mm Mauser trigger.

As the targeted bull was hit, the day erupted into an explosion of noise behind the huntress. Crashing through the thorn bush at quite unbelievable speed was one of the original five bulls. It had become separated from its group and was now storming at the humans. There were no trees for them to climb. Both Margarete and Zaidi remained frozen as the huge animal tore past them to rejoin the other elephants, miraculously ignoring the huntress and her tracker.

The elephant Margarete had hit had not gone down, but had managed to move off in

Left — *Margarete in the field after a hunt for black rhino.*
[Dr Jobst-Ulrich Trappe]

Right —
Urich Trappe
[Baroness Marissa von Firks]

the frightening confusion of the moment and had got behind them, ready to charge! Giant ears flaring and trunk raised, the animal was almost on top of Margarete when she managed to drop it like a lead weight with a shot to the base of its trunk. It was no more than three metres (about ten feet) away from her, its huge frame flattening the undergrowth as it collapsed, sending up clouds of dust in a deafening moment of extreme danger.

When Margarete asked Zaidi afterwards why he had not at least tried to get out of the way of the elephant he replied that there was no point in making such an effort as it was God's will – *amri ya mungu* – whether he lived or died. He went one step further in saying that if something happened to *Yeyo*, then something would happen to him. This sense of fatalism is common in many African cultures.

Such was Margarete's personality and impact on the tribal peoples in particular that stories about her skills and 'magic' were increasingly common. One such story claimed that Margarete was so skilled at approaching elephant that she actually milked elephant cows! It all started during the dry season between July and October in the Iringa region in the southwest of the country where the warlike, statuesque Wahehe tribe dominated. Giant boulders lay scattered across the surface of hills overlooking the Great Ruaha River to the west and a wilderness area replete with fine herds of elephant. This was also baobab country. To the east rose the forested Udzungwa Mountains and the Mufindi Highlands in the south where the Wahehe had held out against the Germans until 1898. Ghosts of the Wahehe warriors were said to stalk the land.

The Wahehe had tipped off Margarete and Zaidi about good ivory to be had in the Iringa district. They spoke of crop-raiding elephant and set the couple on the spoor of some bulls. When within a mere metre or two of one bull, either Margarete or Zaidi unwittingly made a noise, probably by stepping on a dry twig or leaf. The bull, joined by several others, spun round and made for the hunters. Margarete managed to find shelter behind a giant baobab as she witnessed a spectacle she would only see once more in her long life as a huntress – elephants moving with such speed that they appeared to be galloping. The cacophony of tons of moving elephant made the earth tremble as if during a mini earthquake. The noise was such that it resembled several bombs exploding in a confined space. It was over in a flash.

After the excitement and danger of the moment had passed, one of the Wahehe asked Margarete what she had been doing, being up so close to the elephant. Had she been planning to milk them? That did it. The story took wings and took off and a myth was born that simply would not die. Margarete Trappe milked elephants in her spare time. The bush telegraph spread the story well beyond the Wahehe's domain, the story growing as it spread, like all worthwhile myths are supposed to do. *Yeyo* milked elephants.

Margarete had an unusual experience with elephant on *Momella* when going out with two workers to collect a load of firewood. She was driving a small pickup that had been painted bright red. Off she and her staff drove, following a rough track into the bush. Once the firewood had been loaded, the trio made their way back along the same bush track to the farm compound.

Then it happened. Two bull elephants were blocking the track ahead. Margarete, on the lookout for any hint of aggressive behaviour, inched forward, hoping that the sound of the vehicle would coax the animals off the track and back into the bush. One of the bulls did just that, but the other raised its head and began to trumpet as it started down the track towards the vehicle. Margarete put her foot flat and forced the pickup onto the side of the track and into the bush, bouncing over rough terrain, branches whipping the vehicle, the tyres churning up stones and dirt as the humans tried to escape the angry elephant. Escape they did, but the question remained: was it the sound of the vehicle that had annoyed the bull or was it the colour that had jarred its sensitivities?

Another celebrated case of red safari vehicles and the effect on game was recounted in *The Winds of Havoc* A Memoir of Adventure and Destruction in Deepest Africa (New York: St. Martin's Press Inc., 2001), the autobiography of Adelino Serras Pires, one of the veterans of the African safari industry. When he was forced to use a red jeep at one stage, the game stood transfixed, unable to move, as if hypnotised by the colour. The safari clients were able to get out and up close to their quarries during what turned out to be a very successful safari. This was quite the opposite to Margarete's potentially fatal experience.

Concerning elephant in the new millennium, 100-pounders are excessively rare. Wholesale slaughter by international ivory poaching syndicates and the resultant effects on the gene pool in general in the latter part of the 20th century have taken their toll. In the first half of the last century, bulls sporting massive ivory were fairly common in East Africa. In fact, Margarete once came across such a bull stretched out, asleep. She could have shot the animal without further ado, but refused as this would have flouted her ethics as a huntress. Once the bull was awake, on its feet and on the move, Margarete moved in and downed the elephant. Zaidi and no doubt dozens of other tribal people were ecstatic at the thought of so much meat. This latest hunt also gave Zaidi more reason to trumpet his employer's prowess afield. This reinforced all the stories as well as some colourful myths in circulation about Margarete's skill as a huntress.

With time, other legends were woven around Margarete's head. The more time that went by, the more entrenched these legends became. The late Ada Wincza, a remarkable huntress and fêted safari outfitter for thirty years with her husband Laddy in East Africa during the last century, knew Margarete, describing her as 'an exceptionally good professional huntress'. In one of many conversations with the author about Margarete, Ada told of a time when Margarete met resistance from professional hunters when the British wanted to make her an honorary game warden and issue her with a professional hunter's licence. Margarete, annoyed at the bigotry of the times, challenged all the men present to approach a sleeping black rhino and write in chalk on its back the word *pumbavu*, meaning 'stupid' in Kiswahili. Nobody rose to the challenge, but Margarete was reported as having done the deed before some of the very same men who had objected to her inclusion in their cosy little club. Another version has her sticking a stamp on the buttocks of a black rhino.

What with talking to hippo, milking elephants and writing on black rhino rumps, whatever the actual truth of the matter, Margarete was fearless and deeply knowledgeable. She enforced respect from those who did not know any better. This was not based on any misplaced vanity, but on a profound sense of self-worth that comes through hardship and confronting fear. She also did not propagate stories about herself. They merely arose as her fame spread. And spread it did.

Far Horizons

The cattle numbers had risen and the breeding programme was sound; the dairy herd was thriving and butter sales to Arusha had resumed; the barter trade with the tribal peoples was a regular feature at *Momella* and the presence of foreign hunting clients on the property before and after their safaris with Margarete also became common. *Momella* had turned the corner and was moving away from debt and uncertainty. Rolf and Ulrich were proving to be dedicated, skilled hunters who shared the responsibility of running safaris and managing *Momella*. Young Rosie was doing well and Margarete had the support not only of her immediate family, but of her workforce, some of whom had been with her since 1907.

Male and female members of Europe's aristocracy were coming out in increasing numbers to enjoy old-time foot safaris with Margarete and up to one hundred or more porters. This was a word-of-mouth business like no other and the cachet of Europe's fastidious aristocrats was hugely valuable. Margarete was at ease with everyone and exuded confidence and natural authority.

One of the early professional clients was a princess from 'south-eastern Europe'. As Margarete shared with Gerd von Lettow-Vorbeck, this nameless lady was keen to hunt black rhino. She eventually managed to shoot

Margarete with a huntress client. [Yorck-Michael Trappe]

a rhino, but she shot badly and the creature turned and tore towards the terrified princess. Margarete had to put it down or risk a royal funeral. All this did was result in a royal tantrum as the princess expressed her extreme ire that Margarete had killed 'her' rhino. The foreigner had to have it explained to her that whoever had drawn first blood was the rightful claimant to the animal in question. Mollified, the princess completed her safari and departed. It was strange to see this reaction in a European royal who was not a novice huntress. The 'first-blood' tradition was long entrenched and Margarete no doubt puzzled over the princess's tantrum and apparent ignorance.

In between blueblood safaris Margarete once had to interrupt a hunt with a Swiss couple and let Ulrich take over because she had been summoned to a Maasai *manyatta* to hear about a cattle-killing lion that had severely wounded a Maasai. She attended to the tribesman as best she could with the medical kit she always carried, especially when

Margarete, second right, on the verandah of her house at Momella in the mid-1930s with hunting guests and family members. [Emil Karafiat]

on safari. Then the hunt was launched for the lion. It had been wounded by a Maasai spear.

As Margarete recounted immediately afterwards to family and friends and to Gerd von Lettow-Vorbeck many years later, the Swiss hunter insisted on joining Ulrich and the Maasai trackers in following the fresh spoor. The guest wanted to be filmed shooting the lion! The thorn bush, already thick, became even more so and Margarete's sense of alarm rose as the day wore on. The animal turned out to be a lioness and, at about 15 metres (almost 50 feet), the Swiss shot. He shot badly and the animal came for him. Margarete let fly with her rifle and caught the lioness in flight. It dropped into thick undergrowth and all went quiet.

The huntress was not certain the lioness was dead. Ulrich then caught sight of its tail, twitching in the yellow-brown grass. It started to make a strange hissing sound, its head just visible through the grass. Ulrich told the Swiss to get ready and give it the final shot. The man tried to do as he was told but, again, he shot badly and only grazed the animal. It suddenly gathered itself and went for him while Ulrich sat, encumbered with camera equipment, filming! Margarete fired as the lioness charged. The bullet struck as the animal reached the Swiss. In a particularly frightening display of panic, he had begun ejecting all the rounds of his rifle instead of trying to shoot the lioness. It reached him and, as Margarete finally put it down for good, it managed a very feeble half-bite on his leg before dying.

There were four tiny superficial wounds made by the cat's canines. The hunter's leather puttees prevented a serious mauling and Margarete's marksmanship did the rest. She immediately tried to clean and disinfect the puncture marks, taking the Swiss straight to the hospital in Arusha as quickly as she could. There, the English doctor gave the victim a tetanus jab and assured everyone that no great harm had been done.

In the morning, Margarete called on the Swiss at the hospital where he was doing very well. He was scheduled to be discharged the following morning in order to resume his safari. Come the next morning, Margarete was not allowed to see her client. He had developed blood poisoning and was desperately ill. Before the week was out he was dead. The police were informed, but ruled that nobody was to blame. The wife, devastated, left for home and Margarete had to attend to the formalities after the tragedy. She had no time to sink into shock and depression as two German princes were about to arrive for an extended safari.

Kaiser Wilhelm II had given his grandson, Prince Hubertus of Prussia, a present of a two-week big game safari with Margarete. The Prince, accompanied by Prince Friedrich Franz von Mecklenburg-Schwerin, arrived in Nairobi where Margarete and Ulrich, the safari cook, two tracker/gun bearers as well as two camp staff were awaiting them with their lorry. The party left immediately for the first of several hunting regions, Prince Hubertus at the wheel.

The princely pair had a grand safari, hunting for lion and buffalo in particular. Among Margarete's favourite areas was Lake Manyara west of Arusha and, just to the southeast of that, the Tarangire region in the Great Rift Valley wonderland. The Princes entered some of the most spectacular sections of the Valley around Lake Manyara with its prolific populations of plains game, elephant, buffalo and hippo, the shimmering spectacle of many thousands of pink flamingoes on the waters, feeding on algae, and the chance of coming across splendid lion.

A princely story that Margarete knew about was linked to Lake Manyara as the Prince of Wales had hunted around there in 1928. His professional guide was the notorious, debt-riddled *bon vivant* philanderer, Baron Bror von Blixen-Finecke, Karen Dinesen's ex-husband. He had been given a place to live on land at Magara just south of Lake Manyara. This utterly untouched, wild stretch of bush, called Singu Estates, belonged to Colonel Richard Cooper, a wealthy British war hero and Bror's benefactor.

'Blix' and his second wife, Cockie Birkbeck, built a shack for themselves as part of a deal to start clearing some of the bush for an eventual farm. When the Prince of Wales was brought to the estate during his big game safari with Bror, he was shocked to see the conditions under which they lived. In a now famous comment about Blixen-Finecke's housing arrangements, the Prince said: "I say, Blixen, you really oughtn't to let your wife live in such a tumbledown place like this." As for Colonel Cooper ... he was 'bagged' by Ernest Hemingway's 24-year-old ex-mistress, a blonde, leggy American socialite. After the affair fizzled out, the Colonel was found drowned in Lake Manyara.

It was during this intense period of Margarete's life as a professional huntress that Hemingway came out to East Africa on his first big game safari in December 1933. Hemingway also succumbed to the spell of the African bush, spending a protracted period in the Lake Manyara region, in the Serengeti and on the Maasai steppe. This life-changing experience inspired Hemingway to write his celebrated *Green Hills of Africa*, published in 1935, and two major works of fiction within three years of that safari. Margarete would see and also guide an increasing number of Americans throughout the 1930s. There is no doubt that Hemingway's evocative prose was one of the factors propelling his countrymen to come out and see for themselves.

Margarete knew even the most jaded of visitors who had 'seen it all' could never fail to be awed by the sight of Lake Manyara from the top of the escarpment, on the way to the unequalled grandeur of the Ngorongoro Crater and the stupendous Serengeti Plains to the northwest. Giant strangler fig trees, yellow-barked 'fever trees', expansive umbrella acacias and wild date palms were a mere sampling of the extravagant vegetation that could be seen in the vicinity of the Lake. Some baobabs displayed huge indentations in their girths where elephant had been feeding and rubbing themselves. And light: during the dry season between May and October, the setting sun over the mineral and soda deposits in the Lake with its algae and lichen and the hot springs on the western shore shimmered and undulated like a multi-coloured silk fan. The wide fields of vision, the limitless height of the skies and the absence of humans wherever one gazed occasioned a spiritual and physical lightness of being, as if the body were suspended above the entire world, floating, free, ethereal, and infinite.

The vast floodplains and swamps flanking the Tarangire River presented the Princes with a visual extravaganza of massive herds of elephant and buffalo, wildebeest and zebra as eland and fringed-eared oryx, hartebeest and lesser kudu mingled in this wildly beautiful world. Margarete had a way of concentrating her clients' attention on other features of the African safari such as the dragonflies hovering over aquatic plants like squadrons of helicopters with filmy wings; huge termite mounds of fantastically-shaped honeycombed red earth; yellow-billed oxpeckers riding upside down on the stomachs of black rhino, picking out parasites and ticks; cloud-white egrets accompanying buffalo to

Margarete with Sultan Njima, a welcome guest in her hunting camps. [Dr Jobst-Ulrich Trappe]

feast on insects disturbed by the huge animals as they moved; the sound of the breeze as it passed through thorn trees; the unnerving wails and shrieks of bushbabies after dark; the acrid-sweet aroma of rhino middens; the smell of burnt grass in October, ahead of the rains; the feel of night as insects thrummed and the moon grew full; and the taste of chilled water scooped up with both hands as it tumbled over mossy rock in forested shade.

High above birds of prey wheeled as dainty bee-eaters and showy lilac-breasted rollers performed their aerobatics and drew the eye ever forwards and outwards in that world of acacias, huge baobabs and measureless horizons where the sun set each day in fiery satin splendour. Africa's stupendous vistas would follow the Princes home after a very successful safari during which they not only hunted, but also penetrated a little of the mystique of another world. And they spoke of Margarete Trappe.

They spoke of how she had brought alive her Africa, not just a world of big game and hunting techniques, but a world where some very distinctive, remarkable cultures lived. To the west of Lake Manyara, for example, lay Lake Eyasi, a shallow alkaline lake set amid dessicated woodland. Overlooking the lake on one side were heat-loving Euphorbia trees that seemed to grow straight out of giant boulders stained in many places by red-brown lichen. This was home to a mysterious people, the Wahadzabe, who were still practising an undiluted hunter-gatherer way of life at that time. They lived off roots and wild fruits and hunted with five-foot-long bows and arrows with wooden shafts fledged with guinea-fowl feathers. Margarete knew about the deadly vegetable poison the Wahadzabe obtained from the desert rose (*Adenium obesum*) that could grow in the most desiccated of soils. She knew of the centuries-old, nomadic Hadzabe way of life that lived with nature, not against it, and she celebrated their continued existence in the 20th century.

Margarete shared with her guests something of the mystery surrounding this tribe's language whose origins remain unknown to this day. It has several click consonants reminiscent of the languages spoken by the San of the Kalahari Desert in southern Africa, yet the Wahadzabe have no racial affinities with the San. The Hadzabe ancestors also had a rich tradition of rock paintings that could still be seen and that Margarete would take some hunting guests to view.

Some of the areas where Margarete hunted brought her and her clients into contact with the Muslim culture. One old character was a Sultan of some standing in the community. The grizzled old man with hardly a tooth in his head, his face crisscrossed with wrinkles and furrows that spoke of a long life, often welcomed Margarete into his *shamba* when she was in the vicinity. He had a great sense of humour and delighted in sharing his wisdom in Kiswahili. The language is renowned for its heritage of proverbs and wise sayings, revealing the distilled essence of the Swahili culture. When Margarete was with the old patriarch, enriching her life with fresh insights into another world, one proverb comes to mind: *Rahino bora kuliko mali*. Blessings are better than wealth.

One day, Margarete was near his *shamba* and witnessed an extraordinary spectacle of dozens and dozens of the old Sultan's wives gathered together in song, dance and jubilation to welcome him home from an absence of some days. When Margarete commented on the lavish ceremony and its timing, the wily old ruler explained that he always sent a runner ahead to announce his imminent return so that none of his wives could be caught in 'unfaithful' mode and so that he did not have to mete out any punishment. A win-win situation. No *in flagrante delicto* and no recriminations.

There were even instances of individual professional dancers and singers who moved from one *shamba* to the next within the same tribe to entertain. This was an African version of the European court jesters and troubadours of centuries past. In the far south, Margarete and her guests would sometimes meet a tribe of Portuguese East African origin whose women were especially disfigured. They all had wooden discs inserted into their upper lips while very young, the lips then being distended further and further with larger and larger pieces of wooden until the women were grotesque to behold. And that was the point, apparently, to render the women so hideous that the Arab slave raiding caravans of the time would leave them alone. A similar custom was practiced in French Equatorial Africa, around Lake Chad, at the time, although there is still much debate about the core reason for this tradition.

Being a professional huntress meant, amongst other things, being an amateur ethnologist. Margarete knew that the Maasai disposed of their dead by leaving the bodies in the open for scavengers to find. Other tribes indulged in elaborate rituals to mark a death. The passage from youth into adulthood was especially noted in the Maasai culture. Margarete knew of the age group customs and the male and female circumcision rituals. Today, female circumcision is considered as female genital mutilation. Margarete knew how to keep her distance in such matters as it would have served no purpose to injure tribal feelings by expressing disapproval.

Margarete studied her hunting clients and, depending on what she discovered about their interests, she would introduce other elements into the hunting experience. Inevitably, her reputation crossed borders and spread. No stranger to neighbouring Kenya, she was once contacted by the Italian Consul-General in Nairobi who, with his professional hunter, had tried and failed to find a decent lion. Enter Margarete who organized a classic safari with porters and managed to lead the diplomat to a handsome black-maned lion with no trouble in the Maji Moto area near the southern reaches of Lake Manyara. In fact, she made specific mention of this hunt in a letter to relatives in Germany and mentioned how proud she was of the end result.

The Consul-General, greatly encouraged, now wanted to hunt buffalo, but his wife could not cope with the foot safari. The weather was also behaving strangely and a storm was threatening. Margarete took the shortest cut to get the couple back to the base camp on the other side of Lake Manyara by hiring some locals and their canoes. The Italian couple set off as the storm broke, whipping up the waters of the lake. The canoes were pushed across the shallow waters of the soda lake to camp and dry clothes, the drenched diplomat delighted with his safari, footsore wife notwithstanding. News travelled in the already flourishing professional hunter fraternity in British East Africa about the petite German huntress.

Margarete, of course, had to be able to rely on her chief tracker and assistants. Trackers have always been the unsung heroes of the safari industry. Zaidi, her finest *Jagdboy* – assistant hunter – was of the very best and he revered *Yeyo* because he recognized that she was as skilled as he was and that she was able to step into his tracking shoes and take over in a flash. He stuck by her without exception in the most dangerous of hunting

Margarete with two hunting clients, Count Rantzau on her right and Baron Donner on her left.
[Dr Jobst-Ulrich Trappe]

situations. A phenomenal tracker, he remained human, however, and he had his moments. His weaknesses were women and the locally brewed liquor called *pombe*. This was a home-brewed beer that could be made from sugar-cane, honey, fruit or all kinds of grains such as sorghum, millet, barley and maize.

Zaidi once disappeared during a leopard hunt with Count Rantzau. Margarete, knowing his predilections, tracked him into a neighbouring village where she stormed from one hut to the next, her Kiswahili-laced rage audible to everyone, until she found her finest tracker, sprawled in a *pombe*-induced stupor inside one of the huts. He was forced out into the fresh air and made to sober up as fast as possible in order to rejoin the Rantzau safari. Margarete's ire was sufficient to clear the most addled brain.

This was no ordinary safari. Hardly had the said Zaidi got back into tracking mode when a honey badger burst out of the undergrowth and made straight for Margarete's son Rolf. Such was the uproar and movement that Margarete could not risk taking aim at the notoriously aggressive little animal. In stepped Zaidi with a thick *rungu* to bash the creature over its head. Nothing happened. The honey badger went into an even more frenzied mode. Another tracker tossed his spear at the tough-hided badger to no avail as it carried on trying to get hold of Rolf. Margarete was then able to let fly with her firearm, but still the devilish animal continued. When it looked as if Rolf was going to be truly mutilated, his mother was able to get off a clear shot that ended the drama.

Margarete also conducted occasional photographic safaris during this period in her life. Her clients often expressed as much interest in the botanical and ornithological wonders of Tanganyika as they did in its game. In escorting her visitors and their camera equipment during the leisurely safaris of the time, Margarete's detailed knowledge of the land, some of its tribal peoples and the complexity of the natural world ensured that a photographic excursion became a significant experience. In those days, camera equipment was bulky and it was often a battle to keep the equipment safe from extremes in temperature.

Count Plessen and Baron Thilo von Donner were early examples of what is now a mode expression – eco-tourism. They relied on Margarete to bring them up as close as

Margarete behind the wheel of her 1925 Chrysler Phaeton/Tourer on New Year's Day 1932, at the height of her full-time professional hunting career. [Emil Karafiat].

possible to dangerous game such as black rhino. On one occasion, while Margarete was searching for just such an animal for the amateur photographers, one burst out from behind a rocky outcrop. It did not follow through with the charge, for some reason, and the result was a picture of an expanse of rhino hide and a beady little eye. That was how close the guests were to their subject while Margarete hoped she would not have to kill the animal before it killed her visitors.

Fossils and Freedom

Safari means travel and it meant very wide-ranging journeys, much of it on foot, in the 1920s and 1930s in Tanganyika. During a brief break in one such major safari, Margarete went out scouting for game. She came across an elderly tribesman who told her of a dead elephant nearby. Thinking it to be a recent event, Margarete was surprised to discover that the old man was referring to the bones of an elephant he had stumbled on in a dry riverbed.

In scraping away some of the dirt, she discovered what looked like a petrified skull and some molars. The tusks had long been destroyed, but it appeared as if this was some sort of prehistoric elephant. This was in the Great Rift Valley in the northern reaches, not far from the Olduvai Gorge on the Serengeti Plains. The Gorge would become world renowned later on as 'The Cradle of Mankind' because of the millennia-old fossils unearthed by the Leakey family during the 20th century and the fresh light the fossils have cast on the origins of human beings.

There was an early German link to the site through the German entomologist, Wilhelm Kattwinkel, the first European to document the Gorge in 1911. Margarete reported what she had been shown and the location to the competent game warden, but there is no record of any follow-up. It was experiences such as these that brought home to her the as yet unexplored richness of the African wilderness. She was consistently inquisitive about her African home.

In addition to enduring contacts with the tribal peoples, Margarete developed some memorable friendships with missionaries who were stationed in the heart of big game country. One such person was Father Joseph, a Swiss Capuchin monk, the Capuchins being the strictest branch of the Franciscan order. Father Joseph was attached to the Catholic Mission hospital at Ifakara in the far central region. The Mission, which also included a convent for nuns, lay just south of the glorious Udzungwa Mountains and the utterly wild swamp country of the Kilombero River Valley. It was tough, steep terrain in many places, thickly forested from the lower lying woodlands right up to the lush bamboo groves and highland forest canopies.

Red-bearded Father Joseph, who was far from austere, was a hunter. When venison ran low, he would climb on his bicycle and head off into the bush with one of his ornate rifles. His cell was a mini-armory of antique rifles, some of them handmade pieces that would attract intense interest today and probably some very high prices as well. He and Margarete would spend lengthy periods in conversation right there in his cell about game and hunting and he would tip her off about any worthwhile animals believed to be in the region.

Zaidi and some local guides would accompany Margarete by canoe on the stretch of river near the Mission. They would scout the banks for any promising spoor, especially of elephant, and then climb out and start tracking through very high grass and dense river-ine undergrowth. It was tough hunting, not only because of poor visibility, but also because the region was notorious for malaria.

The rivers, naturally, were full of hippo and crocodile. During one such excursion, the local guides pleaded with Margarete to shoot a particular hippo because it had killed many of their people. How one hippo out of dozens was known to be the people-killer was debatable. What was certain was the local enthusiasm for hippo meat. Margarete obliged and goodwill towards her and her assistants spread. Father Joseph and his fellow monks were also remembered when Margarete brought a sizeable quantity of hippo fat back to the Mission to make altar candles!

The country south of Ifakara towards Mahenge and beyond was one of Margarete's favourite destinations, usually for solo hunting safaris as she considered the region too arduous and even too dangerous for all but the toughest and most seasoned of foreign hunters. Not everyone was in Count Rantzau's league and Margarete was very cautious in selecting areas to match her clients and their requirements as best as possible.

Inordinately high and thick grass on marshy terrain south of Ifakara increased the danger of hunting big game. The huntress had experienced on several occasions the heart-freezing moment of coming across elephant and buffalo close to the game paths, their vast bulk almost hidden by the thick high grass. The way animals camouflaged themselves was a source of constant amazement and it was also a warning to Margarete never to let up her guard in the wild. Where possible, she would seek out high termite mounds in order to try to see beyond the dense vegetation. She would even get onto the shoulders of one of her trackers when no other means was available in order to better spot game.

Margarete eventually reached the conclusion that German East Africa/Tanganyika was home to two distinct species of elephant and that they were rarely found in each other's company. Many tribal peoples shared this belief. One type of elephant was smaller in body, had a more aggressive temperament and carried very long thin ivory that was not attractive to the trophy hunter. This kind of elephant predominated in the south and central provinces, whereas the large-bodied elephant with thick, heavy ivory inhabited the northern regions.

Among the more unnerving experiences Margarete had with elephant involved her being tracked by a bull. While out on a solo safari, Margarete and her tracker picked up a series of tracks and concluded that they were those of cow elephant. Although Margarete knew from experience that the bull tended to follow later on, she and her tracker emerged to take a closer look at the tracks as they led into a clearing.

Hardly had they walked into the clearing than they had to retreat into the undergrowth as a bull elephant emerged, its trunk lowered onto the tracks where Margarete and her tracker had been a moment previously. The bull began sniffing like a police dog after a criminal and then began trumpeting, agitated and clearly alarmed. It had picked up non-elephant spoor. That meant danger. It also meant danger for Margarete and the tracker. They withdrew as quickly and as silently as they could. This remained a highly unusual occurrence in her hunting life, but it was echoed later on when she and her trackers were once chased by a bull that had been following *their* spoor. They managed to shake off the animal finally by jumping into a swampy area and crossing over to dry land.

Margarete had other strange experiences while hunting elephant. One involved sand flies that were a huge nuisance in much of the country. She had been tracking a small herd of elephant in very humid conditions. She was safely downwind and had been making good progress in her effort to close the gap and get up close in order to identify the best bull before taking aim. Suddenly, the herd became highly agitated and split up, moving off in a state of alarm in several directions. Margarete had noticed how she and her tracker had been bothered by clouds of sand flies as they swarmed their faces, arms and legs. The sand flies then moved off, as if on cue, to the herd ahead. Margarete was convinced they had taken the human scent with them and that this was what had alarmed the elephant. She had this same strange experience on many more occasions.

Lion once interrupted an elephant hunt in quite dramatic fashion. Margarete had been following up a very good bull and had been sleeping on the track in the process. One night, lion had been inordinately active, roaring repeatedly. The following dawn, Margarete came across a lion with an especially luxuriant mane, but she passed it up as she did not want to send out any alarm signals to the elephant herd she was tracking.

As the day heated up, a lioness appeared next to a small pool of water. It was jumping from one side to the next, highly agitated. Suddenly, with absolutely no warning, it charged like a tawny shell propelled out of a cannon. It pulled up some metres away from Margarete, staring at her. She stared back, not moving and not daring to avert her gaze.

The lioness finally looked away, a sign that it was going to charge again. Margarete remained frozen as she stared the animal down. Again, the animal charged. Again it aborted the attack before moving off at speed into bush next to the pond. Still very shaken, Margarete then saw movement on the other side of the water – lion cubs. The lioness had indulged in all the theatrics in the time-honoured tradition of a mother wishing to distract a potential enemy away from her offspring. Margarete recalled seeing plover adopt such tactics. The elephant hunt had to be called off, but the huntress did not mind at all as the essence of hunting was the journey itself into the wilderness and the special experiences savoured and survived along the way.

Now and again, hunts were unsuccessful and Margarete's trackers sometimes had otherworldly explanations as in the case of the bull elephant that got away. One of the trackers pointed out that the bull was disturbing the ground as it moved forward, digging furrows and then seeming to cover them with branches. The grizzled old tracker warned Margarete that this was a grave for humans and that they had better call off the chase. Margarete tactfully explained that the 'graves' did not apply to the *Wazungu*, but the old chap would have none of it and withdrew. Margarete, never derisive of firmly held tribal beliefs, decided to continue tracking on her own because she was as skilled as any tracker in her employ by then. She too, however, had to call off the pursuit. The bull had vanished.

Illness was inevitable in such climate and given the nature of the work. Malaria came and went, but a chronic attack of lumbago in the middle of a professional hunt was somewhat different, as Gerd Von Lettow-Vorbeck was told when with Margarete in the early 1950s. Not wishing ever to let down her clients or in any way appear weak in that tough world, she arranged for the camp staff to boil water, pour it into a tin bath and then place poles over the bath. She smeared her lower back with a mixture of butter, snuff and red peppers, wrapped herself up in a blanket and then lay on the poles over the steaming water, no doubt replenished at intervals, for the rest of the night. The concoction and the warmth in the makeshift steam bath loosened the muscles, eased the pain and had Margarete back on her feet by dawn. She improvised, found solutions and maintained her calm.

Gold Rush

It was November 1934. Count Rantzau had concluded yet another extensive safari with Margarete when news started gathering pace about fresh finds in the Lupa goldfields of southwestern Tanganyika. The Count and his professional huntress pricked up their ears.

For the first time in over six strenuous years, Margarete could breathe more easily as she started settling the last of her debts and *Momella* had recovered from the disastrous effects of the First World War. Margarete had survived deportation, expropriation of all her property, years of separation from her children and being swindled out of an inheritance. She had had the courage to seek a divorce at a time when it bore a very considerable social stigma and she had re-established herself through full-time professional hunting like no other woman had anywhere in Africa at that time. She had been reunited with her children and her reputation as a fine huntress had been consolidated in the highest circles of European society. A little gold panning seemed in order.

The region where the Lupa goldfields lie is to this day wildly beautiful, isolated, mountainous country that is still relatively poorly known. The Lupa goldfields were situated in the southwestern corner of the country, east of Lake Rukwa and just north of the settlement of Mbeya and the verdant Southern Highlands with their volcanic crater lakes, hot springs, glorious waterfalls, rain forests and dormant volcanoes. The location held the added allure of remoteness that was essential to Margarete's sense of well-being and lifelong adventure.

She had hunted many times in the Ruaha River region to the north of the goldfields. It was known, amongst other things, for its impressive herds of buffalo, greater and lesser kudu and the Defassa waterbuck. Overhead, birds of prey dressed the skies while, below, jewel-like insects, butterflies and beetles shared space with exquisite expanses of wild flowers, even orchids. All thought of discomfort, malaria, tsetse fly and sleeping sickness seemed to dissipate in the presence of this African Eden.

Margarete knew the faraway, desolate Lake Rukwa section of the Rift Valley to the northwest of the goldfields where splendid herds of roan and sable roamed, as did the cinnamon-coloured topi antelope and the puku. The feared African hunting dog also held sway in large packs while falcons, eagles and hawks coasted on the thermals above, in search of the next meal. This was an uncontaminated paradise of wildlife, flanked in the south by the then Northern Rhodesia and by Nyasaland's strikingly scenic Lake Nyasa. The natural world's abundance and beauty belied the dark ravages of the fairly recent past where Arab slaving caravans from the distant coast trawled for fresh victims to haul ever increasing loads of white gold for distant masters.

Word had begun circulating in about 1902 about alluvial gold deposits in the rivers and streams that crisscrossed the region in question. An actual first rush was triggered in 1905 and, as mining activity increased and the gold rush began in all seriousness in 1922, the settlement of Mbeya was established in 1927 to cater to the goldfields and the motley population it attracted. They came by oxwagon and by mule, on horseback and on foot, from titled remittance men to derelicts. The writer, E. Reid, captured the heady atmosphere very well when he wrote *Tanganyika without prejudice; A Balanced Critical Review of the Territory and her People* – London: East African Newspaper Publishers, 1934:

> '... this river had beckoned all sorts and conditions of men and women... cooks' sons and Dukes' daughters, runaway sailors from ships, clerks and counter-hands... big game hunters, public school-boys and 'Varsity graduates, surveyors and cow punchers, actors, hair-dressers and piano-tuners, Dutchmen, Frenchmen and Dagoes, Jews, Gentiles and Pagans. During the period of world depression, scores of planters and farmers, transport riders, white hunters and retrenched civil servants, aye and their womenfolk, too, from Tanganyika itself and other parts of East Africa found in this region a raft or two to tide them over the low waters of those years.'

All German mining enterprises, however modest, that had been conducted in the Lupa goldfields before 1918, were confiscated as enemy property by the British after the First World War. Most of the miners were artisanal miners. Between 1920 and 1925 there was a steep increase in the price of gold and a consequent 'rush' on colonial goldfields. Reef deposits, in addition to alluvial gold, were also discovered at Lupa. The fields were not regulated in that sparsely populated world where prospectors and workers had succumbed to bouts of scurvy and other epidemics a few years before Margarete tried her luck.

By the time Margarete and the Count had acquired their prospecting licence, had organized a labour force and sluice boxes and had actually set up camp in Lupa in November 1934, there were already many hundreds of prospectors there who had staked out their pieces of land in the search for their crock of gold at the end of yet another African rainbow. Food and other supplies were brought in on foot by hundreds of porters from Mbeya.

It was Christmas Eve, 1934 when Margarete's workers struck a seam in their claim. Jubilation engulfed everyone as almost 35 ounces of gold were recovered on that day alone. It then ran out just as suddenly, but not before the news had raced around the fields, bringing tempting offers to Margarete and Count Rantzau. They declined to sell their claim, hoping to make a second find. During those giddy days on the goldfields of Lupa, Margarete had a strange experience. One of her workers came to her to ask for help as he had a brother on another claim who had fallen desperately ill. *Yeyo's* reputation had accompanied her to Lupa. She duly grabbed her medical kit and went off to find the worker in question who was suffering from pneumonia. It was the time of the rains and the atmosphere was damp, even sodden.

The huntress doctored the man to the very best of her ability, warning him not to leave his tent at all. She visited him every day, even several times a day. He was improving. Then, despite all her warnings, the worker left his tent during a thunderstorm. She battled to save him, but he died very quickly, as had other workers and miners on the Lupa goldfields over the years.

The night of the man's death, his brother approached Margarete and gave her a large nugget of gold. He had found it himself and had hidden it. Now, his late brother's spirit had instructed him to give the nugget to Margarete and not to sell it to the Indian traders who had flocked to the goldfields like so many vultures. Nothing Margarete said would dissuade the worker. His gesture revealed the esteem with which he regarded this woman who had tried to save his brother's life.

With her claim now apparently exhausted, Margarete paid her workers and returned to *Momella* with Count Rantzau after an extraordinary adventure on the Lupa goldfields. The nugget brought in sufficient money so that Margarete could clear all remaining debt and settle with her great benefactor, Michael Michalakis, who had been a solid friend at a very bleak time in her life. Not two years later, the Lupa gold rush subsided and the price of gold was fixed at $4.86 to the ounce! In the new millennium, gold mining operations at Lupa are vigorous, today's Tanzania has the third-to-largest gold deposits in all Africa and the gold price has reached unprecedented levels!

Golden Years

The 1930s proved to be golden years for big game hunting in East Africa. It was an age of still leisurely safaris that often lasted for three months. Although the motor vehicle was making increasing inroads into that world and distant hunting grounds were becoming more accessible more quickly, the four-wheel-drive vehicle was still the stuff

of fantasy, as was regular air travel to East Africa. Most roads were usually impassable in the rains and many were still glorified bush tracks anyway. Hunting safaris remained adventurous, expensive and often strenuous affairs involving a great deal of walking and some hardship. Not every camp boasted swanky 'chop boxes' with fine food and wines from Europe served on bone china crockery and in crystal glasses.

Margarete, breathing much more easily now that *Momella* was clear of debt and doing well, also had the advantage of two strapping sons to assist her not only on the estate, but in the field. Rolf and Ulrich, accomplished hunters and amateur naturalists, had been

Margarete, third from right with her son Rolf on her left on the verandah of her house at Momella.

born into the business and had absorbed all the skills from childhood at their mother's knee. As they grew older, they were entrusted with greater and greater responsibilities concerning foreign hunting clients and also concerning the running of *Momella*. The stressful years of separation, loss and financial hardship were now in the past. Margarete would always mourn the loss of *Ngongongare*, but she was a pragmatist to the core and concentrated on conserving and developing what she had managed to rescue, not on what she wished she could have retained.

She epitomized what Ernest Hemingway once wrote:

'Now is no time to think of what you do not have. Think of what you can do with what there is.'

Margarete knew she was an unusual member in the world of big game hunting professional guides at that time. Not everyone was comfortable with the presence of a woman who could organize and conduct lengthy hunting safaris, recruit and maintain a disciplined workforce, speak Kiswahili as if to the manner born, ride and train horses, doctor them and other livestock herds like a trained veterinarian, identify trophy game animals, track and shoot with deadly skill, walk vast distances as a routine, field dress any animal with the best of her male peers under all conditions, and handle a variety of illnesses and accidents in the bush like a military paramedic.

The following details, from a Trappe family source, illustrate one man's 'conversion' after hunting with Margarete. The documentary evidence is of particular interest as so much such evidence concerning Margarete was lost or otherwise destroyed between the late 1930s and the writing of this book in the new millennium. The most regrettable loss was her meticulously maintained journals concerning her hunting clients. If nothing else, this testimony serves as a benchmark of Margarete's abilities.

Ulrich Trappe, clutching a winged spear, is on the left and Baron Hinrich Donner, his hunting client, is on the right holding a short spear. They are sitting on the steps of Margarete's house at Momella with four buffalo trophies. [Dr Jobst-Ulrich Trappe]

Reference Check

One person who had done very careful research before engaging Margarete as his professional huntress-guide was a veteran hunter in the grand European tradition, a certain Colonel August von Spiess. In a lengthy article published in Germany during 1938 in a magazine entitled *Jagd & Hege*, the Colonel revealed how he had heard of this German woman's elevated status. Her remarkable stamina and ability to hunt on foot and on horseback were important pieces of information for the Colonel as he admitted that 'under normal circumstances' one would not expect a woman to have the requisite 'energy' and 'steadfastness' for this kind of activity. He was also intrigued by the fact that Margarete Trappe could hold her own in any conversation about African wildlife, its habits and habitat.

The Colonel learned of the numerous English hunters and huntresses who had engaged Margarete as their guide over the years, as had many other hunters from around the world, all with great success. Margarete's profound experience in hunting elephant and lion as well as her in-depth knowledge of the game fields were reported as setting her apart from other hunter-guides.

The Colonel was so intrigued by details pertaining to Margarete's veterinary skills, her near-mythical renown as a healer of humans and her sound relations with the tribal peoples, especially with the Maasai, that he decided to choose her over a number of male professional hunter guides for his first full-bag African safari in 1936. Another facet of Margarete's character that appealed to this conservative hunter was her reputation for ethical behaviour and absolute adherence to Game Department regulations. The Colonel, already in his sixties, was still very fit and was not about to embark on any major safari with a relatively inexperienced guide.

Colonel Von Spiess, a military man in his youth, mentioned in the article how he was

Momella, v. 2.12.38.

Mein lieber Hans-Ulrich!

Über Deinen Brief habe ich mich sehr gefreut. Aber traurig war ich zu hören, dass Deine liebe Mutter gestorben ist. Wir hören jetzt so wenig von Deutschland, und ich freue mich immer, wenn ich mal einen Brief bekomme. Ich lege Dir paar Marken und paar Bildchen bei. Wenn Du groß bist, musst Du uns mal besuchen. Unser ... ist so schön! Ich gehe noch immer viel auf Jagd und führe auch und bin froh, wenn meine Jagdgäste alles schießen was sie haben wollen, was bis jetzt Gott sei Dank und unberufen auch immer der Fall war. Jetzt bekam ich eine Anfrage, ob ich für ein ... einen Elefanten, einen Büffel und ein Nashorn schießen und präparieren würde. Ob es zustande kommen wird, weiss ich noch nicht. Ich habe wenigstens geschrieben, dass, wenn ich das Geld hierher bekommen kann, dann tue ich es. Denn das Präparieren kostet ja so viel und das Geld ist knapp. Vor 2 Jahren führte ich den Hofjägermeister vom König von Rumänien. Er hat mehrere Aufsätze in Wild und Hund über diese Reise geschrieben und will auch uns in einem Buch über mich schreiben. Na, wer weiss was da rauskommt. Jetzt nächste Woche, will ich mit 2 Herren aus Deutschland auf Büffel und ... gehen ...

Margarete's letter of 2 December 1938 to relatives in Germany in which she mentions Colonel Von Spiess and his intention to write a book about his safari with her. [Gabriële Löhrl]

'reliably informed' of Margarete's 'outstanding services' rendered to General Von Lettow-Vorbeck during the First World War as a mounted reconnaissance operative [...*im berittenen Kundschafterdienst*...]. The Colonel was also informed of her poaching activities after the war and of her struggle to retain what remained of the once very large Trappe estate. He understood her position and why she had had to resort to the very activity she had fought against from the earliest days. He also understood why the British eventually employed Margarete as a game warden.

As was to be expected, Colonel Von Spiess enjoyed a very successful safari with

Margarete. Already sixty-two years old, the Colonel was still exceptionally fit and a consummate marksman. He killed a brace of buffalo with two shots – a right and a left – and also succeeded in hunting two fine-maned lion. When he first heard about Margarete, the Colonel did not know what to expect. Was she '…a muscular truly Germanic farmer's wife or else a lean, blonde athlete…?' He expressed his delight when he met a petite, charming brunette with bobbed hair who conducted his expedition calmly and skillfully throughout. Not surprisingly, Colonel Von Spiess came away with the greatest respect for his huntress-guide.

Left — Margarete taking a break on safari. [Dr Jobst-Ulrich Trappe]

Right — Margarete with Colonel Von Spiess' waterbuck. [Dr Jobst-Ulrich Trappe]

This Colonel, however, was not simply another retired military man, yearning for some adventure in the African bush. He was the former Chief Hunt Master to the Royal Court of the Kings of Romania and Director of the Royal Hunting Department. In fact, the Colonel's safari was a retirement present from the Royal Court! This redoubtable man was a member of the Natural Preservation and National Parks Committee of Romania and an honorary member of several hunting associations in Romania and abroad. A hunter of the old school, he wore his courtly hunting outfits throughout his safari with Margarete, even though they were designed for the freezing winters of the Carpathian Mountains and not for the much warmer climate of Tanganyika!

The fact that such a person from such a rigid, royal background had come out to hunt with Margarete was indicative of her reputation. In fact, Margarete mentioned in a letter written in December 1938 that her Romanian guest was planning to write a book in which he intended to describe his hunt with her. He did just that, devoting over 50 pages of his book to his safari with Margarete. The book was written in Romanian and published in Bucharest in 1942 when Colonel Von Spiess was already in his seventies. The following extract (pages 135 and 137 from D*in Ardeal la Kilimanjaro: Vānātori in Africa* – Bucharesti: Fundatia Regalā Pentru Literaturā Si Artā, 1942), translated by Mr Emil Tudor of the National Library of Romania who tracked down the book in question, reveals just how greatly the Colonel appreciated Margarete Trappe:

> 'This lady knew the country and the people of this equatorial hunting para-
> dise, the various black tribes and the Maasai. Over time, they came to deeply
> appreciate and love her for her courage and her hunting skills but especially
> for the medical assistance she provided the local people when they fell ill
> […] I placed all my trust in her leadership. Those days we spent hunting
> enabled me to return completely satisfied with the trophies I had wanted. I
> also had a chance to meet an intelligent woman with sound knowledge of

the natural world. Her cordial and consistently correct behaviour made my first trip to Africa very successful and instructive. I owe, therefore, all my respect and gratitude to this lady, not only as a hunter and naturalist but also as someone who was sociable throughout the time we spent together in the forests and bush and on the grassy plains of Africa.'

Margarete at Lake Khanzee on the Momella property, a favourite of hers. [Emil Karafiat]

The weeks spent hunting with Margarete in the exceptional surroundings of Tanganyika and the honest simplicity of life in the wilds contrasted very starkly with the court connivings and scandals of the Romanian Royal Family. As many professional hunters and huntresses can attest today, their guests tend to unwind and confide by the campfire in the intimacy of the bush, far from the strictures of their normal lives.

So it was with the Colonel. Romania had been ruled first by King Carol I, then by King Ferdinand and, after a strange succession debacle, by the scandalous playboy King Carol II whose life was replete with mistresses, elopements, supplanting of successors and illegitimate offspring. Colonel Von Spiess had seen it all. Hunting and the natural world predominated around the campfire with Margarete and her sons, affording the Colonel a real escape into healthy reality. When his licence was filled, the Colonel returned to Romania with a leopard skin for the King, a zebra skin for the Queen and a baboon skin for the Crown Prince. One wonders about the hierarchy of gifts to Romanian Royals.

The East African Professional Hunters' Association (EAPHA)

During the period between both World Wars, Tanganyika and, indeed, the rest of colonial Africa, was an overwhelmingly male-orientated world, run on the paternalistic conventions of the day. This never fazed Margarete. She was too busy surviving and supporting a family and workforce to pay attention to other people's prejudices. Everyone associated with hunting in Tanganyika and the rest of East Africa, in any case, knew of the 'little lady at *Momella*' and the broad sweep of her extraordinary life. Her clientèle alone kept the bush telegraph busy in East Africa as she consistently attracted the upper echelons of European society with its centuries' old hunting traditions, high expectations and intolerance of mediocrity.

On 12 April 1934, the East African Professional Hunters' Association (EAPHA) was formed in neighbouring Kenya at the iconic Norfolk Hotel. Since the end of the First World War, the game fields of East Africa were becoming more and more widely known and frequented. President Theodore Roosevelt's landmark 1909/1910 big game hunting and collecting expedition in British East Africa had been a major factor, and the increasing number of hunters and settlers was now starting to exert new pressures on game and habitat alike.

Some of the prime objectives of the EAPHA were '...securing the general adoption of a high and sportsmanlike conception of wildlife and the hunting of game', 'the preservation of the fauna and flora of Eastern Africa, in accordance with the practice of the profession of hunting' and 'to keep the sport of big-game shooting clean and wholesome.' This organization introduced and fearlessly promoted a whole array of game laws

THESE ARE THE NAMES OF MOST OF THE PROFESSIONAL HUNTERS EMPLOYED IN EAST AFRICA BETWEEN 1903 AND 1977. WHERE STATED THEY WERE CHAIRMAN OR VICE CHAIRMAN OF THEIR PROFESSIONAL ASSOCIATION.

Aagaard Finn.	Carlyon, Jack.	Foran, Major Robert.	Kingsley–Heath, John.	Nurk, Capt. Carl, M.C.	Senior, J.C.
Adamson, George.	Carr–Hartley, Brian.	Forgan, Neil.	Klein, A.J. Vice-Chairman	O'Brien, Tony.	Seton, Alec.
Alexander, John.	Carr–Hartley, Mike.	Foster, Bob.	Kolowicz, W.	Ommanney, David.	Seth–Smith, Donald.
Allan, Torr.	Carr–Hartley, Roy.	Fourie, Ben.	Kuhle, Bror.	Outram, Major George.	Seth–Smith, Tony.
Allen, Anton.	Catchpole, Guy.	Fowle, Col. Andrew.	Lang, Franz.	Paddock, L.R.	Shaw, Dan.
Allen, Bunny.	Catchpole, Tony.	France, Tony.	Lawrence, M. St. John. Chairman & Vice-Chairman	Palfrey, Ray.	Sheldrick, Major David.
Allen, David.	Cedergren, Sten.	Gaymer, Barry.	Lawrence–Brown, Stan.	Palmer, Lionel.	Sheldrick, Ken.
Anderson, Major H.G.	Cheffings, Joe.	Gilbert–Hopkins, Patrick.	Lawrence–Brown, Geoff, Chairman	Palmer–Wilson, Richard.	Smith, G.L. O.B.E.
Anniere, John.	Clark, Ken.	Giraudo, Lee.	Level, Ken.	Palmer–Wilson D.E.	Smith, P.H.
Angelides G.W.	Cleland-Scott, S.R.	Grant, Guy.	Lindstrom, s.	Palmer–Wilson C.W.	Smith S.J.
Ambrose G.J.	Coles, W.J.	Gregory, A.R.	Lithgow, Tom, Vice-Chairman	Pelizzoli, Alfredo.	Stautmeister J.
Archer, Tony, Vice-Chairman	Collins, Major Dougie.	Guex, J.G.	Lockwood, David.	Percival, Philip, Chairman	Steyn, Hermann.
Aschan, Kris.	Coleman, Brian.	Hammond, Jackie.	Loolpapit, R.K.	Petrosley, Rev. C.	Stewart, Ken.
Atthow, Ian.	Cook, John.	Hartley, Lionel.	Lowis, R.A.	Pitcairn–Holmes, J.	Sutton, John, Vice-Chairman
Auersperg, Prince Alfie.	Coreth, Count Maurice.	Hartley, Lionel.	Lucy, Jack.	Pollman, K.H.	Swan, Nick.
Awan, W.N.A.	Cormack, Keith.	Hassan, S.I.	Luies, Chris.	Poolman, Fred.	Tamagnini P.
Ayre, A.F. Pat.	Cottar, Charles & Sons.	Henley, Tony.	Lunan, David.	Poolman, Henry.	Tarlton, Leslie.
Ayre, W.H.	Cottar, Glen.	Henley, Henry.	Luthy K.	Pretorius, H.J.	Tatham–Warter, Major Digby, D.S.O.
Babault, Rene.	Courtney, R.J.C.M.C.	Herne, Brian, Vice-Chairman	Lynn, Liam.	Prettejohn, Mike.	Temple–Boreham, Major Lyn M. C.
Barrington, George.	Craig, Ian.	Hessel, Jens.	Lyon, Chris.	Pretorius B.P.	Tippett, Mike.
Bashir, Mohammed.	Crofton, R.M.	Hill, Clifford.	MacAlpine-Leny, Major Roy.	Price, Alan.	Tornielli, Count Max.
Bartlet, Fred.	Cunninhame, R.J.	Hill, Harold.	Macdonald, Ian.	Prickett, R.J.	Torrens, Kevin.
Beaumont, A.J.N.A.	Da Cruz, C.	Hissey, Mike.	Malewsky, H.	Pridham, Bill.	Trappe, Margarete.
Becker, Peter.	Danhauser B.	Hoey, Cecil.	Mambrioni, Francesco.	Prowse, Harold.	Trappe, Rolf.
Behr, Peter.	Davey, Peter.	Hoey, W.H.	Marriot, Col. Tiger.	Raitray, Andrew.	Trappe R B.
Bentley, Victor.	Dawson, Jock.	Holmberg, Anders.	Martin, E.R.	Ray, Bunny.	Trutzschler, Baron Max. von.
Barkenheger Ingo.	De Beer, J.N.R.	Home, Roy.	Mason M.O.	Read, Norman, Chairman	Turner, Dauncey, M.
Beverley, Pip.	De Bono, Edgar, Vice-Chairman	Hook, Col. Hilary.	Mathews, Terry, Vice-Chairman	Rees, O.M.	Turner, Myles, M.B.E.
Bisleti, Count Francesco.	De Metio, Peter.	Hopcralt, Richard.	Mathews, G.	Reitnaur, Bob.	Ulyate, K.
Black, Alan.	Destro, Reggie, Vice-Chairman	Hornyhold, Marquis, Ralph.	Maxtone–Mailer, Tony, Vice-Chairman	Ricci, Giovani.	Van de Slegen, Count Rudi.
Blacklaws, Jack.	De Wet, W.	Horsley, Mike.	McCallum, Owen.	Ritchie, Capt. Archie, M.C.	Van Dyke, W.F.
Bleazard, Stan.	Dickinson, Col. Dicker, C.B.E.	Howard–Williams, Mark.	Mc.Callum, Danny.	Roberts, Boyce.	Von Rooyen, Father and sons.
Blixen, Baron von Bror.	Dhillon, S.	Hulett, Capt. H.	McClinton, Peter.	Roberts, Alec.	Wagner, Ludwig.
Blunt, Commander David.	Dugmore, John.	Hunter, J.A.	McKeand, Julian.	Roberts, Barry.	Wali Mohamed, Habib.
Blunt, Nicky.	Dunn, Derek, Vice-Chairman	Hurt, Robin.	Mead, David.	Roberts, G.C.	Wali Mohamed, Hamid.
Bonnett, L.H.	Dollisca G.B.	Iqbal, M. Bali.	Meran, Count Franz.	Robotham, Mike.	Walmsley, E.
Bousefield, Don.	Dove, George.	Irwin, Terry.	Michaelides, Chris.	Rungren, Eric.	Waller, Sydney.
Bousefield, Jack.	Dove, Mike.	Ismail, M.	Miller, Frank, Chairman	Rungren, D.E.	Ward, Freddie.
Bowker, Douglas, Russell, Vice-Chairman	Downey, Syd.	Jakobsen, O.P.	Miller, Gerard.	Runton, George.	Ward, Capt. Vivian, Chairman
Bowman, Frank.	Dyer, Tony, Chairman & Vice-Chairman	Jenkins, Peter, M.B.E.	Mills, Capt. E.C.	Russell, John.	Webley, Mike.
Bowring, R.C.	Dyer, Sqd. Ldr. John A.F.C. D.F.C.	Jenvey, Bill.	Miller N.T.	Ryan, Bill, Vice-Chairman	Welier, J.F.
Boy, Ronnie.	Elliot, Chris.	Jespersen, Ken.	Miller E.J.	Salahud Din, M.	Whitehead, Peter.
Boyd, Robin.	Evans, Peter.	Jones, Walter.	Morkel, Bill.	Samaras L.	Williams, David.
Branham, Bud.	Evans D.W.J.	Joesch, J.	Muhangia, Kamau	Samaras T.	Wilson, J.G.
Branham, Mike.	Fangoudis, E.A.	Judd, Bill.	Muller, Harry	Sanchez-Arino, Tony	Wincza, Capt. Laddy, Vice-Chairman
Brown, Bob.	Faull, Peter.	Kawawa, S.	Murray–Smith, Capt. Tom, Chairman	Sapieha, Prince Stash	Winter, Bill.
Brown, David.	Fawcus, A.	Keily, Mike.	Nagy, Dr. Andreas von.	Saw, Peter.	Woodley, Major Bill, M.D.E. M.C.
Brown, Monty.	Fey, Venn.	Ker, Donald, Chairman & Vice-Chairman	Newby, J.R.	Schindelar, Fritz.	Woodruff, Louis.
Burton, Miles.	Finch–Hatton, Lt. Col. The Hon. Denys, D.S.O.	Kibiego, Henry.	Nicholson, Brian.	Seed, Freddie.	Zashow Captain J. von
Cardozo A.T.	Fletcher, John.	Kingdom, Major Jack.	Northcote, John.	Selby Harry	Zwilling, E.A.

Compiled and Presented as a token of esteem by Tony Maxtone–Mailer

MARCH 1990.

The scroll compiled in 1990 and made available to the International Professional Hunters' Association. It lists 'most of the professional hunters in East Africa between 1903 and 1977'. Margarete's name can be seen in the column on the extreme right, followed by the name of her son Rolf and his son Richard – three generations from the same family and the only woman on the entire scroll, although she was never allowed to become a member of the East African Professional Hunters' Association because of her gender.

`

aimed at conserving habitat and wildlife. All ethical hunters and huntresses are true conservationists as they understand with particular clarity the consequences of ignoring sustainable use of renewable wildlife resources. Margarete already had first-hand experience of strict game ordinances introduced decades earlier in the former German East Africa.

The motto of the EAPHA was *Nec timor nec temeritas* – Neither fear nor foolhardiness. Membership as a fully licensed professional guide was subject to exceptionally stringent requirements, the founding members representing a veritable who's who of early big game hunting personalities. They conducted safaris throughout the vast East African region, from Kenya into Tanganyika and Uganda – the 'Golden Triangle' – down to Northern Rhodesia and Nyasaland, northwards to Sudan, Somalia and Ethiopia and westwards into the Belgian Congo. Arusha had become a pivotally important part of the safari business as clients, mostly from Europe and Great Britain between the two world wars but, increasingly, from the United States of America, stopped over on their way to the unparalleled game paradise of Tanganyika.

Margarete was never allowed to become a member of that august fraternity. It is deeply ironic, consequently, to note that Margarete's name was included anyway on a special scroll, compiled in 1990 and destined for the Nairobi Museum Library, listing most of the professional hunters active in East Africa between 1903 and 1977 when hunting was closed down in Kenya. Margarete is the only woman on the scroll. She was the embodiment of the EAPHA motto: she was fearless, but never foolhardy. The Anglo-Saxon 'gentleman's club' ethos has come and gone while Margarete's reputation survived for posthumous inclusion on the EAPHA scroll.

She would have enjoyed that, just as she would have understood the mindset of some authors writing about the African safari industry in the last century. They either completely ignored Margarete Trappe or they made brief, even anaemic mention of her, much as one pats a child on the head. One author, a German, in a clear reference to Margarete, wrote that 'her reputation in the profession is very high…'. Curiously, the author could not bring himself to name her in his book! One cannot help but recall the words of Arthur Blayney Percival, a Kenya Colony pioneer and esteemed veteran of over 22 years in the Game Department, who eventually became the colony's Game Warden. He averred in the 1920s that safari was 'no trip for a woman'. It would take time for this outlook to change and for women to cease being semi-invisible in the game fields of Africa where they were usually depicted in secondary roles. Today, in the new millennium, they are a growing force throughout the safari industry.

The Wind Shifts

Since her return to Tanganyika in 1925, Margarete had not only reconnected with people who had been part of her life before her deportation; she had also cultivated new friendships as the years passed. The predominantly German character of the country disappeared and was replaced by an increasingly British atmosphere as some place names changed and British subjects assumed the reins of government and occupied all administrative roles. English-speaking missionaries were becoming more common, as were English-speaking farmer-settlers. A series of newspapers began to appear in English, some lasting while others folded very soon after the first edition. Arusha had also experienced a steady increase in safaris from the Anglophone world.

Margarete was a realist who had long learned one of the basic lessons of human

Margarete, far right, in 1936 with her daughter-in-law, the Countess Erika con Donner, third from left. Seated on the extreme left is Colonel August Roland von Spiess Braccioforte zum Portner und Höflein, the former Chief Hunt master to the Romanian Royal Court. [Emil Karafiat]

survival in that all life is a compromise somewhere along the line. She was highly adaptable and was on good terms with everyone. She met most of the hunting person-alities of the day, was consulted as a matter of course and was always ready to share information about areas and game. As long as she could retain *Momella*, provide her chil-dren with a home and stability, and continue to live and work in peace and freedom in one of the most astoundingly beautiful places on earth, she felt fulfilled and thankful to have survived as she had. It could indeed have been much worse.

The wind, however, was beginning to shift and Margarete sensed it. The Great Depression had ravaged the world between 1929 and 1933 and news from Germany was becoming more and more disconcerting. The devastation of the country after the First World War and the savage effects of the Versailles Treaty had resulted in economic collapse and had given rise to a series of events that were already incubating a second world war, although few could have imagined such a prospect at that time.

When Adolf Hitler became the new German Chancellor in 1933, he acquired inordi-nately wide powers that propelled a growing reign of terror. Come 1935, the Versailles Treaty was repudiated and compulsory military service introduced. There was something foreboding about this renewed militarisation. A totalitarian state with new and terrifying legislation under the Nationalist Socialist Party was emerging that filled many inside the country with dread and that began triggering signals of growing alarm elsewhere in the world. Margarete sensed the unease as surely as she sensed when dangerous game was about to follow through with a charge. She still had relatives in Germany and knew that their world was becoming inexorably more dangerous.

All was not well with the British either. In 1936, King George V died and was succeeded by his son who was to reign as King Edward VIII. This was the same engaging Prince of Wales who had been on safari in Tanganyika in 1928 and who had passed close by *Momella* as he proceeded on a big game expedition. The Prince abdicated to marry the American divorcée, Wallis Simpson, causing outrage and scandal that reverberated in the African colonies. His younger brother, Prince Albert, Duke of York, then assumed the throne as George VI. The British Prime Minister, Neville Chamberlain, subsequently sought to

Margarete's letter of 20 July 1939, on the eve of the Second World War, in which she reveals her anxiety and exhaustion. [Gabriële Löhrl]

appease Hitler and Benito Mussolini of Italy in order to secure 'peace in our time'.

Margarete experienced some respite from the tension and uncertainty when her son Ulrich married Countess Erika von Donner in 1936. The couple settled on their property, Simba Estate, in the west Kilimanjaro foothills, not too far from *Momella*.

That same year saw Spain descend into civil war. A mood of trepidation was taking root in Europe. By 1938 Germany had marched into Austria and had occupied Czechoslovakia.

There was even talk in some circles of Germany eventually recovering her African colonies. As the situation became more ominous, Margarete had other more immediate matters to attend to. In December 1938, as she wrote in a letter to relatives in Germany, the 'house elephants' on *Momella* were misbehaving:

> 'The elephants, unfortunately, are often very brazen ... Every night we try to chase them off with flares and blanks but they have become so used to them that they simply move some ten metres away from us and carry on quietly munching. Yesterday, 48 elephants put our cattle herds to flight. A bad elephant is hanging around here. It has already killed several natives... Hopefully I'll get it soon.'

Already approaching her mid-fifties, Margarete showed no signs of slowing down. Although the situation in Europe was becoming more and more foreboding, the moneyed classes still travelled and hunted and Margarete's reputation assured a steady flow of well-heeled clients. As for the local European population, Margarete had become increasingly aware of a change in attitude towards her by some of the British in the region. Most remained the same steadfast, open people who knew and admired her. The shift in mood among some was quite subtle at first, but as the news from Europe grew more ominous, the mistrust and unspoken antagonisms of people towards those of German origin in Arusha and in the surrounding region became more noticeable. Margarete found herself withdrawing more and more into *Momella*. She sought a new kind of refuge in her family and in the tribal peoples who had long accepted her.

Although it was inevitable, changes had started becoming more apparent among the tribal peoples over the last couple of decades or so. Margarete, however, was still routinely consulted when disputes arose and her advice was usually accepted because she was seen as evenhanded and honest. And yet.... there did not seem to be the same frequency of song and dance as before. Maybe the increasingly sombre mood of mistrust among the white settlers was beginning to infect the usually carefree nature of the tribes. They sensed something was brewing with the *Wazungu*.

In a letter dated 20 July 1939 to relatives in Germany, Margarete reveals this anxiety:

> '... everything here is still so uncertain... I am often away from home for months, hunting...there are many problems... I have had little desire to write. It is often so hard to be a guide. You cannot imagine just how exhausting it is for me.'

Margarete could never simply sit back and relax. She had a reputation to uphold and a business to conduct. Ulrich and Rolf, now grown men, were of great assistance to their mother while Margarete's sister, Tine, was an irreplaceable part of her life. Although Ursula was long married and out of the home, Rosie, her 'late lamb', was still at school and the joy of the household.

Margarete experienced a bitter-sweet solace when out in the wilds, far from other human beings, purveyors of as yet undefined threats and hostility. When she contemplated the timeless outlines of the great mountains of her world and looked over the eternal valleys with their lakes and rivers, she wondered what other human-engendered catastrophes would be played out in their presence, how many more of her kind would be sucked into a situation not of their making. These same mountains and valleys, lakes and rivers watched and waited as they had for millennia. This too would pass, but at what cost and when?

The Trappe farmstead on Momella, in the foothills of Mount Meru. [Dr Jobst-Ulrich Trappe]

PART FOUR

"Let him who desires peace prepare for war"

FLAVIUS VEGETIUS RENATUS

A Time of Darkness

"I am speaking to you from the Cabinet Room at 10 Downing Street. This morning the British Ambassador in Berlin handed the German Government a final note stating that, unless we hear from them by 11 o'clock that they were prepared at once to withdraw their troops from Poland, a state of war would exist between us. I have to tell you now that no such undertaking has been received, and that consequently this country is at war with Germany."

Neville Chamberlain, British Prime Minister
11H00, 3 September 1939.

The new Zenith model radio with its distinctive black dial in the handsome walnut case had been readied for this fateful broadcast when word started doing the rounds of an imminent and significant announcement out of London. Chamberlain's measured words were like stabbing shards of ice to anyone that day who heard them, but especially to someone like Margarete Trappe who had already lived through one world war, had possessions expropriated, been interned, deported, separated from her children, suffered financial ruin, endured divorce and been forced to borrow money and work for long, exhausting years to recuperate only part of her former life.

The gradual, palpable chill she had felt recently in her dealings with some of the surrounding British-born community had grown in tandem with the darkening reports from Europe. They were placed in very sharp relief that morning as Neville Chamberlain spoke. Although Margarete had been held in the greatest esteem for her courage, hard work, honesty and multitude of skills, clearly this was now suddenly not enough for some people. The attitudes said it all: Margarete Trappe was German-born, wasn't she? She had relatives back in Hitler's Third Reich, didn't she? Her hunting guests were mostly from the old country, weren't they? Yes, she had become a naturalised South African citizen and carried the passport of a British dominion country, but…

Suspicion, increasing uncertainty, rising anxiety and creeping fear now consumed households in the highlands as more news came in that same fateful day. Australia, New Zealand, France, India and South Africa all declared war on Germany before midnight, 3 September 1939. Canada did likewise very soon afterwards. It was going to be another world war and it was inevitable that it would involve Tanganyika. Germany had invaded Poland on 1 September 1939 in a massive show of military might. Now, 48 hours later, Margarete could already feel the ice-like grip of renewed world war. She could already sense the implications of Chamberlain's words on her life, on the lives of her children and on the lives of all those who lived and worked at *Momella*. She sensed in a flash serious risks now threatening all she possessed in the world, rooted in the soil of Tanganyika. She felt a huge threat towards her home of the last thirty-two years, forced absences notwithstanding. The news was a catastrophe.

A terrible sensation of *déjà vu* was inescapable. Hardly had Margarete or any other German-born resident of Tanganyika had a moment to try to absorb this shocking new development when official proclamations started appearing in all colonial newspapers, stating:

> 'Any person who, although now a naturalised British subject, was at any time a citizen of any state with which the King is at present at war or a person who expresses sympathy with any power against which Britain is now at war ... would be considered an enemy alien.'

> And 'Warning all enemy subjects within the colonies to register details of their birth, passport and property owned, surrender all arms, ammunition and yourself to the member-in-Charge of the nearest police station.'

There it was, in black and white. Despite all that she, like so many other settlers, had endured in the First World War, despite having an irreproachable reputation and despite having had no involvement at all in any event that had resulted in this fresh horror, Margarete would be considered an enemy alien, like all other German-born settlers in Tanganyika, regardless of age, gender or circumstance. Her South African passport would mean nothing. She was German-born. She would be rounded up, sooner or later, like German-born people all over the world.

Margarete's world went quiet, like the strange quiet before an African thunderstorm rips open the heavens, slashing the skies with jagged lightning as thunder cracks overhead and torrents of rain come gushing down, sweeping away everything like a gigantic river gone mad. The spectre of fresh anguish and destruction hung in the air. How long? How long before this new world war would explode right over *Momella*?

While she waited for consequences that were sure to come, Margarete carried on as before, running her farm, hunting for the pot when necessary and looking after her family and workforce. Renewed war effectively killed all prospects of further hunting clients from Europe. The tribal peoples, of course, knew that another big war had been declared by the *Wazungu* on one another and they knew that the *Wajeremani* – the Germans – who used to rule over their country, were involved in this new war.

Such was the situation that people were more cautious in their efforts to try to obtain reliable information. Nobody as yet had ordered Margarete to report to any military authority, hand over her firearms and ammunition or herself. She kept wondering how or if her South African passport would somehow protect her from internment and, horror of all horrors, eventual deportation back to Germany, or what would remain of that country after another world war.

Somehow, it was less nerve wracking to track dangerous game in the high *matete* grass or face a full-blown charge by a bull elephant than to wait in silence, trying to cope with a faceless threat, wondering when the axe would fall as fall it would. Over 4 000 Germans at Iringa in southwestern Tanganyika had already been detained before the end of 1939 and sent off to internment camps. The men were sent to the Union of South Africa and the women to Southern Rhodesia, thereby compounding the stress through separation of spouses and families for what could be years.

Christmas 1939 came and went as the war escalated and country after country in Europe succumbed to the Third Reich's forces. By early May 1940, it was clear that this war was going to be lengthy and terrible. A taste of renewed fear came in May 1940. All of a sudden, Margarete's son Ulrich, who carried a German passport, was rounded up at Simba Estate, his own beautiful property in the western foothills of Mount Kilimanjaro, and sent off to an internment camp for enemy aliens in distant South Africa. It was particularly distressing for Margarete to see her child, although now a grown man, taken away as she stood by, helpless. There was more to come, much more.

Not eight weeks later, in July, the British authorities suddenly appeared at *Momella* and detained Margarete's sister, Tine. She, too, was taken off to an internment camp as an enemy alien. Tine had been a second mother to Margarete's children and the source of unshakeable companionship and comfort during very tough times since the First World War. Just four weeks later, in August 1940, Margarete's first-born, Ursula, who also held a German passport and was married to a German, was detained and interned as an enemy alien. Then it was Rolf's turn. He was detained and sent to an internment camp at Alt Shinyanga in the central province.

Margarete's British friends in the region rallied around and tried to help her as she saw three of her children and her sister detained and driven off to internment. The very well-known sisters, Margot and Gladys Rydon, who owned flourishing coffee estates as well as the new Safari Hotel in Arusha and who were influential in the 'right' circles, stepped into the ring to fight for Margarete and her family. Margarete was a very welcome guest at Margot Rydon's wonderful estate just east of Arusha, overlooking the beautiful Lake Duluti, a crater lake fed by the underground springs from Mount Meru. Margarete was a valued friend whose courageous life and accomplishments overrode any residual English reservations about Germans and Germany. Nothing the Rydon sisters said or did, however, was of any use.

Margarete now only left *Momella* to visit her remaining child, Rosie, who was a boarder at the English-language Christian Mission Society School in Arusha. When she went over in October that year to see her child, she collapsed because of the relentless anxiety, stress and solitude in facing this situation. She had finally succumbed to nervous exhaustion.

Margarete began to recuperate at the school under the care of the then headmaster, the Reverend William Wynn-Jones, a remarkable man from Wales. He was the first head-master of that co-educational school and had developed a wonderful name for his empathy with all people. His school was a mini-League of Nations. When war broke out, Wynn-Jones gathered the non-German pupils together and advised them that the school was one large family and that everyone was to remember this and treat fellow pupils accordingly. He advised one and all not to poison the atmosphere at school by referring to the war and by transferring attitudes from their parents to fellow pupils who happened to be German, English or any other nationality for that matter. The headmaster also vigorously promoted the teaching of Kiswahili and had an open door policy to all. Margarete felt welcome and safe and she knew her daughter was well cared for at the school.

With no forewarning, a police vehicle abruptly drove into the school grounds. Margarete was ordered to return with the police that minute to *Momella*. Despite the Reverend Wynn-Jones' stern protests, the police insisted and Margarete, still shaky, had no choice but to comply. Her daughter witnessed it all.

On driving onto her property the first thing Margarete saw was another police vehicle, parked right in front of the entrance to her home, a British official in uniform standing ready with a sheaf of papers in his hand. So much for her supposed British subject status! They had finally come for her too.

Interned

Margarete was sent to Alt Shinyanga, the same camp in the central province where her son, Rolf, was interned. There were several more such camps scattered about the colony. Elsewhere in Africa, other internment camps were being prepared to receive enemy aliens and also many of their own citizens deemed sympathetic to the Nazi cause. This was especially true of the Union of South Africa where there was indeed quite widespread support among the Afrikaners – formerly known as the Boers – for the Germans. The pro-Nazi *Ossewa Brandwag* [Sentinels of the Oxwagon] movement had been founded in 1939 and had attracted enough support to be a cause for concern to the South African Government of the day that had decided to enter the war against Germany. In addition, the catastrophic effects of the Anglo-Boer War were still very much in raw, living memory and many Afrikaners carried personal scars of that war and deep antipathy towards anything British.

Margarete refused to succumb to the British official's orders and enter her house under guard like a felon to select extra clothing and personal belongings for the internment. Still shaky after her collapse a couple of weeks earlier in Arusha, Margarete poured scorn on the official, there to detain her as an enemy alien. She merely held onto the clothing she had taken with her to Arusha, turning her back on her home and all it contained, and getting into the police vehicle for a ride into fresh uncertainty, fresh torment.

The workforce, obviously, had gathered when they saw the police vehicles driving onto the property, one containing *Yeyo*. They watched in renewed dismay as they saw their employer and consistent helper in times of need and ill health being driven off. The British official made no attempt to remove two of Margarete's dogs that leapt into the vehicle with her and refused to budge. Dogs weren't people and didn't qualify as 'enemy aliens'. Her large, beautifully managed estate was now being abandoned. Again.

It was inevitable that the Maasai would flood back in with their cattle and that the estate would be vandalised. With no central, tough authority in residence to enforce discipline, it would be a free-for-all. The cattle and horses as well as all the other smaller livestock, acquired with such difficulty in the wake of the First World War, would be vulnerable to neglect, theft and disease. As for the crops, orchards, vegetable and flower gardens, the weeds would take over in a blink. The buildings, their contents, including books and records of hunting guests, and all farm equipment faced the same prospect of neglect, theft and deterioration. Margarete knew that no wartime caretaker presence on her estate would ever exercise the same care and diligence as she and her workforce had done. As for her status as a British Dominion subject through her South African passport, it counted for nothing or she would not have been rounded up and driven off to an internment camp.

The internment camps in Tanganyika adhered to reasonable standards of housing, hygiene, nutrition and medical care. There was a camp hospital and meals were regular, if Spartan. Internees were able to write and receive letters and parcels, but they were, of course, strictly censored. No Gothic script was allowed to be used in correspondence. Unless one is used to reading this elaborate script it can be difficult to decipher. Roll call, sick parade, a total prohibition on all radio equipment, cameras and firearms, and the barbed wire, guards and watchtowers meant not simply internment but imprisonment, as if the internees had committed serious crimes and been duly convicted. Despite a ban on all animals, Margarete managed to be allowed to bring in two of her dogs, the ones

MOSHI INTERNMENT CAMP.

C A M P   R E G U L A T I O N S.
======   =======================
(To come into operation on September 10th 1939.)

1. <u>Sections</u>. The Camp is divided into Sections of 21 people including the Section Leader who is responsible for the discipline of his Section. Each Section is designated by a letter.

2. <u>Section Leaders</u> will hold their meetings in the large Office.

3. <u>Camp Office</u>. Internees may bring their personal matters before the Camp Authority in the Office from 12.00 to 1.00 daily.

4. <u>Personal effects</u>. A complete list of articles in the possession of Internees (including all clothing) must be entered in the Inventory Form which has been supplied to them. These Inventories will be kept in the Camp Office.

5. <u>Prohibited articles</u>. The following are not allowed in the Camp:-
    Firearms and ammunition,
    Wireless sets and equipment,
    Cameras and photographic materials,
    Animals.

6. <u>Meals</u>:-   Breakfast,   8.30 a.m.
               Dinner,   1.00 p.m.
               Tea,   5.30 p.m.

7. <u>Correspondence</u> must be censored and must be written in Latin characters: if written in Gothic script it will be returned to the sender.
    Correspondence must be placed in open envelopes giving the name and address of the writer as well as the addressee.
    <u>Outward</u> correspondence must be placed in the Postbox at the Notice Board in the Mess-room.
    <u>Inward</u> correspondence must be placed in the Postbox outside the Main gates.
    Correspondence will be distributed at Roll Call.

8. <u>Parcels</u> will be inspected at the Camp Office and must be labelled with the name and address of the sender as well as the addressee.
    <u>Outward</u> parcels must be handed into the Camp Office from 12.00 to 1.00 on Tuesdays and Fridays only. The Camp Authority cannot undertake to deliver these parcels. They will be sent through the post (if fully stamped by the sender) or handed to Visitors to deliver.
    <u>Inward</u> parcels will be received at the Main gates from 2.00 to 3.00 p.m. daily, and will be distributed to the addressees at 3.00 p.m. daily in the Camp Office.

9. <u>Roll Calls</u> will be held at 8.00 a.m. and 9 p.m. daily.

10. <u>Sick Parade</u>. Section Leaders must report to the Camp Hospital at 10.00 a.m. if anyone in their Section requires medical attention. The Camp Hospital will send a Sick Report to the Camp Office daily.

11. <u>Notice Boards</u> are placed in the Mess-room and outside the Main gates. Only the Camp Authority can place and remove

Typical internment camp regulations to which Margarete and all fellow German-born internees were subjected.
[Dr Jobst-Ulrich Trappe]

that had simply jumped into the police vehicle and that had refused to leave their mistress.

The real cancer in an internment camp was the uprooting of people and separation of families, crushing boredom, lack of any outside news, limitless days of waiting and not knowing what would eventually happen or when. This mental anguish and fear of an unknown future could be a killer. Margarete, a petite but very tough woman, refused to succumb to creeping, corrosive depression, lassitude and defeat. She took up running. Every day of the week she would start out with her dogs and run the lengthy perimeter fence of the internment camp. She kept up what became a murderous routine until she came down with pleurisy, an inflammation of the membrane lining the lungs and covering the thoracic cavity. This was followed by a series of malaria attacks. Her immune system had weakened under the stress, but not her resolve. Never her resolve!

A New Camp

In April 1941, Margarete and her son were transferred to another internment camp called Oldeani where better conditions prevailed. It was closer to Momella which was about 125 miles away. Margarete was free within the confines of the camp, but her health had taken a serious knock and she was the proverbial skin and bone.

The war was spreading. Germany had invaded Norway, Denmark, the Netherlands, Belgium, Luxembourg and France before the end of 1940. The massive evacuation of Allied troops from the beaches of Dunkirk had since taken place, the Battle of Britain had begun and London had been bombed. The New Year saw the Germans enter the Balkans and invade Russia. The cataclysmic Japanese attack on Pearl Harbour in December 1941 finally catapulted the Americans into the war.

As the news of outside events trickled into the camp, Margarete wondered who would pay any attention at all to a lone woman in Tanganyika and her battle to hang onto her property and try to secure something for her family's future, whatever that was going to be. She had already been given the shocking news that *Momella* and all its contents were to be auctioned off to the highest bidder. Anyone detained in an internment camp, even if they had the financial means to enter the bidding, was prohibited from participating. This seemed like theft by stealth.

Again, Margarete found herself fighting unseen forces and fighting alone. When she thought that all was permanently lost, the auction was suddenly called off and she was informed that a decision had been taken by the Custodian of Enemy Property to restore *Momella* to her. There was a catch, however: she would have to settle all debts that had accumulated in the meantime!

It did not matter how Margarete tried to fathom the logic of this latest *diktat*. She was also told that she could not set foot on the property until these 'debts' had been fully paid. In hindsight, one wonders what the real reason was for the venom behind this decision to burden Margarete with debts not of her making. The British authorities were definitely aware of her near-legendary status in the eyes of the tribal peoples, and of her special assignments during the First World War under General Von Lettow-Vorbeck. Were these facts somehow poisoning the minds of the Custodian of Enemy Property? Was this some sort of belated white tribal 'settling of accounts'?

In the end, the only person to whom Margarete could turn at this blackest time in her whole life was Michael Michalakis in Dar es Salaam. Once again, this generous-spirited man came forward and helped Margarete when nobody else could or would. The British, in a peculiarly sour reaction, on seeing that the 'debts' had been settled, informed Margarete that she could indeed now visit *Momella* once every four weeks for a couple of days to 'work' her property, but that she was to report back to the internment camp without fail – rather like prisoners in a chain gang being allowed out of prison during the day to work.

The Road Home

The Custodian of Enemy Property and his fellow officials had dismissed most of the *Momella* workforce. As Margarete neared her home in the still-magnificent Mount Meru foothills, she had no idea what to expect. Would anyone at all who had worked for her for years even be in the vicinity now? In what state of neglect was her farm? What had been stolen, damaged, or destroyed? What had happened to her cattle and horses? And her other dogs? What would the attitude be of even the oldest and longest serving of her workers, if they were still in the district? After all, this was not the first time that she had been forced out and away, effectively abandoning dozens of people who relied on her for their livelihoods and safety. They, in particular, were on the periphery of this latest *Wazungu* madness, but had been sucked into the fight and pushed off *Yeyo*'s land, their home too.

In a replay of another time of separation, loss and despair, followed by return, renewal and hope, Margarete reached *Momella*. Neglect cloaked the farm like fungus on a damp wall. Weeds ran riot over once meticulously maintained gardens and all the buildings spoke of abandonment and silence where there had so recently been a vigilant presence and constant human activity. Her pedigreed dairy herd had disappeared, as had much of the farm equipment. Everywhere Margarete looked, she saw waste, neglect and theft. It was worse than she had feared. What had the Custodian for Enemy Property done to her home? Before rage and shock had a chance to tighten their grip, something exceptional happened that far-off day in the shadow of Mount Meru.

Like the first rays of dawn after dark night, Margarete's workforce began re-appearing on *Momella*. The word had got out and travelled as surely as a satellite phone call travels today: *Yeyo* was back! Their mother figure was back again, after what seemed like a time of deadly drought when the earth and all that lived on it were dying. *Yeyo* was back! It was an extraordinary sight: dozens of tribal people, some of whom had been with Margarete since the very early days, began streaming onto the farm, jubilating and ululating at her return.

Questions, answers, laughs and shouts filled the air as Margarete explained her current situation and the impossibility of being able to pay anyone anything until she was free of the internment camp. Only when she was able to return to *Momella* and try, yet again, to pick up the threads of a life whose fabric had been ripped apart by distant forces could she try to find money to pay the people something. She explained how she would not be able to start recuperating the property without the consistent help of all present.

The people spoke with one voice: it did not matter. *Yeyo* had always helped them and now they would help her. They would work for nothing and help re-establish *Momella*. *Yeyo* could start paying them when she was able to do so. They would return to live on the property that day and they would carry out any task given them. Margarete was told she could rely on her workers in her forced absences, just as they had been able to rely on her for help in times of suffering.

And so it was. After a couple of strenuous, hugely upsetting days, Margarete reset the *Momella* compass for courageous hard work, purposeful living and honour in the face of wrong. She had her headman in place and a 'chain of command' under him to do the work and achieve basic goals until her return a month later. She then had to go back to

Oldeani Internment Camp, but she was returning with the one ingredient that makes any life worth living – a spark of hope for the future. Here, the words of Gerd von Lettow-Vorbeck are recalled in his book *Am Fusse des Meru* when he wrote that General Von Lettow-Vorbeck described Margarete Trappe as having *Schneid für drei Männer* – the guts or courage of three men! The General was never known for frivolous speech, on or off the battlefield.

Every 30 days, Margarete returned to *Momella* and every time she saw progress as her workforce carried out her instructions, improvising along the way and making steady, noticeable improvement at what had been their home as well. Not once did they break their undertaking to *Yeyo*. The vegetable gardens were beginning to 'take' and every time Margarete returned for those precious couple of days, the workers would present her with some little gift such as fresh eggs and chickens or even flowers that were now also being cultivated once more on what had been one of the finest estates in the country. Progress was visible and it was constant.

Released

After two years and four months in internment camps, Margarete was suddenly informed in February 1943 that she was free to leave the Oldeani internment camp and return permanently to *Momella*. News came in that same month of the catastrophe suffered by the Germans at the Battle of Stalingrad, viewed now as a key turning point in the Second World War. Margarete had been released during this dark time, fair enough, but she could never feel truly free as long as the war raged on and the sword of deadly uncertainty hung over her head and over the heads of her entire family and of all those who had always depended on her. Only the animals were truly free.

After living behind barbed wire, never knowing when she would be released, Margarete travelled the all-too-familiar route back to her farm, but she experienced everything with heightened sensation. The skies over Mount Meru were that much higher and brighter, the birds that much more audacious in their flight patterns, the horizons that much more expansive, the sweet smell of damp earth after rain that much more fragrant, the breezes on the skin that much more cooling, the raucous calls of the crimson-feathered turaco that much more joyous, and the taste of food, however meagre, cooked in her farmhouse on *Momella* that much more gratifying. If truth be told, being released from the contagious presence of so many other despairing people, ravaged by loss and bitterness, was also a liberation all on its own.

Back at *Momella*, the tribal people stood shoulder to shoulder with Margarete as they continued to regenerate and rebuild the farm. Her youngest child, Rosie, had completed her schooling in Arusha and was now at home. Margarete felt renewed hope as she saw life once more through the eyes of a young girl. Gerd Von Lettow-Vorbeck gave a profoundly touching description in his book when he spoke of a Wameru woman welcoming Margarete back and presenting her with a banana tree to plant. When Margarete wanted to pay her for the tree, the woman refused, saying that she had never forgotten how Margarete had sent her food after the birth of her son thirty years previously!

Soon, Margarete had several big dogs back on the property. Through barter trade she started building up a cattle herd all over again and she also had to resume her vigilance against cattle rustling. She acquired a few young horses and began training them to saddle for essential patrol work on the property and supervision of the workforce.

Margarete was almost sixty years old. Riding was second nature to her and, somehow, being on the back of a horse brought her into closer, more natural contact with the vast and beautiful world that was her home.

Hunting took a back seat. There was far too much hard work to be done in battling to re-establish the farm, look after the workers and try to plan for a still highly uncertain future. The allied forces were gaining ground against the Germans and as Tanganyika was a British mandated terri-tory, there were sure to be fresh repercussions when this war ended, as end it surely would. Margarete concen-trated her energies on *Momella*. This was an unnerving replay of what she had been forced to do years earlier in the later stages of the First World War and thereafter. News of the war, nevertheless, made its way to her.

As the farm became more organised and Margarete had the comfort of her daughter's presence to cope with the constant worry about the future and about her other chil-dren who were still interned, another occurrence helped boost Margarete's morale. The elephant had started to visit *Momella* again – as in raiding the vegetable gardens and generally making their presence felt. Margarete was overjoyed. It was as if these huge animals had resumed their visits as a way of letting her know she was not forgot-ten, that while the world of humans had proved to be

treacherous, the animal world had proved otherwise. Margarete had never forgotten the circumstances of Rosie's birth and she would happily spend cold nights on the perime-ter of her vegetable gardens and young crops, scaring away the elephant with noisy rattles and a barking dog than even think of using a firearm again to fire a warning shot into the air.

Margarete with her daughter Rosie. [Emil Karafiat]

In May 1944, just a few weeks before the Allies invaded Normandy on 6 June, signalling the beginning of the end of the war, Margarete had the joy and relief of welcoming back home her son Rolf. He was a huge blessing to his mother, working side by side with her and with the workforce. Now Margarete longed to see her daughter Ursula, her son Ulrich and her sister Tine released from internment and back in Tanganyika, ready to resume living.

It was at that time that Margarete also established a bond with one of the internment camps for Polish people at a place called Tengeru, just a few miles east of Arusha, close to Lake Duluti. She would throw open *Momella* to the young Poles and invite them on walks of discovery through the bush, telling them about the animals and birds and their habitat and sharing with them the wild beauty of her home.

When one recalls that this took place during the war, Margarete's generosity of spirit takes on a particular significance. It was as if she were trying to use the healing powers of the natural world to compensate for the inevitable dislocation and loss that war brings and to bridge a chasm of hatred and suffering in the wake of that fateful day on 1 September 1939. This was a lifelong characteristic – the rejection of grudges and the abil-ity to reach out and understand. Little did Margarete know that one of the lovely young girls, Halinka, who came to *Momella*, would one day marry Rolf.

The war finally ended with Germany's unconditional surrender on 8 May 1945. The trauma suffered for so long by so many people throughout Europe and elsewhere in the world during the most ruinous war in recorded history, reached right into a corner of East Africa. There, Margarete Trappe would still have further battles to fight before she could finally know some peace after years of torment.

Fresh Storms

After the end of the war, Margarete, Rolf and Rosie steadily and doggedly worked at restoring their home. There was still no word of Ursula, Ulrich and Tine. The enervation of waiting turned in a flash into cold shock in November 1946 when a British police officer drove out to *Momella* to hand over a deportation order from the authorities in Dar es Salaam to Margarete and all her family. They were to prepare to return to Germany. There was a problem, however. The Trappe home in Silesia no longer formed part of Germany as it had been incorporated into Poland after the Potsdam Conference that ended on 2 August 1945. There was no home to which Margarete Trappe could return, yet the British authorities would not allow her or her children to remain in Tanganyika.

In survival mode once more, she approached the chief of the Wameru people for help in interceding with the authorities. She also had the complete support of several dozen British settlers in the region who had known her for decades. All approached the authorities and implored them to leave the Trappe family in peace. They were ignored. Instead, a fresh order from Dar es Salaam came to Margarete, prohibiting her henceforth from selling anything from *Momella* until she and all her relatives were sent back to Germany. This meant that Margarete had no way of generating any income at all. It also meant she could not pay her workforce at all.

The workforce, once more, told *Yeyo* that they would not abandon her and that they would work for nothing until this latest problem was resolved. The British authorities had other ideas and promptly dismissed Margarete's entire labour force, ordering them off *Momella* and issuing orders that all activity on the farm cease. Confronted all over again by disaster, Margarete succeeded in obtaining permission to sell all but five of her horses, thereby generating sufficient money to hang on.

After six agonising months, the deportation order, like the auction sale of *Momella* and her sudden release from the internment camp, was abruptly withdrawn and Margarete once more had full rights over *Momella* restored to her. It has never been discovered why the British overturned their decisions concerning Margarete. She was faced once more with a property in a state of shambles, but her workforce came back the moment the word was out that *Yeyo* was going to be allowed to remain after this never-ending *Wazungu* war.

Like some biblical curse, an epidemic scythed through her cattle herd, killing most of the animals. Margarete had almost no money left from the sale of her stud and was also remortgaged to the hilt. Then came the news in May 1947 that her daughter Ursula, her son Ulrich and her sister Tine were all being sent back to Germany from the internment camps. Ulrich lost his beautiful property on the western slopes of Mount Kilimanjaro. Rolf, who married his Polish fiancée Halinka in mid-1948, was also deported to Germany but only in February 1949.

In the interim, there was some sunshine to lift the gloom: Rosie had met and married a Swiss professional hunter, Emil Karafiat. She subsequently gave birth to her first child, Yvonne, on 29 April 1949 in Margarete's bedroom at *Momella*. Now, with her grandchild, fresh hope was in the air for a new life for all.

But facts had to be faced: Margarete was on *Momella*, strangled by debt and her family was fragmented all over again. It would take several years to overcome the financial situation, but an income had to be generated in the meantime.

Photographic and Film Safaris

Margarete entered an entirely new phase of her extraordinary life when she began concentrating exclusively on photographic and film safaris for paying guests. She had an illustrious precursor in wildlife photography, Carl G. Schilllings. A German big game hunter and brilliant naturalist, ornithologist and trained scientific observer, Schillings had already produced two remarkable books by 1907, the year Margarete sailed for Africa. They were entitled *With Flashlight and Rifle: A Record of Hunting Adventures and of Studies in Wild Life in Equatorial East Africa* (1906 in English) and the two-volume *In Wildest Africa* (1907 in English). These substantial volumes with their profusion of wildlife photography and outstanding ethnographic studies in German East Africa were hailed for their unique character. None other than President Theodore Roosevelt urged, after seeing the first book: "His book should be translated into English at once."

Margarete knew these books and Schillings' pioneering accomplishments in telephoto-lens photography in the wilds as well as flashlight photography of wildlife at night. By the time she began her photographic safaris in earnest four decades later, camera equipment had evolved so dramatically as to be unrecognizable when compared with the clumsy, primitive equipment Schillings and his battalion of porters humped about through swamps and rivers, over mountains and down into heat-soaked plains. Today's miniature cameras, digital photography and instantly available full-colour pictures were still the stuff of science fiction.

From short excursions to the nearby forests and lakes to elaborate filming in distant locations, Margarete handled it all. She no longer had any desire to conduct big game hunting safaris or, indeed, to hunt by herself for herself. This is a common experience among veteran big game hunters who go through several stages in their hunting lives. From the early days when the exhilaration of the hunt in wild country dominates in a deeply personal way and is characteristic of vigorous youth and as yet unrequited hunting ambitions, the hunter gradually moves into another gear as the years go by, experience in the field accumulates and that initial thrill and the high level of expectation mellow. The hunter then experiences the need to participate in a different way, to give back to the natural world on a different plane.

What is certain is that Margarete no longer felt the irresistible urge to go off into the blue for weeks on end to hunt. It was not only the passage of time and the inevitable decrease in energy and interest. It was also a change within her spirit. She had endured prolonged stress and had witnessed too much ending of life and ways of life in various forms for her to continue in the same vein and with the same drive characteristic of her youth. It was as if she were seeking to avoid the confrontational aspect of the hunt and replace it with a more contemplative, unobtrusive activity that left the natural world as she and her guests had found it.

Margarete had no idea how many of the big five she had personally hunted. She did not keep personal boast files of trophies. What is sure is that this indomitable huntress had accumulated vast experience of all phases of the hunt for every species available in German East Africa/Tanganyika over about four decades by the time she launched her photographic and film safaris. Her fund of stories, based on personal observations in the field and her profound knowledge of animal and bird life and their ways, was testimony to that.

Among Margarete's first guests were Americans who helped spread the news very quickly about this petite German lady, already in her sixties, a veteran big game huntress with nerves of cast iron, who enabled her guests to get up very close to dangerous game for exceptional photography and filming.

A safari with Margarete Trappe was a journey into Hemingway's green hills of Africa; it was a journey into several worlds, such was the variety of the human and geographic landscape. Healthy numbers of black rhino and large herds of elephant were still common sights on *Momella*'s doorstep. In fact, one of Margarete's guests, a Swiss, had been particularly keen to film black rhino. He saw about 58 of them over a three-day period!

The new venture became very successful and, once again, Margarete was able to generate an income and retain her beloved *Momella*. Individuals and groups, schoolchildren, industrialists, laymen and scientists from around the world started coming to *Momella* for an extraordinary wilderness experience. Camping out, far from any other humans and under heavens of sooty velvet embroidered with millions of stars, was the hors d'oeuvres. The main course entailed coming to within a few metres of a massive bull elephant having a sand bath, or spotting a tricky-tempered and always dangerous black rhino in the shade of a giant candelabrum euphorbia, being close to hundreds of buffalo at a waterhole, observing lion on a kill as scavengers stared from a distance, seeing rivers with pods of hippo heaving in the sunlight, their crocodile neighbours motionless on tongues of rock and sand, and luxuriating in the sight of flights of waterbirds coming home to their roosting places on the lakes at sunset. These were life-changing encounters for many of the guests as they listened to Margarete's stories. In fact, she was living and propagating the eco-tourism ethos decades before it became the fashionable activity it is today.

The continued absence, however, of her children and sister who had been forced back to a shattered country made it impossible for Margarete to be happy. She was like a small boat at sea, struggling to come into harbour, but continuously thwarted by squalls and storms. She was in survival mode, once again.

So it was that when Christmas came in 1949, Margarete felt little joy. That was until she, the Karafiat family and Halinka were greeted on Christmas Eve by a wonderful procession of her Wameru workers and their families, singing and dancing as they came up to the farmhouse bearing gifts of poultry and eggs and all kinds of other trinkets to celebrate. Most of all, they brought themselves in a show of solidarity with and understanding of this lady from a far country who had made her home in Africa and who had had to fight her own wars in the process. While the Wameru sang, Margarete's dogs howled and barked in joyous unison. It was enough to lift anyone's spirits!

Homecoming

Nothing compared with the joy Margarete, Rosie and Halinka felt when Rolf was allowed back into Tanganyika in August 1951. The Wameru and the other tribal peoples at *Momella* pulled out all stops that day, arriving *en masse* at the farmhouse with gifts, singing and laughing in excitement as the motor vehicle came into view. One old man and his son, who had worked for Rolf, had saved money – a small fortune for them – and insisted on handing it over to him as their way of celebrating his return after two

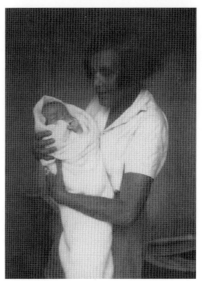

and half years' absence. Hardly had dawn broken the next day and the tribal people were back, ready to continue with the jubilation. Rolf was held in great esteem by the various tribes who had worked with him. He had also inherited his mother's natural aptitude for getting on with all people and for embracing different cultures.

Tine, the adored *Tante Tintel*, also returned, never to leave *Momella* again. Ursula, known as Ussi in the family, had had a rough time in Germany. Her marriage did not survive the traumas of wartime and the hostility of her husband's family. A divorce ensued and she returned to *Momella* as well. Ursula eventually married an Italian engineer from Bergamo, Mario Sirtoli, who had served as an engineer in Mussolini's forces in Abyssinia. They developed a farm on the western slopes of Mount Kilimanjaro. As neither spoke English, Mario spoke no German and Ursula no Italian, they spoke Kiswahili to each other! It was a long, happy union, but there were no children.

Ulrich did not return to Tanganyika as he had no desire to become a British subject in order to be allowed to try to recover his farm in the foothills of Kilimanjaro. He had rejected an offer of British naturalisation, remaining an unflinching individualist to the end. Ulrich, who had been born under the Southern Cross and who had grown up in the very heart of the African wilderness where he absorbed all the bush lore and knowledge about the natural world from his redoubtable mother, simply could not contemplate returning to a shadow of his former life. After years of internment, a shattered family life – his marriage to Countess Erika Von Donner had been dissolved during the war – and alienation from all that was familiar, there simply was no going back for him.

Top left —
Margarete with her
granddaughter
Yvonne and her
grandson Richard.
[Emil Karafiat]

Top right —
Margarete with her
grandson Emil.
[Emil Karafiat]

Left — Margarete
with her grandson
Rolf Junior, known
as Puci.
[Emil Karafiat]

Rolf Senior and his
son Rolf Junior
(Puci).
[Emil Karafiat]

Ulrich came out to South Africa in 1949 before moving on to Angola and Mozambique where he worked between the years 1950 and 1953. Margarete was destined to see her first-born son only once after the war when she travelled to Mozambique to be with him for a short while. She understood her son's decision. He eventually went to the former German South-West Africa where he met his second wife, who was also German. They married there in 1955 and became the parents of two sons.

Rosie brought fresh joy to her mother when she gave birth to a son in 1951, named Emil Armin Hans. Rolf and Halinka had two sons, Rolf Junior and Richard, both of whom would one day become well-known professional hunters. With the grandchildren injecting fresh joy and life into *Momella* and with the proximity and support of her children and sister, Margarete began to breathe more easily after years of relentless anxiety.

Rolf resumed conducting hunting safaris as normalcy returned to international travel. Arusha could be reached by air from 1948 onwards, boosting the safari business as a whole, be it photographic or hunting. Peace and better travel facilities saw an influx of Americans in particular as they entered the new golden age of African safari after the Second World War.

In neighbouring Kenya, safari clients were now arriving in increasing numbers by air – albeit usually a four-day trip aboard Sunderland amphibious aircraft. The war years had seen the arrival of the first four-wheel drive vehicles in the region. These and an increasing prevalence of other motorized vehicles, adapted for photographic safaris and for better conveyance of hunting clients to the great game lands of East Africa, brought about significant changes to the safari industry. One such change was the greater ease, comfort and speed with which people could reach Tanganyika by road from Kenya.

The poetic essence of the old-time, leisurely three-month foot safaris, such as Margarete had conducted, and the hard hunting they entailed in the heart of the African bush receded as transport improved and the world started living by the clock as never before. The upside was the increased turnover in motivated visitors and in the resultant cash flow through safari coffers.

One of Margarete's most memorable photographic safari clients was Prince Frederick of Prussia, a grandson of the late Kaiser Wilhelm II. Prince Frederick came out to *Momella* in February 1953 with his wife, the former Lady Brigid Guinness, daughter of the Earl of Iveagh, heir to the Guinness brewery fortune. The couple enjoyed 'a glorious holiday' with Margarete on a photographic safari during which the Prince was able to film black rhino, amongst other species. Prince Frederick and his wife also witnessed a tremendous spectacle of elephants stripping maize fields, no doubt at *Momella*, with Margarete looking on in blissful enjoyment at the sight of her favourite African animal cavorting in safety.

Needless to say, the Tanganyika Standard newspaper featured this visit and spoke of Margarete as 'the well-known Arusha settler, Mrs Margaret Trappe' and that she 'came to Tanganyika before the First World War and in the past entertained the Prince's late brother'. *Momella* is described as being 'on the slopes of Meru in big-game country'.

Margarete and the Prince recalled in detail the safari that his late brother, Prince Hubertus, and Prince Friederich Franz von Mecklenburg-Schwerin undertook with her and her son Ulrich between the two World Wars, during the historic period when

Margarete became the first full-time professional huntress in Africa.

After the sojourn in Tanganyika with Margarete, the princely pair spent a few days back in Kenya at the renowned Treetops Hotel at Nyeri in the Aberdare Mountains. This was where Princess Elizabeth and the Duke of Edinburgh spent an idyllic two days just a year previously. Treetops became world famous during that visit because Princess Elizabeth ascended the ladder into the treetops hotel as a princess, but came down the following day as the next Queen of Great Britain because her father, King George VI, had died during the night.

The Prince and his wife then flew south from Kenya to visit their 75 000 acre sheep station in South-West Africa, a former German colony. It had been a time of great nostalgia as Margarete reviewed with her distinguished guests the tumultuous events of the preceding 25 years.

An Echo from the Past

One of the great experiences in Margarete's unusual life found an echo in her memories in February 1953, straight after the Prince Frederick photographic safari. General Von Lettow-Vorbeck, just one month away from his 83rd birthday, accompanied by his daughter Heloise, returned to Africa to revisit some of the people and places that had featured so prominently in his extraordinary life. Margarete had been apprised of his programme.

The General had just enjoyed a deeply nostalgic reunion with former comrades-in-arms and military personalities in Cape Town, South Africa. During a fairly extensive tour of the country, the General also called on Field Marshall Smuts' widow at her historic home in Irene, just south of Pretoria. Smuts had died in 1950. There was so much to share with his widow.

Field Marshall Smuts had invited his chivalrous former foe on the battlefield to London in December 1929 as guest of honour at a most historic *Festessen* or banquet held to celebrate the former East African Expeditionary Force. The two men had become firm friends after the First World War, Smuts and the unforgettable Colonel Richard Meinertzhagen helping the General with food parcels through terrible times after the Second World War. Mrs Smuts knew all about the General's plight at the time.

Hitler never forgave the General for refusing to serve as his ambassador to the Court of St. James and he effectively ruined the rest of Von Lettow-Vorbeck's military career when he declined to be part of the Hitlerian scheme of things. He was persecuted and abandoned during those dark years, eventually losing both his sons in the war. The Von Lettow-Vorbeck family had lost several of its finest men to both world wars. The General's home in Bremen was destroyed by Allied bombs and he knew real destitution and malnutrition before his prestige was restored under the Federal Republic of Germany that accorded him military and parliamentary pensions. Field Marshall Smuts even arranged a pension for him from the victors! Von Lettow-Vorbeck spent the final years of his momentous life in a flat in Hamburg where the equally unforgettable Karen Dinesen of *Out of Africa* literary fame visited him.

After paying a brief visit to South-West Africa where he had been stationed almost 50 years previously, the General and his daughter boarded ship in Durban for the voyage up the east coast of Africa to Dar es Salaam. When the boat docked in Dar es Salaam, General Von Lettow-Vorbeck was greeted by British dignitaries and former *Schutztruppe* comrades who had managed to return to Tanganyika.

ape Argus

SPEC

VN, WEDNESDAY, JANUARY 14, 1953   REGISTERED AT THE G.P.O. AS A NEWSPAPER

FLOOD | 1914-1918 WAR COMRADES MEET GEN. VON LETTOW-VORBECK

OLD COMRADES AND A FORMER ENEMY met the German commander of the 1914-18 East African campaign, Maj.-Gen. P. von Lettow-Vorbeck, when he arrived in Cape Town by air to-day. From left are Capt. G. W. T. Garrood (former R.F.C. pilot), Miss Heloise von Lettow-Vorbeck, Cpl. T. Kloss (German Army), the general, and Maj. E. Mueller (the general's former A.D.C.).

General Von Lettow-Vorbeck, second right, and his daughter Heloise, in Cape Town on 14 January 1953.

A deeply emotional meeting was then arranged between the General and some 400 former *askaris* who were still alive and residing in the greater Dar es Salaam region. Old, often frail *askaris* surged around their former commander-in-chief, filled with emotion at seeing once more the man they had been prepared to follow to the ends of the earth in the Great War. As General Von Lettow-Vorbeck wrote on page 55 of his very scarce booklet, *Afrika: Wie ich es wiedersah* [Africa: How I saw it again] (München: J.F. Lehmanns Verlag, 1955):

'For me, the meeting with the old Askaris was the highlight of the entire trip.'

There are few words capable of describing such an event. Tears flowed as old men gathered, recalling times of camaraderie and courage in the face of death and of great hardships thereafter. The *askaris* also still recalled their German drill commands, many retaining the ability to converse in basic German.

The General had sent word to Margarete at *Momella* to try to meet him in New Moshi, near Arusha, where he would be arriving for a stay of only a few hours. In a most unfortunate turn of events, the two old comrades missed each other that day, but they were in touch by letter shortly afterwards.

One wonders how Margarete and Von Lettow-Vorbeck found the words to describe what had befallen them both in the intervening decades. The General had never forgotten the young woman on a black horse who had served under him with such tenacity, albeit in a strictly unofficial capacity, and who was never caught during the missions she carried out for him. He never forgot the feisty huntress from the foothills of Mount Meru who helped look after the military horses in her area, who supplied his troops with food and who knew no fear as she took part in special operations as a mounted reconnaissance operative far from home.

General Von Lettow-Vorbeck wrote the following about Margarete of the above-mentioned booklet:

S.A. veterans will 'dine' ex-German general

MAJ.-GEN. Paul Von Lettow-Vorbeck, German commander in East Africa in World War I, stepped from the Skymaster at Wingfield Airport to-day and embraced his former *aide-de-camp* and adjutant, Maj. E. Mueller, who lives in Cape Town. The general and Major Mueller last met in 1936 at the Olympic Games in Berlin.

Next he turned to shake hands with two old, bearded former comrades, Capt. F. N. Debertshauser and Cpl. T. Kloss.

The general, a man of 82, fresh complexioned and still retaining a soldierly bearing, is accompanied by his daughter Heloise.

Asked where he had spent the last war, General von Lettow-Vorbeck said: 'In Bremen to start with. I was too old to take part in the war, but my sons did.

'BOMBED OUT'

'My wife, daughter and I were bombed out of our home and moved to Schleswig-Holstein. We now have a flat in Hamburg.'

After a few days in Cape Town the general intends to fly to South West Africa. On his return to the Cape, Capt. G. W. T. Garrood, a former member of No. 26 Squadron (S.A.) R.F.C., which fought in East Africa, will organize a dinner to which veterans of the East African campaign, including Germans, will be invited.

On February 10 the general and his party are due to sail from Durban to visit the East African battlefields.

It is probable that General von Lettow-Vorbeck will meet the Prime Minister (Dr. Malan) on his return to the Peninsula from South West Africa.

Left — The article in The Cape Argus on 14 January 1953 concerning General Von Lettow-Vorbeck's arrival in Cape Town.

Top right — General Von Lettow-Vorbeck, left and Field Marshall Jane Smuts in London in December 1929.

Above — The cover of General Von Lettow-Vorbeck very scarce booklet, Afrika: Wie ich es wiedersah, in which he describes his visit to Africa in 1953.

'She is an old friend, the greatest and finest huntress I know ... conserving game and taking care of it... During the war, the South Africans had already broken through and the troops had to withdraw; she personally brought through yet another herd of cattle to the troops across enemy lines.'

When the General died on 9 March 1964 in Hamburg, at the age of ninety-four, he was buried with full military honours. Several of his former *askaris* were brought over from Tanzania to attend his funeral which was also attended by representatives of the West

German Government and the British Government. Soon afterwards, clearly in honour of this legendary leader, the West German *Bundestag* approved a fund to provide all the back pay owed to those *askaris* who were still alive.

About 350 old men gathered at the appointed meeting place at Mwanza on Lake Victoria to prove their role as *askaris*. Some had pieces of their original uniforms while a few had the certificates, now tattered bits of paper, which had been given to them as proof of service. Many had nothing by way of proof, but when given a broom handle and ordered in German to carry out the appropriate drill, they all did so without fault. That was proof enough and all the former *askaris* were paid out in full.

The Sunset Years

Rolf had become increasingly active as a professional big game hunter, escorting foreign clients on full-bag safaris that took him away for protracted periods of time. His work brought in money for *Momella* and eased the strain on his mother who turned

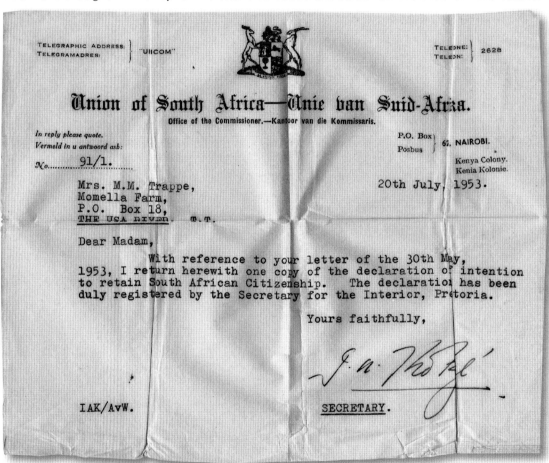

Confirmation that Margarete had renewed her South African citizenship in 1953.
[Yorck-Michael Trappe]

seventy in August 1954. The estate was still encumbered, but life was easier and certainly much happier. Rolf's wife Halinka and the children resided on *Momella* where Margarete could enjoy seeing her grandchildren develop in the bracing climate and scenic magnificence of the high country. She especially looked forward to weekends and holidays when she could spend time with little Yvonne in particular who had started school in Arusha.

It was a curious replay of her early days with her own children, seeing her grandchildren learning to ride and absorbing the languages and bush skills of their African wilderness home.

Speaking of black rhino, Margarete revealed to one of her special safari guests in the early 1950s, Maximilian von Rogister, that although there were about one hundred of these iconic animals on *Momella*, this was about half the number that once roamed in the immediate region before the outbreak of the Second World War. No explanation was given in Von Rogister's book *Momella: An African Game Paradise* as to the cause of this decline. It was years before the scourge of very sophisticated poaching syndicates and their assault rifles took root in Africa and started decimating black rhino for their horn and elephant for their ivory.

Margarete and her Polish daughter-in-law Halinka, married to her son Rolf, taken in the early 1950s. [Emil Karafiat]

Margarete and Rolf forbade any further hunting of black rhino at *Momella* after 1951. This was before the arrival of an American guest on a hunting safari with Rolf. Margarete had come down with malaria. While waiting for the safari to begin in earnest, the American wished to go for a stroll. He had been instructed to accompany one of Margarete's top black assistant hunters and to listen to him at all times. The guest, unfortunately, ignored this advice and wandered off into the bush by himself.

He stumbled on a black rhino cow with her calf, a potentially lethal situation. The rhino charged and the American had to shoot it to save his life. When Margarete heard about the dead female rhino and the abandoned calf, she must have exploded, although there is no surviving written record of this. What is known is that the calf was found that same day, brought back to *Momella* and raised with all the love and skill for which Margarete and her family had become known.

The baby rhino, named *Momella*, bonded with Margarete and wandered about the estate, letting Margarete's granddaughter, Yvonne, ride it like a miniature pony. It played hide-and-seek with Ursula and with one of the grooms and generally had the run of the estate. Before long, however, it started maturing and becoming too strong and, eventually, too dangerous to have around.

Margarete arranged for the young rhino to be shipped to a game park in England with another bull calf. The money generated paid for a tractor and ploughshare that were sorely needed on the estate. Despite this inevitable parting of the ways and the fact that a tame rhino calf could not have survived had it been set free in the Tanganyikan wilderness, Margarete always carried a twinge of guilt over the transaction. She rejected out of hand all commercial game capture operations as being akin to animal slavery.

Today, the capture and relocation of game animals to repopulate suitable wilderness areas in Africa and, indeed, to be introduced to appropriate habitat, game parks and zoos around the world is accepted conservation practice. Conservation and diversification of gene pools through captive breeding programmes are very skilled, scientifically-driven, essential undertakings in a world of shrinking natural habitat and exploding human population growth. South Africa, for example, made world headlines as far back as the late 1950s with Operation Rhino under Dr Ian Player who pioneered new capture methods to relocate white rhino to many foreign countries. From a few hundred surviving white rhino, they now number well over 12 000 animals in the new millennium.

Left — Yvonne Karafiat with the orphaned baby black rhino 'Momella' and one of Margarete's farm employees. [Emil Karafiat]

Right — Yvonne Karafiat on the baby black rhino 'Momella' in the early 1950s. [Emil Karafiat]

Harry Tennison of Fort Worth, Texas, founder of Game Conservation International, a great friend of Dr Player and who had vivid memories of meeting Margarete in Arusha in 1955, also made history in this regard. His personal mission saw the relocation of black and white rhino breeding stock from the former Southern Rhodesia and from the Republic of South Africa nearly four decades ago to a series of private ranches in Texas where they have flourished ever since.

Margarete, now increasingly aware of the decline in rhino numbers in her part of the world, once had to make an exception to the rhino rule when a particularly aggressive bull rhino attacked several grazing cows on the *Momella* pasture lands. It was a frequent visitor to the estate and had become a danger to the workforce. Rolf was called in to put it down. Not an ounce of the meat or hide was wasted and there is no doubt that the horn generated funds.

Now, when only the ghosts of black rhino wander over the former Trappe estate, it is hard to imagine just how prolific these huge animals once were. In fact, one of Rolf's domestic workers, a man named Selimani, was attacked by a rhino while making his way back to his kraal on *Momella*. He suffered severe injury to his left leg, but managed to drag himself back to the perimeter of Rolf's house where he cried out for help. Rolf and Halinka raced to his aid and were able to transport the poor man in their Land Rover to the hospital in Arusha. Selimani underwent an operation and spent nearly nine months recuperating in hospital before being able to return to *Momella*.

Selimani's left leg was several centimeters shorter than his right leg and this forced the man to hobble about with a crutch of sorts. As Margarete recounted to Gerd von Lettow-Vorbeck, one of her personal friends and house guests at the time was Baroness Anga Bodenhausen. When she saw the extent of Selimani's disability, she promptly took a few measurements and contacted the former Chief Shoemaker to the late Kaiser Wilhelm II to make a pair of orthopaedic boots for Selimani, obviously with a built up heel for the

Margarete and Halinka with their German shepherd dogs, taken in the early 1950s. [Emil Karafiat]

injured leg so that he could walk a little more easily and reduce the strain on his hips and spine.

Some months later, a package arrived in Arusha, addressed to *Herrn Selimani in Momella*. The package named as sender the 'Chief Purveyor to Their Majesties the Kaisers and Kings'. It contained the handmade, 'bespoke' leather orthopaedic boots that Selimani was wearing when Gerd von Lettow-Vorbeck visited *Momella* in the early 1950s and it is to Von Lettow-Vorbeck that one is indebted for recording this charming story about good-will and kindness across cultures.

Trouble Nextdoor and Implications at Home

Margarete's life had been marked by triumph and disaster and by death and rebirth of various kinds ever since she set foot in East Africa. Her acutely developed sixth sense had been picking up a change in the air since the end of the Second World War.

Tanganyika, a League of Nations Mandate territory under British administration after the First World War, became a United Nations Trusteeship territory from 1946 onwards. Plans were afoot to promote greater participation by the tribal peoples in the governing structures of their vast country. With no more than about 20 000 whites living in Tanganyika by the early 1950s, many of them not British, no vigorous anti-British senti-ment developed in Tanganyika.

Margarete noted over time how the tribal peoples had undergone changes of their own in the previous four decades as they came into increasing contact with Western cultures, lifestyles and dress. Something of the simplicity and joy of life and the innate pride in their tribal identities had changed, as their clothing styles changed. New pressures had entered their lives and more and more members of the strictly rural communities were coming into urban settlements where ties with their very traditional rural homes were loosening. Those tribal peoples who had left the country before and during the Second World War and who had lived in Europe and fought in the war, returned with new perspectives about nationality, self-rule and emancipation from colonial government.

Between August 1951 and August 1952, however, news had been spreading in East Africa at an increasing tempo of an anti-British, militant African nationalist movement in neighbouring Kenya, known as the *Mau Mau*. The main purpose of this secret organisa-tion, dominated by the Wakikuyu tribe, was to end British colonial rule and remove all European settlers. By August 1952, and after much violence against those blacks who did not wish to join the *Mau Mau*, curfews were enforced in the greater Nairobi district. The security situation deteriorated to such an extent from then on that British troops were sent out to Kenya in October of that year, the government in Kenya declaring a state of emergency on 20 October. The *Mau Mau* leaders then declared open rebellion against British colonial rule before the end of that November.

Attacks on white settlers began in 1952, starting with assaults and violent home inva-sions and degenerating into indiscriminate slaughter. *Mau Mau* suspects were arrested in increasing numbers, signalling the beginning of a huge escalation in hostilities, mass arrests and more deaths on both sides. The iconic Treetops Hotel where Princess Elizabeth and the Duke of Edinburgh had stayed in February 1952 and, a year later, Margarete's guests, Prince and Princess Frederick of Prussia, was burned down by the *Mau Mau* in May 1954, sending fresh shock waves through the country and into Tanganyika.

Margarete noted these developments with concern as the safari industry was sensitive

Margarete and a friend with Margarete's granddaughter Yvonne game-viewing on Momella. [Emil Karafiat]

to any situation that potential guests could view as threatening. She knew that an association had been formed in Tanganyika in 1929 called the African Association to promote Black African solidarity. It was initially a social welfare organisation that developed into a social and cultural forum for the Black urbanized intellectuals. Come 1948, it was renamed the Tanganyika African Association with a more focused, political orientation. Julius Nyerere, a school teacher who had been educated in Britain, became its first president in 1953.

The next year, Nyerere and Oscar Kambona changed the name to the Tanganyika African National Union (TANU). Margarete knew that this was now an overtly political organisation and that this was the beginning of the struggle for independence from foreign rule of any kind – be it via the United Nations or Great Britain. She could not have failed to ponder the implications for her of this incubating movement.

Except for a handful of incidents since her arrival in Africa almost fifty years previously, Margarete had not experienced any kind of antagonistic behaviour by her workforce or by any of the tribal peoples with whom she came into contact. In fact, when she thought back on her time with General Von Lettow-Vorbeck she recalled how there had been no rebellion of any sort by the indigenous peoples of German East Africa against the Germans in the war against the British-led forces. One of the most noteworthy characteristics of the *askaris* was their iron-clad loyalty to Von Lettow-Vorbeck who led from the front to the very end of the war. Now, there was also no sign of a Tanganyika-style *Mau Mau* developing. Race relations in the country were generally sound, but the events next door in Kenya and the deaths of over 10 000 *Mau Mau* activists by early 1956 in that country indicated that sociopolitical changes were inevitable in Tanganyika.

Margarete had a son, two daughters and four grandchildren living near her and she knew a degree of peace and support as she entered her 72nd year. *Momella* and all that it had meant to her for almost 50 years was still her home and she had the loyalty and enduring goodwill of tribal people whose fathers and, in a few instances, even grandfathers had worked for her. She could not start fighting fresh wars of survival merely on fears of what might transpire as a result of the *Mau Mau* guerrilla warfare in Kenya. She would cross that bridge when she came to it – as she had done ever since arriving in Africa. In the meantime, there was an unusual event in the offing that required her attention.

A Royal Occasion

The British subjects in Tanganyika were in a state of great excitement in October 1955 when Princess Margaret, the Queen's beautiful younger sister, paid a visit to the country as part of a five-week state visit to Mauritius, Zanzibar, Tanganyika and Kenya.

Margarete Trappe would find herself participating in rather unusual fashion.

Interest was intense as it had been exactly one year since Princess Margaret's announcement that she had decided to call off plans to marry divorced Battle of Britain war hero, Group Captain Peter Townsend. The relationship had electrified the Empire and all eyes were now on the pretty, vivacious 26-year-old princess and her next move. News from 'home' was never so exciting.

Margarete and five of her employees who had worked for her for at least 30 years. They are standing in front of Margarete's house on Momella. Taken in 1955 during Princess Margaret's state visit to Tanganyika. [Baron Christian von Lettow-Vorbeck]

The Royal Britannia yacht docked in Dar es Salaam with all due pomp and ceremony. A special 'Princess Margaret' wing had been freshly built at Government House and the capital was decked out in Union Jacks as royal fever gripped the country. Crowds lined the roads, cheering as the princess and her entourage, accompanied by Sir Edward Twining, the Governor-General of Tanganyika and member of the Twining Tea family, drove past in splendour that hot October day.

On 16 October 1955, Princess Margaret was welcomed in Arusha by thousands of schoolchildren from all communities, waving a sea of miniature Union Jacks. Masses of indigenous people in tribal regalia lined the route as part of a huge, exotic reception for the Queen's sister.

After visiting the school that Rosie Trappe had attended during the war years and after a picnic at the very scenic Duluti crater lake just east of Arusha, Princess Margaret was taken up to visit the Ngurdoto Crater – Little Ngorongoro – very close to the series of lakes on *Momella*. From the crater's rim she feasted on the wildlife spectacle below in the vast volcanic caldera with its huge herds of elephant and buffalo.

The next day, Princess Margaret was the honoured guest at the farm of August Künzler, a longstanding and very well-known Swiss resident in the greater Arusha region. He was godfather to Yvonne Karafiat, Margarete's grandchild, and a good friend of the Trappe family as a whole.

Künzler invited Princess Margarete to pick out two zebra foals as presents for Prince Charles, heir to the British throne, and for Princess Anne, his little sister. The Princess obliged and when asked by Sir Edward as to the address to be used for the dispatch of the zebra, Princess Margaret replied: "Home." One presumes that meant Buckingham Palace!

A special agricultural exposition had been arranged in Moshi to coincide with the Princess's two-day visit. Her Royal Highness would officially open the exposition. The call had gone out to farm employers to bring to the Moshi show any workers who had been in their employ on the same farm for at least thirty years so that they could each receive a decoration from the Princess for their loyalty to the Crown. Up stepped Margarete Trappe with five of her staff who had worked for her for three decades and, indeed, much longer.

The Princess, of course, and many others present that day could not have understood the underlying message or the irony conveyed by Margarete and her loyal staff. They had stuck with her through terrible times when she had refused to buckle under the pressure exerted by the British after 1916. As for her workers, they had refused, time and again, to desert her, even when she had no means to pay them and after they had been hounded off *Momella* twice by the British authorities. Their loyalty had nothing at all to do with the British Crown or with some distant monarch of whom they knew nothing at all. Their arrival that day with *Yeyo* to be presented to the most senior representative of the British Empire to visit the northern region since the Prince of Wales's fleeting visit in 1928, was testimony to the exceptional loyalty of the workers towards Margarete Trappe. They *knew* her and they were proud to stand with *Yeyo* that day in Moshi, proud of their lifetime with the lady from a far country who had never harmed them.

Last Days

Rolf was away for lengthy periods as a professional hunter. Margarete, although now entering her 73rd year in 1957, continued to try to manage *Momella* in Rolf's absence. It was a struggle for her to try to maintain standards, but she persevered, shouldering

Margarete in her seventies and still in the wilds, close to the animals. [Yorck-Michael Trappe]

heavy responsibilities into old age. She continued to help the local people with their problems and medical ailments and to supervise the dairy herd and the horses. Trade with the tribal peoples still took place as did trips into Arusha to attend to other business. Margarete would take the old Land Rover and go about her property, where possible, checking on livestock and humans alike. She was always accompanied by some of her dogs as she shouldered her tasks. Orders were firm as this still remarkably youthful woman tried to keep control of her refuge as best she could with the means at her disposal.

Europe was now distant, but Margarete would reserve a special place in her memories of her childhood and youth in Germany with her father, hunting and riding together and sharing the dream of one day going out to Africa. She had become increasingly contemplative. In the late afternoons, she was in the habit of walking down with some of her dogs to her favourite spot on *Momella* where she would look across at a massive outcrop in the foothills of Mount Meru and enjoy the twilight as it enveloped the countryside.

She would catch the familiar sounds of the African night as it approached and recall her lifetime spent under the Southern Cross with the wild creatures of that world and with the tribal peoples who had been her greatest source of support and loyalty. Scenes of the first, tough but exhilarating years in Africa filled her thoughts, as did the birth of her four children and several grandchildren and the joy they had brought her.

Vignettes would flow before her mind's eye of war and of her time with General Von Lettow-Vorbeck's forces, taking risks and facing danger; the tough years in South Africa and then the relief of coming home to Mount Meru; turning professional guide and hunting with guests from around the world; gold prospecting and that one lucky strike; another war, internment, eventual peace and starting over; the exceptional people who had inhabited her world, from humble tribal women and their babies to European royalty she had guided on hunting expeditions and photographic safaris . Ever present was the wildlife in whose domain she had always felt secure. It had been a life well lived.

In May 1957, Margarete's health began to fail. She became increasingly frail and took to her bed. A window looked out over *Momella* as the land fell away to the valley below, Mount Kilimanjaro dressing the distant horizon as it had done for millennia. At night, the moon could often be seen rising over the mountain to join skies awash with stars.

There were small herds of elephant that were usually resident on *Momella*. These 'house' elephants meant everything to Margarete. Now, a herd had moved close, gravitating between the fringes of the forest and a clearing near Margarete's window. At night, they could be heard as they rumbled their communications to one another, foraging about on the edge of the forest. Their great grey-black bulk could be seen, picked out by moonlight, trunks sometimes testing the air as they watched and waited. These excep-

tionally intelligent animals clearly sensed something was not as it should be.

Margarete's condition then worsened. One of her workers of long standing, Phillipo Stephano Pallangyo, was instructed to drive to Arusha to fetch a doctor. It took almost five hours before he and the doctor were able to get back to the farmhouse, but it was already too late.

After a life of extraordinary challenges, of great highs and terrible lows, of intense joy and profound sorrow, of magnificent accomplishment and dark defeat, Margarete slipped away on her final safari on 5 June 1957. The news spread like a runaway bush fire. Soon, the bereft family was joined by throngs of tribal people who gathered about the

What is believed to have been one of the last photographs taken of Margarete. She is pictured on Momella with her dogs at her favourite spot, opposite the massive outcrop in the Mount Meru foothills.
[Dr Jobst-Ulrich Trappe]

house, numbed. They then witnessed an unusual scene – several elephant that had been milling about no more than ten metres away from the house, began trumpeting as if to convey the news throughout the land that their *Yeyo*, too, had now gone to rest. The elephants were still there two days later and they remained close by when Margarete was buried that week on *Momella*. They seemed sensitive to the grief of the family and of the tribal people at large who had gathered to mourn the passing of this valiant lady. She was now eternally at rest in the only place on earth she had never wanted to lose or leave.

The family reunion at Margarete's house on Momella in early 1962 with detailed caption. [Emil Karafiat]

Back row standing: Emil Karafiat, Rosie Karafiat, Tine Zehe (Margarete's sister), Martha Trappe (married to Ulrich), Yvonne Karafiat.
Back row sitting: Mario Sirtoli, Rolf Trappe, Ursula Sirtoli
Front row sitting: Emil Karafiat, Richard sitting on Halinka Trappe's lap, Ulrich Trappe, Rolf Trappe Junior (Puci)
Front: Jobst-Ulrich Trappe

Afterword

A process that had been launched in 1958, soon after Margarete's death, resulted in Tanganyika's independence from British rule on 9 December 1961. In 1964, after a blood-soaked uprising on the island of Zanzibar and the massacre of thousands of Zanzibaris, mostly Arabs, a union was formed between the mainland and the island resulting in the birth on 26 April 1964 of the one-party state of the United Republic of Tanganyika and Zanzibar. This was changed later that year to the United Republic of Tanzania.

Millions of rural dwellers were subsequently relocated in stages, willingly and then by force, into communal villages to grow cash crops and food for the market on a communal basis. Influx control measures were also introduced to prevent people from flocking to urban areas. By the late 1970s, almost 80% of the entire country's population had been resettled in these communal villages – 'the largest mass movement in Africa's history' to quote Martin Meredith on page 255 in his book *The State of Africa: A History of Fifty Years of Independence* (London: The Free Press, 2005). This homegrown form of socialism was called *ujamaa*, a Kiswahili word President Julius Nyerere translated as 'familyhood'. This policy, coupled with widespread nationalisation, triggered a political and economic crisis whose effects were felt for decades afterwards.

It was at this juncture that Ulrich Trappe, his wife and two small sons packed up their lives in South-West Africa where they had been living for several years. They then packed a Volkswagen Beetle and drove across Africa, from Windhoek to *Momella*, a distance of several thousand kilometres. The magnetic pull of Ulrich's birthplace was overwhelming. He had never stopped yearning to see his home again and all the places where the first twenty-seven years of his life were anchored.

The Trappes were hoping to be able to build a new life under a new government amid surroundings of profound personal significance. Ulrich met his brother Rolf, his sisters Rosie and Ursula and Aunt Tine again on *Momella* after almost twenty-two years of separation. Young cousins also met one another for the first time. The nostalgia was overpowering, as were the inevitable thoughts of what might have been, had Tanganyika somehow been able to escape the contagion and consequences of world war.

The homecoming proved bitter-sweet: circumstances were such that Ulrich and his wife felt it advisable to return to Germany for good in 1962. By 1970, and in the wake of very unfortunate events concerning title to the estate, the 63-year-old association of the Trappe name with *Momella* was permanently terminated when the Tanzanian Government nationalised the property and incorporated it into the Arusha National Park.

Had Margarete still been alive, she would have received no financial compensation at all for her property in the late evening of her life. She was spared seeing the dire economic effects of further nationalisation throughout the country, the banning of all hunting safaris from late 1973 until 1982 and even the closure of the border with Kenya in the latter part of the 1970s. She was also spared witnessing the results of the unbridled slaughter during the 1980s of elephant and black rhino by poaching gangs over vast regions of the country. The tide began to turn in the 1990s and fresh hope returned to

Left — Lazaro Samual Mafie, a longtime employee of Margarete, photographed in November 2006 at the age of 83. [Lars Hauck]

Right — Philippo Stephano Pallangyo who worked for Margarete during the last years of her life. [Lars Hauck]

Tanzania for the long-term conservation of game and habitat. The superabundance of wildlife Margarete knew, however, no longer exists.

Today, Margarete's spirit is at peace and it is as free as the tawny eagles that still coast on the thermals in the dramatically beautiful region that was her home for half a century and where she knew her greatest freedom and joy. Her legacy was one of courage in the face of adversity, endurance in the face of loss, empathy for others and the fortitude to start all over again.

In November 2006, the Ziegler Film Company of Berlin came out on location to Tanzania to film a two-part documentary on the life and times of Margarete Trappe. The German Broadcasting Corporation screened the film to acclaim in January and February 2007 in celebration of the centenary of Margarete's arrival in German East Africa and also to coincide with the 50th anniversary of her death.

Several of the tribal people who had worked for Margarete and who were all in advanced old age were interviewed on film and recalled her with intense pride. One of Margarete's former employees, Mirau Lodumare, who was a house servant and a gardener from 1934 onwards, recalled: "She was a good woman. I had a problem with my leg and was ill for three years. She took care of me for the entire time until I had recovered. This is why I shall remember her for my whole life."

Kisiwa Nanyaro, who was one of Margarete's assistant hunters from 1934, recalled how Margarete provided living space on *Momella* for many Maasai as well as grazing for their cattle. When the British took over in the region, many of the newly arrived British forced the Maasai and their cattle off their newly acquired properties. "She liked the Maasai. When the cattle were sick, she would help them," recalled Kisiwa Nanyaro.

Phillippo Stephano Pallangyo, in Margarete's employ during the last years of her life and the person who drove in all haste to Arusha to fetch a doctor on the day Margarete died, said: "When there was a problem in the kraal, we would wake her in the middle of the night. When anyone was ill or if a woman was about to give birth, she would come and help."

Another very old man stated simply: "She kept her word. There was no one else like her.

Margarete's house on Momella, now a state guest house, in the shadow of Mount Meru. [Bernd Reufels]

The former swimming pool on Momella, Novemver 2006. [Bernd Reufels]

Top — Margarete's grave.

Bottom left — The grave of Rolf Trappe.

Bottom right — The grave of Ursula Sirtoli.

I shall never forget her." His sentiments were echoed by Massawe Pallangyo, another of Margarete's longtime employees who said: "Nobody could say anything bad about that lady. The people loved Margarete Trappe and still admire her."

———————

The author was invited to take part in the filming and it was during this time that she was accompanied to see Margarete's Trappe's grave on what used to be her *Momella* estate. The grave lay at the bottom of a fairly steep incline immediately in front of the house where she died and that is now a state guesthouse, used for guests of the Tanzanian Government.

The grave lay amid quite thick undergrowth, close to the once-lovely cement and rock swimming pool. The little gate and remains of the fencing that used to enclose the pool area could still be seen embedded in the bush. A well-used, fresh game path went right past Margarete's gravestone that was overgrown and only partially visible. It was flanked on one side by her son Rolf's gravestone and on the other by her daughter Ursula's final resting place that was unmarked except for some large stones that traced the outline of the grave. Rolf had died in 1984 and Ursula, the first-born, in 1998 as she entered her 89th year. Rosie, Margarete's much-loved 'late lamb', died tragically young at thirty-eight in 1964 from cancer. She was buried in Arusha. Ulrich, who died in 1997 after a lengthy battle with cancer, lies buried in Germany.

During the filming of the documentary, the author was based at the beautiful Hatari Game Lodge located on part of the former Trappe estate. The head guide employed by the Lodge at the time was Charles Urio, a member of the Wameru people. He accompanied the author to visit Margarete's grave. After hacking out a path through the dense undergrowth and down a fairly steep incline, the guide stood next to the grave and confided the following: "My grandfather worked for Margarete Trappe. We still speak of that lady today. When she died, our people lost a mother as well. In my language we had a special name for her, *Mangaroi*. It means 'Great Woman'. She was a great woman."

Charles Urio and Fiona Capstick in what was once Margarete's house at Momella.

Giraffe in the Momella area. [Marlies and Jörg Gabriel]

Postscript

Professor Emil Karafiat

Moenchaltorf, Switzerland, September 2011

When we were asked by the Ziegler Film Company what memories we had of our grandmother, I was amazed at how much more my dear late sister Yvonne remembered than I did – of course, Yvonne was eight, I was only six when our grandmother passed away in 1957.

So different were our memories of Momi, as our grandmother was called by the whole family, that it seemed almost as though we were remembering two separate women.

Born in 1949, the first-born of her own much loved 'late arrival' Rosie, Yvonne was Margarete's pearl, a source of joy and distraction from the ever-recurring worries relating to the farm, the government and her sons, Ulrich and Rolf, whom she missed dearly.

This lively little tot soon had the run of her house. She was her absolute darling, allowed to do whatever she liked, and Margarete was the one person she could count on if there was 'trouble' with her mother, such as the occasion when Rosie, for reasons of hygiene, wanted to wash Yvonne's linen rag. This rag was Yvonne's permanent companion, which she chewed, dragged through the dust and took to bed with her. Yvonne refused to let go of it, threw a tantrum and ran to Momi, who consoled her by giving her a mysterious, furry little claw, set in silver to hold and to look at. This had the effect of a tranquillizer and sparked off a strong sense of wonder. She drifted off into a world of strange creatures and soon fell asleep. She had won a victory over her mother. Family history does not relate whether or not Rosie subsequently managed to get the rag washed.

In her later years, Margarete often took Yvonne with her on walks to her favourite spots, such as the big rock or one of the lakes. Yvonne remembered some of the sounds her grandmother used to make to attract hippos from the water. Once Momi had to come to her rescue when she found herself covered in siafu – those aggressive forest ants. She took off Yvonne's clothes and finally managed to shake them off.

Before she died in 2007, Yvonne told me that those first eight years, in which she enjoyed Margarete's unconditional love, were by far the happiest time of her life.

My memories are somewhat different. I recall Margarete once catching my cousin and me smoking twigs for cigarettes. What an uproar that caused! She gave us a telling-off in the Prussian tradition – much to the amusement of those present on her veranda – in her shorts and her knee-high riding boots, stamping one foot on the cement floor to enhance her words. In retrospect, I feel sure this was more of a dramatic performance than an outburst of real fury, for I recall a mischievous glint in her eyes. At the time, however, I was thoroughly awed and felt it wise to keep my distance. She showed her gentle side, however, when I was once involved in a severe argument with her servant's children. We appealed to Margarete, and, smiling, she intervened to the satisfaction of both factions. There was no telling-off this time. My role, however, was that of second or even third or fourth fiddle – for in the meantime Rolf's two boys had joined the crew of grandchildren. Yvonne, however, always remained the number one.

Emil Karafiat, photographed in 2006 at home in Switzerland. [Bernd Reufels]

Yvonne, Emil's sister, who died in 2007 soon after being interviewed for the documentary film. [Bernd Reufels]

The last scene I can remember was that of Margarete, lying peacefully in her coffin. Ursula, her oldest child, lifted me to the rim of the coffin so I could catch a last glimpse of my grandmother. The atmosphere was heavy with grief. No talking. Utter silence. She was dearly loved and mourned by everybody in Momella.

From a historical perspective Margarete was born into one of the cruellest periods of history, one which had lasting effects on Africa – effects all too evident even today. The belief in the predominance of the white race over all others prevailed even before one madman in the middle of civilised Europe 'went wrong', to quote Joseph Conrad in *Heart of Darkness*. This belief and the greedy determination of European countries to virtually 'help themselves to the black continent' was perverted into an ideology that was cynically dressed up as a humane cause: those who went out to the dark continent saw themselves as servants of the universal will, bringing Christianity to the primitive corners of the earth. In fact they brought destruction, exploitation and more than a century of suffering to Africa, thereby betraying the very civilisation they had come to spread.

From a modern perspective these imperial atrocities are clearly inexcusable. Only once that view is established can we turn to those exceptional figures – and Margarete was one of them – who, despite being part of the imperial machinery, led lives characterised by human understanding and dignity, treating the peoples of German East Africa with respect and understanding, showing that each side could learn and profit from the other. This is what the author has successfully shown in this remarkable book.

Margarete's story also shows how connected ('globalized' would be the modern word) the world already was. Events in Europe inevitably had repercussions in the far corners of the world. What an immense change of thinking Margarete must have undergone from being an active German patriot in 1914 to becoming a British dominion subject in the end, thereby proving that her love of Momella was what counted and all else was secondary. I have little doubt that she would have tried to acquire Tanzanian citizenship, had she lived on, if only to be able to stay in her beloved country.

Friends of Kisimiri, KME Switzerland – an NGO

This non-profit organization was founded in 1996 by Emil Karafiat in order to support the state school system of Tanzania, especially the schools in Momella and neighbouring Kisimiri. The projects are all based on the principle of integration of the local community. This has two benefits: first, it allows the available funds to be used as efficiently as possible and, second, it stimulates the enthusiasm of the local people by affording them an active role. The organisation's motto is: Helping others to help themselves. The provision of education is perhaps the most elementary and lasting form of co-operative Third World aid. Hence the work of "Friends of Kisimiri" is to be seen, not as an alternative, but as a complement to other forms of emergency and Third World aid. The organization's greatest achievement so far has been the creation from scratch of a state-sector secondary and high school which provides post-primary education to some 700 boys and girls whose educational careers would otherwise have ended after primary school with a standard school-leaving certificate.

More details are available at: www.kisimiri.ch.

Emil Karafiat, founder of The Kisimiri Foundation, with some of the children at the secondary school his Foundation established, close to his grandmother's former home at Momella.
[Bernd Reufels]

Select bibliography

Unpublished sources

A variety of handwritten letters from Margarete TRAPPE to her relatives in Germany as well as associated documentation and an appreciable amount of correspondence over several years between the author and the subject's grandsons, Emil Karafiat in Switzerland, Dr Jobst-Ulrich Trappe and his brother Yorck-Michael Trappe in Germany on the life and times of their grandmother. The grandsons provided photographs and much essential information without which this book would have been impossible to write.

Conversations over several years with the late Ada Wincza, a renowned huntress and safari company owner with her husband Captain Laddy Wincza, the last Vice-President of the East African Professional Hunters' Association. Ada knew of the writer's particular interest in Margarete Trappe as a pioneer in colonial African hunting history. The Winczas lived for three decades in East Africa where Ada came to know Margarete TRAPPE in the last years of her life. Ada provided excellent background material on the then Tanganyika in particular, on the Maasai people about whom she wrote, and on an array of issues that facilitated better insight into the exceptional life of Margarete Trappe.

Interaction with Bernd Reufels, the well-known German freelance filmmaker specialising in documentary films. He was the director and scriptwriter of the acclaimed two-part documentary film on the life of Margarete Trappe, filmed on location in Tanzania in November 2006 and released in January 2007 to celebrate the centenary of her arrival in the then German East Africa. Bernd was exceptionally generous with his time, knowledge and research.

Published sources

Ahlefeldt-Bille, Count G. – *Tandalla: A Danish Game Warden's Study of Native and Wild Life in Kenya and Tanganyika* – London: Routledge and Kegan Paul, 1951.

Ayittey, George B.N. – *Africa Betrayed* – London: The Macmillan Press Ltd., 1994.

Ayittey, George B.N. – *Africa in Chaos* – New York: St. Martin's Griffin, 1998.

Appiah, Kwame Anthony and Gates, Henry Louis, Jr., (Editors) – *Africana: The Encyclopedia of the African and African American Experience* – New York: Basic Civitas Books, 1999.

Boyes, John – *The Company of Adventurers* – London: "East Africa" Ltd., 1928.

Brown, James A. – *They Fought for King and Kaiser. South Africans in German East Africa 1916* – Johannesburg: Ashanti Publishing (Pty) Limited, 1991.

Burger, John E. – *African Jungle Memories* – London; Robert Hale Limited, 1958.

Buxton, Edward North – *Two African Trips with Notes and Suggestions on Big Game Preservation in Africa* – London: Edward Stanford, 1902.

Capstick, Fiona – *The Diana Files; The Huntress/Traveller Through History* – Johannesburg: Rowland Ward Publications, 2004.

Capstick, Peter Hathaway – *Death in the Silent Places* – New York: St Martin's Press, 1981

Cranworth, Lord – *A Colony in the Making: Or Sport and Profit in British East Africa* – London: MacMillan and Co., Limited, 1912.

Dyer, Anthony – *The East African Hunters: The History of the East African Professional Hunters' Association* – Clinton, New Jersey: The Amwell Press, 1979.

Dyer, Anthony – *Men for All Seasons; The Hunters and Pioneers* – Agoura, California: Trophy Room Books, 1996.

Dyer, Anthony – *Men for All Seasons and Legendary Ladies* – Johannesburg: Rowland Ward Publications, 2008.

Farwell, Byron – *The Great War in Africa* (1914-1918) – Middlesex, England: Viking, 1987.

Fetner, P. Jay – *The African Safari: The Ultimate Wildlife and Photographic Adventure* - New York: St Martins Press, 1987.

Fox, James – *White Mischief* – London: Penguin Books, 1984.

Fraser, Sean – *National Geographic African Adventure Atlas* – Singapore: Tien Wah Press (Pte) Ltd., 2003.

Grzimek, Bernard & Michael – *Serengeti shall not Die* – New York: E.P. Dutton & Co., Inc., 1973

Huxley, Elspeth – *White Man's Country; Lord Delamere and the Making of Kenya* – London: Macmillan and Company, 1935.

Inhülsen, Otto – *Wir ritten für Deutsch-Ostafrika* – Leipzig: Koehler & Amelang, 1941.

Josephy, Alvin M. (editor) – *The Horizon History of Africa* – New York: American Heritage Publishing Company Inc., 1971.

Kittenberger, Kálmán – *Big Game Hunting and Collecting in East Africa 1903-1926* – London: Edward Arnold & Co., 1929.

Meikle, Robert S. and Mrs M.E. Meikle – *After Big Game. The Story of an African Holiday* – London: T. Werner Laurie Ltd., circa 1917.

Meredith, Martin – *The State of Africa: A History of Fifty Years of Independence* – London: Jonathan Ball Publishers, 2005.

Miller, Charles – *The Lunatic Express; An Entertainment in Imperialism* – New York: The Macmillan Company, 1971.

Miller, Charles – *Battle for the Bundu: The First World War in East Africa* – London: Purnell Book Services limited, 1974.

Moore, E.D. – *Ivory: Scourge of Africa* – New York: Harper & Brothers, 1931.

Moorehead, Alan – *The White Nile* – London: Hamish Hamilton, 1960.

Puxley, F.L. – *In African Game Tracks: Wanderings with a Rifle Through Eastern Africa* - London: H.F. & G. Witherby, 1929.

Nicholson, Brian – *The Last of Old Africa: Big-Game Hunting in East Africa* – Long Beach, California: Safari Press, 2001.

Paice, Edward – *Lost Lion of Empire: The Life and Times of Cape-to-Cairo Grogan* – London: HarperCollins Publishers, 2001.

Paice, Edward – *Tip and Run* – London; Weidenfeld & Nicholson, 2007.

Pakenham, Thomas – *The Scramble for Africa: The White Man's Conquest of the Dark Continent from 1876 to 1912* – New York: Random House, 1991.

Pieterse, H.J.C. – *Baanbrekers in die Maalstroom: Dagboek van Mev. Abel Pienaar Moeder van Sangiro* – Kaapstad: Nasionale Pers Beperk, 1942.

Read, David – *Barefoot over the Serengeti* – London: Cassell Ltd., 1979.

Reid, E. – *Tanganyika without Prejudice: A Balanced Critical Review of the Territory and her People* – London: East African Newspaper Publishers, 1934.

Reader, John – *AFRICA: A Biography of the Continent* – London: Penguin Books, 1998.

Schillings, C.G. – *Flashlights in the Jungle: A Record of Hunting Adventures and of Studies in Wild Life in Equatorial East Africa* – New York: Doubleday, Page & Company, 1905.

Schillings, C.G. – *In Wildest Africa* (two volumes) – London: Hutchinson & Co., 1907.

Serras Pires, Adelino and Capstick, Fiona (co-authors) – *The Winds of Havoc: A Memoir of Adventure and Destruction in Deepest Africa* – New York; St Martin's Press, Inc., 2001.

Von Höhnel, Lieut. Ludwig – *Discovery of Lakes Rudolf and Stefanie: A Narrative of Count Samuel Teleki's Exploring & Hunting Expedition in Eastern Equatorial Africa in 1887 & 1888* (two volumes) – London: Longmans, Green, and Co., 1894.

Von Lettow-Vorbeck, Gerd – *Am Fusse des Meru: Das Leben von Margarete Trappe,*

Afrikas grosser Jägerin – Hamburg: Verlag Paul Parey, 1957.

Von Lettow-Vorbeck, General Paul – **My Reminiscences of East Africa** – London: Hurst and Blackett, Ltd., 1920.

Von Lettow-Vorbeck, General Paul – **Afrika wie ich es wiedersah** – München: J.F. Lehmanns Verlag, 1955.

Von Rogister, Maximilian – **Momella; An African Game Paradise** – London: Odhams Press Limited, 1957.

Von Wissmann, Dr Hermann – **In den Wildnissen Afrikas und Asiens** – Berlin; Paul Parey. 1901.

Wincza, Ada and Laddy – **Bush and Plains** – Clinton, New Jersey: Amwell Press, 1983.

Woods, Gregor – **Rifles for Africa: Practical Advice on Rifles and Ammunition for an African Safari** – Long Beach, California: Safari Press, 2002.

Younghusband, Ethel – **Glimpses of East Africa and Zanzibar** – London: John Long Limited, 1908

Newspapers and Magazines

Hamburger Nachrichten, 1 May 1910
Illustrierte Landwirtschaftliche Zeitung, 6 November 1912
New York Times, 11 November 1918
The Cape Argus, 11 May 1931
Jagd und Hege, 1938
The Cape Times, 5 May 1950
The Cape Argus, 14 January 1953
Tanganyika Standard, 2 March 1953
Visier, February 2004
Jagd und Hund, June 2005
Newsletter of the International Council for Game and Wildlife Conservation, March 2008
Meinerzhagen Zeitung, 1 May 2008
Wild und Hund December 2009

Appendix

Game ordinances for German East Africa taken from Edward North Buxton's book *Two African Trips* (London: Edward Stanford, 1902) Pages 203-208.

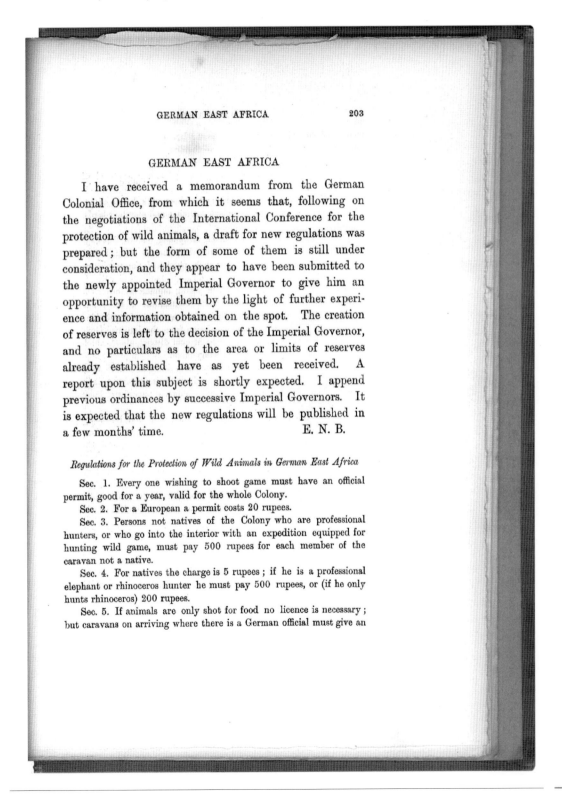

GERMAN EAST AFRICA

I have received a memorandum from the German Colonial Office, from which it seems that, following on the negotiations of the International Conference for the protection of wild animals, a draft for new regulations was prepared; but the form of some of them is still under consideration, and they appear to have been submitted to the newly appointed Imperial Governor to give him an opportunity to revise them by the light of further experience and information obtained on the spot. The creation of reserves is left to the decision of the Imperial Governor, and no particulars as to the area or limits of reserves already established have as yet been received. A report upon this subject is shortly expected. I append previous ordinances by successive Imperial Governors. It is expected that the new regulations will be published in a few months' time.   E. N. B.

Regulations for the Protection of Wild Animals in German East Africa

Sec. 1. Every one wishing to shoot game must have an official permit, good for a year, valid for the whole Colony.

Sec. 2. For a European a permit costs 20 rupees.

Sec. 3. Persons not natives of the Colony who are professional hunters, or who go into the interior with an expedition equipped for hunting wild game, must pay 500 rupees for each member of the caravan not a native.

Sec. 4. For natives the charge is 5 rupees; if he is a professional elephant or rhinoceros hunter he must pay 500 rupees, or (if he only hunts rhinoceros) 200 rupees.

Sec. 5. If animals are only shot for food no licence is necessary; but caravans on arriving where there is a German official must give an

204   GAME LAWS

account of the animals shot, with particulars as to their nature and number, and proof of the necessity of shooting them.

Sec. 6. Nor is it necessary to have a licence in order to shoot animals trespassing on cultivated ground; but the approval of the local official must be obtained.

Sec. 7. Nor is a licence necessary to shoot apes, beasts of prey of all kinds, wild pigs, all birds except ostriches and secretary-birds, and reptiles.

Sec. 8. It is forbidden to shoot all young, calves, foals, young elephants (without tusks, or with tusks less than 3 kilog. in weight), females so far as distinguishable as such, except of the species named in section 7.

Sec. 9. It is permitted to catch young animals in order to send them to zoological gardens and scientific institutions. If this is pursued as a trade, permission must be obtained on payment of a suitable sum.

Sec. 10. Without express permission from the Imperial Governor it is forbidden to shoot zebras in the Moschi district, eland, antelopes, giraffes, buffalo, ostriches, and secretary-birds.

Sec. 11. Without express permission it is forbidden to use nets, fire-drives, or drives on a large scale. If there is imminent danger of damage from the depredations of wild animals, provisional leave can be obtained from the local official.

Sec. 12. The following charges are levied on non-natives :—

100 rupees for the first and 250 rupees for every subsequent elephant bagged, and 50 rupees for the first rhinoceros, and 150 for every subsequent rhinoceros killed.

Sec. 13. Special game preserves will be established and special Regulations made therefor.

Sec. 14. Infractions of the above Regulations are punishable with a fine of 50 to 1000 rupees, in case of fraud by a five-fold to twenty-fold licence fee.

The animals unlawfully killed, or parts of them (tusks, horns, etc.), are confiscated.

In cases of repetition of the offence the right to shoot can be withdrawn for a time or altogether.

Sec. 15. This Order comes into force from to-day.

(Signed)   DR. VON WISSMANN,
                            The Imperial Governor.

DAR-ES-SALAAM, *May* 7, 1896.

GERMAN EAST AFRICA   205

No. 45

Circular of the Imperial Governor of German East Africa to the District and-Sub-District Offices and Stations in the Interior

(Translation.)

By the enclosed amended Game Ordinance, which is based upon the results of practical experience, the Ordinance of the 7th May 1896 respecting the protection of game in German East Africa, and its supplements, are repealed. This is to take effect from the day of public notification in each district.

I empower the local administrative authorities, especially in frontier districts, to issue provisional Regulations altering this Ordinance when necessity arises; they must, however, in this case apply for confirmation of their decisions by the Government without delay. For the establishment of game reserves the sanction of the Government must be previously obtained. Those already existing remain.

It may at times also be found necessary to refuse the issue of hunting licences to natives altogether, or to forbid entirely the killing of certain species of game. In view of the diversity of the conditions of existence of game in the several districts of the Protectorate, and the small knowledge of the subject which we at present possess, it is impossible to introduce a general close time.

I shall be glad to receive reports without delay as to the feasibility and desirability of the following measures :—

1. Licences to hunt elephants shall no longer be issued to natives.

2. The Station shall grant to one or more trustworthy "fundi" the exclusive right of elephant-hunting in the district.

3. Guns and ammunition shall be supplied to these men by the Station, for themselves and for their followers, in return for which they shall enter the service of the Station as foresters and gamekeepers.

4. Of each elephant killed they shall deliver one tusk—to be chosen by the Station.

These privileged hunters will be induced by their own interest to report every case of unlawful killing of an elephant; and, above all, they will learn to hunt in a sportsmanlike manner.

(Signed)   LIEBERT,
The Imperial Governor.

Dar-es-Salaam, *January 17, 1898.*

No. 46

Ordinance respecting the Protection of Game in German East Africa

§ 1. Every person who wishes to kill game must provide himself with a game licence, which is issued by a District or Sub-District Officer, or by a Station, for a particular person and for a period of one year from the date of issue. Such licences are valid for the whole Protectorate.

§ 2. The fee for a licence for Europeans is 10 rupees. If they are professionally engaged in hunting, the fee is 500 rupees; and if they proceed into the interior with an expedition specially organised for hunting, the fee shall be 800 rupees for each non-native participator. For native members of such an expedition, the lesser game licence described in § 3 must be obtained.

§ 3. A game licence for natives is subject to a fee of 5 rupees. If they are professionally engaged in hunting elephants or rhinoceros, they must pay 500 rupees in order to obtain a licence. If the people are trustworthy, the payment of this fee may be deferred.

§ 4. For hunting Associations, the native leader or entrepreneur ("fundi") must take out one greater game licence under § 3, and also one lesser licence under § 3, for each native member of the Association. These assistants, whose number must be determined when the greater game licence is issued, and must not exceed thirty, are subject to the provisions of § 10.

§ 5. A licence is not required when the game is killed merely for the purpose of obtaining food on the march.

§ 6. No game licence is required for killing monkeys, all carnivora, wild boar, amphibians, and reptiles.

For the killing of adult lions a premium of 30 rupees, for adult leopards a premium of 20 rupees, will be paid on application by the competent local authorities.

§ 7. The killing of sucking elephants is prohibited.

§ 8. The capture of young animals for breeding purposes, or for transmission to zoological gardens and scientific institutions, is permitted. If this kind of capture is carried on professionally, the greater game licence must be taken out. This permission can at any time be revoked if its exercise results in a considerable reduction of the head of game.

§ 9. Without express permission, game may not be hunted with nets, fire, or large battues. In case the game is causing considerable damage to crops in migration, the local authorities may grant this permission.

§ 10. A tax of 100 rupees shall be levied for every elephant killed. The hunter may avoid the payment of this tax by the surrender of one tusk, and the total amount of such taxes paid by any one hunter during the year shall not exceed the fee paid for the greater game licence.

§ 11. In districts where great Chiefs have a customary claim to one of the tusks of each elephant killed by a native hunter, the tusk surrendered shall in future be due alternately to the Station and to the Chief, so that if two elephants are killed, the hunter will get two tusks, the Station and the Chief one each.

§ 12. Infractions of the provisions of this Ordinance shall be punished by fines up to 500 rupees, or, in case of non-payment, by imprisonment up to three months. In case the dues are fraudulently withheld, from twice to twenty-five times the amount of such dues shall be levied as a penalty.

Of all moneys received in consequence of this Ordinance, one-half shall be paid in to the Government, the other half shall be devoted to the purposes of the public service at the District Office or Station where the licence is issued or the fine levied. Game unlawfully obtained, or parts of the same, may be confiscated.

In case of a repetition of the offence, the permission to hunt may be withdrawn for a time, or permanently.

(Signed)   LIEBERT,
The Imperial Governor.

Dar-es-Salaam, January 17, 1898.

ORDER OF THE IMPERIAL GOVERNOR RELATING TO THE SHOOTING OF ELEPHANTS IN GERMAN EAST AFRICA

§ 1. The export of elephant tusks which weigh less than 11 ratli (5 kilog.) is prohibited from the 1st April 1901.

§ 2. On and after the 1st April 1901 elephant tusks as above

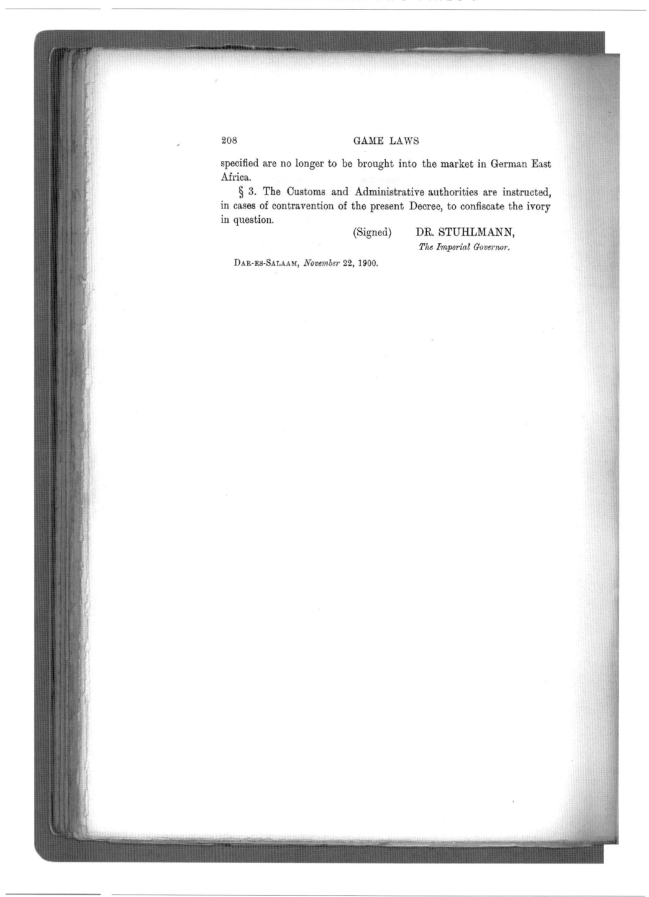

208   GAME LAWS

specified are no longer to be brought into the market in German East Africa.

§ 3. The Customs and Administrative authorities are instructed, in cases of contravention of the present Decree, to confiscate the ivory in question.

(Signed)   DR. STUHLMANN,
The Imperial Governor.

DAR-ES-SALAAM, *November 22, 1900.*

Index